Land Reform and Democracy

CLARENCE SENIOR

Land Reform and Democracy

GREENWOOD PRESS, PUBLISHERS
WESTPORT, CONNECTICUT

Library of Congress Cataloging in Publication Data

Senior, Clarence Ollson, 1903-
   Land reform and democracy.

   Reprint of the ed. published by University of Florida
Press, Gainesville.
   Bibliography: p.
   1. Land tenure--Mexico. 2. Mexico--Rural condi-
tions. I. Title.
[HD325.S42 1974]   333.3'0972   74-8261
ISBN 0-8371-7563-1

Originally published in 1958 by University of Florida,
Gainesville

Reprinted with the permission of University of Florida Press

Reprinted in 1974 by Greenwood Press,
a division of Williamhouse-Regency Inc.

Library of Congress Catalog Card Number 74-8261

ISBN 0-8371-7563-1

Printed in the United States of America

Preface

> *Nothing was left for the peasant; he owned neither earth nor water nor fire, nor even the air he breathed. . . . Suffering came to him from all quarters—from man, from nature, from himself. . . .*
>
> *Then, when his sufferings grew unbearable, Jacques Bonhomme rose in revolt. Behind him lay centuries of fear and resignation, his shoulders had been hardened by blows, his heart was so broken that he did not realise his degradation. He could be beaten for a long time, famished, robbed of all his possessions without being driven out of his shell of caution. . . . He could go on thus until one last injustice, one last pang made him suddenly leap at the throat of his masters like a tamed animal that had been maddened by overbeating. Again and again, century after century, the same desperate uprisings took place. . . .*
>
> —The Martyrdom of Jacques Bonhomme, from *Earth,* by Emile Zola

ZOLA'S SEARING PHRASES describing the calvary of the earthbound people of France may seem "dated" to most of us living in the comfort of the modern world. The echoes of African and Asian peasant revolts, the news of land reforms in Bolivia and Guatemala, reach our ears only faintly. But farsighted analysts of the world scene show no complacency on agrarian matters, which is one of the fundamental aspects of "the world revolution of our time." Associate Justice William C. Douglas of the United States Supreme Court even proposes that this country promote "peasant revolutions" in underdeveloped areas to end "economic serfdom" and open the way to democracy. We, as a nation, are committed to "further the secure growth of democratic ways of life" by the 1950 Act for International Development and subsequent policy decisions.

v

Millions of peasants have been involved in land reform movements in recent years; all indications are that such movements will continue. If people in the "developed" areas are to understand most of the peoples of the other two-thirds of the world, their attempts at land reform, and the difficulties they encounter in building democracy must be understood. This study attempts to make a contribution to such understanding.

Probably the most widespread aspect of land tenure reform is an attack on latifundia and an attempt to destroy the rural feudalism which usually accompanies large-scale landholdings. This was a major element in the Mexican Revolution as a whole and specifically in the application of Mexican agrarian laws to the Laguna region in the north-central Mexican states of Coahuila and Durango. Some 30,000 peasant families were given land on October 6, 1936, in the greatest single agrarian move in the history of the Revolution. They were organized into some 300 ejidos, farm groups in which the land was communally owned and cooperatively worked.

The Laguna land reform was announced in the interests of "greater democracy," as are so many others throughout the world. The Mexican Revolution itself is generally referred to as having promoted "greater democracy." Since for many years I had been a participant in movements for "greater democracy," I set out to follow the Laguna experiment in the hope of learning at first hand how democracy grows after the destruction of feudalism.

I have been fortunate in being able personally to study the Laguna region at frequent intervals from March, 1937, six months after the expropriation, to August, 1952. I have spent periods ranging from three weeks to three months in the region on twenty-one different occasions. For three years it was my pleasure to help organize and participate in the work of college and university students from the United States who spent their summer vacations in the region helping the peasants build rural schools, dig irrigation ditches, and erect a cotton gin, under the auspices of the American Friends Service Committee. Several visits, including the original one, were made for the purpose of preparing reports for the Southern Tenant Farmers Union (now the National Agricultural Workers Union, AFL-CIO). One was made in the interests of research in connection with the Latin American Regional Resources Development project of the National Planning Association. I organized four

conferences on the Laguna experiment for which local participants
in various aspects of the agrarian movement prepared papers which
were read and discussed by social workers, teachers, labor leaders,
newspapermen, civic leaders, and government officials from both
the United States and Mexico.

Such activities helped gain the confidence of individuals in many
ranks of life. I believe I was able to talk with hundreds of persons
and share in numerous group discussions without being treated as
an "outsider." The documentary sources quoted are made more
meaningful by peasant and union meetings attended, and by work
side by side with local people in building rural schools or arranging
educational conferences.

It early became apparent that the abundant "good intentions"
of the agrarian authorities and the peasant leadership might, alone,
be no more than the paving blocks on the road to disaster. It became
apparent to many of the participants in the Laguna experiment also,
but usually they called upon experts too late in the agrarian process.
Other times the experts they called upon were highly trained specialists in their own fields but too limited in their vision of how
extensive a job of social reconstruction was required to achieve
the democratic aims of the agrarian reform.

Work in the field of population and economic development took
me away from Mexico to Washington, Puerto Rico, Costa Rica,
Chile, Brazil, Jamaica, and the United Kingdom. Everywhere questions about land reform arose in connection with a wide range of
social, economic, and political issues. Inequities in land tenure
arrangements many times were found to be a major factor in discouraging immigration into countries which officially announce that
they want settlers. Disequilibrium between population and developed resources is obviously one of the "push" factors in those areas
from which there is migration—when that is politically feasible—or
in which dangerous population pressures build up when it is not.
Demographic considerations had been completely ignored in the
structuring of the Laguna experiment. How important was that
factor in the failure of some of the ejidos?

This and many other questions in my mind finally crystallized
around three major issues of land reform:

1. How are those who want the reform going to secure the
power to carry it into effect?

2. How is democracy going to be achieved during and after the land reform?

3. What kinds of technical problems must be solved?

I have tried to view agrarianism, democracy, and social change scientifically, and to apply some of the concepts of sociology to these issues. Moves made in La Laguna to build new social institutions embodying equalitarian ideas in the country with a powerful heritage antagonistic to democracy are examined and their relative success or failure assayed. Lasswell's "eight goal values of democracy" are utilized in this endeavor as the organizing schema: power, wealth, well-being, skill, enlightenment, affection, rectitude, and respect.

Geographic, economic, and historical factors in the development of the Laguna region and in Mexico as a whole are related to the process of building democracy following land distribution. Special attention is paid to demographic factors which have militated against the achievement of greater economic advance and have hampered the democratic reorganization of the social structure of the region.

The study ends with some "sociological generalizations" which it is hoped will be helpful to policy-makers in the agrarian field or those who deal with or comment upon agrarian movements. The principal conclusion is that the building of democracy must extend far beyond the agrarian institutions directly involved and be expressed in the structure and functions of all major social institutions if a fundamentally sound democracy is the aim.

My deepest gratitude is due dozens of Mexican peasants, workers, government officials, teachers, and business and professional men for the unfailing good will with which they have answered questions and helped in investigations and other activities. Thanks for innumerable valuable criticisms and suggestions are also due Dr. Clarence Jones, formerly director of the National Planning Association's Regional Resources Development Project, Professors Robert S. Lynd, Arthur MacMahon, Robert K. Merton, Frank Tannenbaum, and William Vickrey of Columbia University, Kingsley Davis (now of the University of California), and the late Paul K. Hatt, while at the Social Science Research Center of the University of Puerto Rico. The organization of the Laguna conferences during 1939, 1940, and 1941 was made possible by the sponsorship of Dr. Albert Sprague Coolidge of Harvard; his interest in the improvement and extension of democracy has always been a source of inspiration to me. Ing. Gonzalo Blanco Macías and Miss Mary Louis and Miss Peggy Doherty have been most helpful in keeping me in touch with events during absences from Mexico. The study would never have been completed without the unfaltering assistance and encouragement of my wife, Ruth, who for over 20 years intermittently has lived in and with La Laguna.

Obviously, the author alone is responsible for what he has done with the information and interpretations furnished by his friends and colleagues, for errors of omission or commission, for interpretations and for viewpoints.

CLARENCE SENIOR

Columbia University

Contents

Preface v

List of Tables xii

List of Figures xiii

1. LAND REFORM—A WORLD ISSUE 1

2. THE MEXICAN REVOLUTION: DESTRUCTION AND
   RECONSTRUCTION 13

3. THE REVOLUTION REACHES LA LAGUNA 47

4. GEOGRAPHIC AND ECONOMIC FACTORS IN REGIONAL
   DEVELOPMENT 68

5. THE FRAMEWORK FOR AGRARIAN DEMOCRACY 89

6. PROBLEMS AND PROGRESS IN BUILDING AN AGRARIAN
   DEMOCRACY 118

7. POPULATION PRESSURE AND AGRARIAN PROBLEMS ... 166

8. DEMOCRACY COMES TO A COTTON KINGDOM 182

Notes 213

Appendix 239

Bibliography 253

Index 267

Tables

1. PROPORTION OF WORLD POPULATION IN AGRICULTURE, 1949 _____ 3
2. MEXICO: CHANGES IN CLASS STRUCTURE, 1895-1940 _____ 41
3. ACQUISITION OF TITLE, BY METHODS: LA LAGUNA _____ 54
4. MEXICAN COTTON PRODUCTION, AREA, YIELD, 1925-1926 TO 1954-1955 70
5. COTTON: TOTAL AREA CULTIVATED, PRODUCTION AND YIELD,
   LAGUNA REGION, 1930-1931 TO 1953-1954 _____ 71
6. VALUE OF COTTON DESTROYED BY DISEASE AND PESTS:
   LA LAGUNA, 1936-1937 TO 1940-1941 _____ 77
7. WHEAT: TOTAL AREA CULTIVATED, PRODUCTION, AND YIELD:
   LAGUNA REGION, 1930-1931 TO 1953-1954 _____ 79
8. EXAMPLE OF *Ejidal* FINANCIAL TRANSACTIONS: EJIDO BARCELONA,
   STATE OF DURANGO, 1939 _____ 102
9. LEGAL MINIMUM WAGE INDEX: LAGUNA REGION, 1942-1955 _____ 145
10. LEGAL MINIMUM WAGE AVERAGES, 1936-1955 _____ 146
11. BEDS, SEWING MACHINES, AND RADIOS PER 100 PERSONS: MEXICO,
    COAHUILA, DURANGO, AND LA LAGUNA, 1939 _____ 147
12. LITERACY: MEXICO, COAHUILA, AND DURANGO, 1900, 1910, 1921,
    1930, 1940, 1950 _____ 155
13. PRIMARY SCHOOLS: MEXICO, COAHUILA, AND DURANGO, 1927,
    1937, 1940, 1950, 1952 _____ 156
14. LITERACY: LA LAGUNA, 1900, 1930, 1940, 1950 _____ 157
15. CURRICULUM, SCHOOL OF PRACTICAL AGRICULTURE: SANTA TERESA,
    COAHUILA _____ 159
16. CRUDE BIRTH AND DEATH RATES AND NATURAL INCREASE OF
    POPULATION: MEXICO, COAHUILA, DURANGO, AND LA LAGUNA,
    1940 AND 1950 _____ 169
17. INFANT MORTALITY: MEXICO, COAHUILA, DURANGO, AND LA
    LAGUNA, 1930, 1940, AND 1950 _____ 171
18. INVESTMENTS AND RETURNS OF LAGUNA EJIDOS ACCORDING TO
    DEGREE OF MECHANIZATION, 1939 _____ 174
19. PER CENT OF POPULATION GAINFULLY EMPLOYED:
    LAGUNA REGION, 1940 AND 1950 _____ 179
20. COTTON: AREA CULTIVATED, PRODUCTION, AND YIELD,
    PRIVATE PROPERTIES AND EJIDOS: LAGUNA REGION,
    1936-1937 TO 1945-1946 _____ 189
21. WHEAT: AREA CULTIVATED, PRODUCTION, AND YIELD,
    PRIVATE PROPERTIES AND EJIDOS: LAGUNA REGION,
    1936-1937 TO 1945-1946 _____ 190
22. YIELDS, WHEAT AND COTTON, COMPARISON OF *Ejidal*
    WITH PRIVATE PROPERTY: LA LAGUNA, 1945-1946 _____ 192
23. LAND DISTRIBUTED, NUMBER OF EJIDOS AND *Ejidatarios*:
    MEXICO, 1916-1954 _____ 239
24. OWNERSHIP OF IRRIGATED LAND, BY SIZES: LA LAGUNA, 1928 _____ 240
25. PROPERTIES LEASED, RENTED, OR SHARECROPPED, BY *Municipio*,
    NUMBER, AREA, AND VALUE: LA LAGUNA, 1928 _____ 241
26. PROPERTIES WORKED OR ADMINISTERED BY OWNERS, BY
    Municipio, NUMBER, AREA, AND VALUE: LA LAGUNA, 1928 _____ 241
27. MEXICAN COTTON PRODUCTION, AREA, YIELD: PRINCIPAL
    REGIONS, 1944-1945, 1949-1950, AND 1953-1954 _____ 242

xii

28. WHEAT: TYPES OF CULTIVATION, COSTS, YIELD, AND PROFIT:
LA LAGUNA _____ 243
29. WHEAT: COSTS OF VARIOUS OPERATIONS: FLOODING BY RIVER,
TWO IRRIGATIONS BY PUMPS, AND USE OF TRACTOR AND MULES:
LA LAGUNA _____ 244
30. WHEAT: COSTS OF VARIOUS OPERATIONS: FLOODING BY RIVER
AND USE OF TRACTORS AND MULE-DRAWN EQUIPMENT:
LA LAGUNA _____ 245
31. DISTRIBUTION OF CREDIT SOCIETIES BY AREAS WORKED
AND MEMBERSHIP: LA LAGUNA, 1937-1938 _____ 246
32. NUMBER OF BUILDINGS AND PERCENTAGES BY MATERIALS:
COAHUILA, DURANGO, AND LA LAGUNA, 1929, 1939, AND 1950 _____ 247
33. HOUSING, DRINKING WATER SUPPLY: MEXICO, COAHUILA,
DURANGO, AND LA LAGUNA, 1939 AND 1950 _____ 248
34. CHURCH BUILDINGS: MEXICO, COAHUILA, AND DURANGO,
1929 AND 1939 _____ 248
35. COTTON INVESTMENT AND OPERATIONS: LAGUNA EJIDOS
WITH LIGHT MECHANIZATION, 1939 _____ 249
36. PROFITS FROM COTTON CULTIVATION, DISTRIBUTED BY BANCO
EJIDAL, 1937-1938 TO 1954-1955 _____ 250
37. AVERAGE ANNUAL EXCHANGE RATE, PESOS TO DOLLARS, 1927-1957 ____ 251

Figures

1. LOCATION OF THE LAGUNA REGION—MEXICO _____ 48
2. RAILROADS, ROADS, AND PRINCIPAL POINTS—LAGUNA REGION _____ 57
3. PRINCIPAL CANALS—LAGUNA REGION, 1942 _____ 62
4. ANNUAL WATER FLOW OF RÍO NAZAS, 1891-1943 _____ 64
5. SAMPLE LAND TENURE PATTERN, 1943 _____ 92

Chapter 1

LAND REFORM—A WORLD ISSUE

*T*HE ESSENCE of the "world revolution of our time"[1]*
for perhaps the majority of the people of the world
is the demand for land. This is not new, nor should it be strange
to those of us who are the heirs of centuries of major social
struggles, most of which were concerned with questions of land
ownership.

"Land to the landless" is a slogan at least thirty centuries old.
"Plutarch tells us that the free peasant disappeared in the second
century B.C. . . . the Gracchi . . . tried to restore the old order of
society based on a more equal distribution of the land."[2]

THE SIGNIFICANCE OF LAND REFORM

Most of the fundamental social changes which have molded our
own culture in Western Europe and North America have had land
reform aspects: The fall of the Roman Empire, the peasant wars,
the Protestant Reformation, the agrarian revolution (which required
three centuries in England and about three decades in France, where
it formed the mainspring of the French Revolution), the American
Revolution, the Industrial Revolution, the Civil War, and the Russian
Revolution, to mention only the most broad-scale. One scholar has
counted 1,622 peasant revolts in medieval and modern times; all
had the "land problem" at their base.

*Notes to this chapter begin on page 213.

1

RECENT AGRARIAN MOVES

Current agrarian movements are reflected in practically every issue of the daily press: "Philippines Eyes Agrarian Reforms," "Guatemala Plans Seizure of Lands," "Big Estate in Iran Is Divided by Shah," "Egyptian Proposes New Land Reform," "Kashmir Confiscates All Large Estates," "Indian State to End Peasants' Bondage," "Burmese Peasants to Get Bigger Role," "Collectives Take Yugoslav Farms," "Land Distribution is Pushed in China" headline only a few of the clippings from the *New York Times* during part of the year 1952. One story was headed, "Wide Land Reforms Laid to U.S. Urging." A "selective bibliography" on land reform around the world, confined to major items appearing from 1940 to mid-1951 in English, French, and Spanish, lists nearly 500 entries.

We deal not with past history, however; not even with recent history. We deal with current events. The Bolivian land reform started in earnest in 1953; President Ramón Magsaysay launched "the Philippine Answer to Communism" in 1954; a British Royal Commission proposed, in 1955, widespread improvements in inequitable land tenure relationships in Kenya, Tanganyika, and Uganda; and 1956 saw the United States government financially helping both the Bolivian and Guatemalan people work out agrarian problems.

Agrarian reform may be peaceful: witness, among others, the "land gift mission" carried out by India's "walking saint," Vinoba Bhave. Or it may be drenched with blood, as in the case of the Mau Mau or the forced collectivization in China.

In any case, most of the time, on both sides of the "Iron Curtain," land reform is verbally linked with democracy.

COLONIALISM AND AGRARIANISM

Two factors stand out clearly when recent reports are analyzed. First, most of the "reforming" occurs in the colonial or semicolonial areas or those only recently achieving release from their colonial status. Second, the "reforming" is largely concentrated in those areas where the proportion of the population engaged in agricultural pursuits is high. A comparison of the items in the *World Land Reform* bibliography with Table 1 indicates that the two categories of areas overlap considerably.

Africa, possibly the most explosive of the colonial areas today, had in 1950 given rise to enough recent articles on land tenure to fill a 156-page annotated bibliography.

Flesh is put on the bibliographic bones by the statement of a Christian student leader from Kenya at a recent religious conference in Ohio:

Africans are in revolt, not against white society, but rather against paternalism, racialism, economic and political domination by a small white minority.

Mau Mau is only a mild protest compared with what may occur in Kenya unless this revolution is accepted as a genuine effort by those who are denied any channel of self-expression to secure rights, dignities, freedoms and opportunities which go along with acceptance of democratic ideas.[3]

The clouds which hang over Africa become more meaningful when we place alongside the above statement the progress report of Lieutenant General Gerald Lathbury, in charge of "security" in Kenya, as quoted in the *New York Times* of June 24, 1955: "He said the terrorists, pledged to drive the 30,000 white settlers from this sun-baked British colony, were being eliminated at the rate of 500 a month. . . . Since the emergency was declared, troops and

TABLE 1

PROPORTION OF WORLD POPULATION
IN AGRICULTURE, 1949

(in millions)

Area	Total Population	Agricultural Population	Agricultural Population as Percentage of Total
World	2,177	1,285	59
North America*	163	33	20
Europe	391	129	33
Oceania	12	4	33
South America	107	64	60
Central America†	50	33	67
Asia	1,255	878	70
Africa	198	146	74

Source: Food and Agriculture Organization of the United Nations, *Yearbook of Food and Agriculture, 1950* (Rome: Food and Agriculture Organization of the United Nations, 1950), p. 15.

*Canada and the United States.

†Including Mexico.

the police have killed 8,883 terrorists, General Lathbury disclosed. In addition, 932 others were captured wounded, 24,188 were captured or detained as suspects and 1,538 surrendered."

Recent books on Asia and Latin America devote major space to agrarian problems, although they usually carry no such gruesome news.

Why the Present Interest? — Why, in the light of the long and varied history of agrarian revolts, is there now such a great interest on the part of many persons not directly involved? Traditionally, the people of the United States have sympathized with the struggles of other peoples for independence and for economic advancement. The "Fourteen Points" of President Wilson, the "Four Freedoms" of President Roosevelt, and the Atlantic Charter represent outstanding expressions of such interest. None of them, however, mentions agrarian reform.

United States delegates sponsored resolutions before the United Nations and the Economic and Social Council using the theme, "there are sound and pressing reasons for the practical consideration by the United Nations of problems of land reform at this time."[4] The United States Army introduced land reform in Japan, where absentee landlords as a class disappeared,[5] and in Korea, where "a total of 700,000 peasants acquired farms of their own in a period of five months."[6] The reforms were carried out to further the development of democracy.

The International Bank for Reconstruction and Development, among many other international bodies, has testified to the urgency of land tenure changes:

. . . the maintenance in a number of countries of inefficient and oppressive systems of land tenure militates against increase in agricultural output and improvement in the general standard of living.[7]

The Roman Catholic church, among the nongovernmental organizations, has organized four international congresses on rural problems, including land tenure, in the past few years. The three most recent were held at Manizales, Colombia, January, 1953, at Panama, April, 1955, and at Santiago, Chile, April, 1957, each attended by representatives of twenty-three nations.[8]

The importance of world-wide action to acknowledge and even to aid agrarianism has been recognized by the United States government, by the United Nations, FAO, ILO, and many nongovernmental organizations only within the past few years. Among the factors impelling interest would seem to be the following: the revolt against colonialism, the new economic position of the United States, and the ideological struggle for the world. Even a short discussion of each would take us too far from our major purpose.[9]

Agrarian reform will play, for millions of people, a major role in the resolution of the ideological struggle underlying the "coexistence" of democracy and Communism.

Cultural Limitations in Understanding Agrarianism. — The current interest on the part of the "have" nations is encouraging. It is not enough. There must be willingness to see and understand each agrarian movement within the framework of its own culture. Each must be judged in the light of its own historical roots—and without forgetting our own.

"Democracy," as a shibboleth, will aid no peasants to resolve their agrarian problems.

Justice William O. Douglas found agrarian unrest throughout the Middle East, arising out of the daily struggle for existence against hostile social institutions which had existed for years. One of his peasant friends gave him a significant reaction:

Please tell the people of America not to lecture us about democracy. Don't tell our people that they must choose between democracy and communism. The people of this region are not free to make the choice. They are slaves. They are illiterate. They have no present escape from their misery. There is no such thing for them as liberty.[10]

We, and others of the more "advanced" nations, do lecture peasants about democracy, however, and we do prejudge agrarian movements in what seems to this author a most unrealistic manner. This was spotlighted in a clear and evidently self-contradictory statement of the First World Land Tenure Problems Conference, held in Madison, Wisconsin, a few years ago. The steering committee of the conference pointed out the ubiquitous "concentration of ownership in a few hands" and found it "necessary to emphasize that ownership rights, especially in the Orient, are of dubious origin and legally and morally not well established." However, the steering committee then attempted to separate "the sheep from the goats" in agrarian movements in the following manner:

What distinguishes the democratic from the totalitarian approach to the question is whether or not the reform is sought to be accomplished by due process of law and is subject to judicial review. If the legislation authorizing purchase has been passed by a democratically constituted legislature and respects the person and individuality of the divested parties, the extent of compensation, though of course vital, becomes less crucial.[11]

Democracy's representatives, in effect, say to the peasant whose land hunger has become one of his major preoccupations, "You cannot build a democratic society without land reform, but you cannot get land reform without using the methods of democracy." The methods are then defined as those which are strange to the experience and thinking of probably most of the peasants of the world.

Undoubtedly, everyone would be happier if land could be distributed on a sunny Sunday afternoon with the ceremonies followed by pretzels and beer, or hot dogs and soda pop, or *tortillas* and *pulque*, or rice cakes and *sake*. An analysis of past agrarian movements indicates that, in general, they have not displayed this idyllic character. One summary refers to them as "cruel, disastrous, orderless, undisciplined."[12] Another finds that the majority of revolts and uprisings of the agricultural classes have been marked by "a purely elemental, programless, objectiveless character."[13]

The stress on compensation would be understood by some who know the history of the United States as indicating a repudiation of part of our own heritage. A far more realistic attitude was taken by the late Henry G. Bennett, Administrator of the Technical Cooperation Administration, when he said:

The restlessness of an increasing number of families without land was one of the factors that led to the American Revolution. The colonies had inherited the land laws of the mother country. Large holdings passed from father to first son, and vast estates were kept intact by entailment. The manorial system persisted until the colonies won their independence. Individual colonists of poor or moderate means found it hard to buy land.

Among the first results of the Revolution was the confiscation of large Royalist estates. Feudalistic quitrents were abolished, and laws that protected large estates were repealed.

This sharp break with the past enabled the young Nation to create a new legal framework for land ownership.[14]

It will be recalled that the abolition of chattel slavery in the United States brought no compensation to the "vested interests" whose livelihood was based on ownership of slaves and on commerce in them.

It is to be feared that equating democracy with the legal forms created by or on behalf of the great landowners in those countries facing agrarian reforms plays into the hands of the Communists. The World Land Tenure Problems Conference statement could easily be interpreted by the enemies of democracy that, as an export commodity, it is only a hollow form.

The peasant whose whole being cries out for land is to be given a stone labeled "due process of law." The Communist appeal is much more simple and direct: "What exists is evil; therefore, smash it! The landlord has what you need: take it from him!" It does little good to tell the landless peasant that the Communist program is only a propaganda trick; that soon after he is given the land it will be taken from him.[15] This, while undoubtedly true in Russia, and in China, Poland, and other "satellite" areas, is geographically a culturally distant and an "iffy" argument to the landless peasant. "Sufficient unto the day is the evil thereof" is a folk saying with variants in many cultures; "We'll cross that bridge when we come to it" is another. The representatives of democracy must be aware of the danger of falling into the trap of judging the aims of agrarian movements in other cultures by the criteria they have absorbed from their own culture.

Agrarianism Viewed Sociologically. — "Agrarian reform" may cover many aspects of the process of changing land tenure arrangements: improvement of leasing or renting arrangements, protection of sharecroppers, legalization of peasant organization, consolidation of small strips into efficient-sized farms, or breaking up of large estates and distribution to the landless peasants. The latter is the aspect which most concerns us here, since we are to examine an area in which the chief problem was concentration of land ownership in the hands of a few persons. It was chosen, however, because it displayed many of the characteristics reported from other areas of the world.

The sociologist is interested in social systems and social relationships and in how they change. Agrarian institutions are among the most important parts of the social system, their importance rising with the proportion of the population living directly from agricultural pursuits.

Changes in land tenure patterns are one of the major items on the world's agenda of social problems. A sociological analysis of a specific project of land reform and its background in the widespread social change of the Mexican Revolution should help us understand what is happening in various parts of the world and what may happen in the future.

The key concept in understanding social change, according to Merton, is "that of strain, tension, contradiction, or discrepancy between the component elements of the social and cultural structure."[16] Specifically, in order to understand changes in land tenure arrangements, a sociologist would expect to find at least the following elements present:

1. Peasant dissatisfaction with existing agrarian institutions;
2. A determination to act on that dissatisfaction;
3. A goal (even though it be hazily formulated) toward which to work; and
4. Organization to carry out that determination and work toward the goal envisioned.

These elements are capable of formation into a large number of combinations. The structure and functions of the agrarian institutions themselves are influenced by other institutions of the society involved: religious, commercial, technological, military, political, educational, and familial. Geography enters into the picture, since rural feudalism is more apt to be found in relatively isolated spots not reached by the free flow of ideas made possible by modern communications. Institutional, geographic, and cultural factors influence the conditions under which the peasants may act and the means which they will use. New ideas and ideals adopted or adapted from other cultures or ideas and ideals revived from the real or imagined past of the peasants also may deeply influence the group.

Merton's key concept is helpful in understanding Mexico, which started its third major social upheaval in a century in 1910. The resultant eleven-year civil war and the advanced 1917 Constitution caused repercussions throughout Latin America, and gave rise to a considerable library of polemics and apologia as well as to a number of sound works of description and interpretation.[17] *Tierra,* it is to be noted during all of the Mexican Revolution, has been prior to, but always linked with, *libertad*. The influence on Mexican agrarianism of the Indian, Spanish, and Mexican cultural streams, plus the role of new ideas from France and the United States, will be examined in the coming pages.

MAJOR ISSUES OF LAND REFORM

There are three broad major questions connected with land reform in its relation to democracy. The first is, "How are those who want the reform going to secure the power to carry it into effect?" Second, "Does democracy grow spontaneously after land is distributed or must it be deliberately sought and planned for during and after agrarian reform?" Third, "What technical problems must be solved?"

The first question is seldom raised or discussed in the circles of the United States Department of State, the United Nations General Assembly, or the Economic and Social Council. Land reform is usually treated as if it were a question of technology, solvable by persons with the proper technical training and experience. That it is being discussed in Western circles, anyway, largely by those who are the beneficiaries of at least five centuries of broad-gauged social changes (both violent and peaceful) seems hardly to occur to those discussing it.

The second question—the achievement of democracy after land reform—is usually also treated as a technological problem depending on credits, advice, education, and similar governmental programs. It seems to be sufficient to say with Dean Acheson, "Our democracy has its roots in a sound land policy."[18] The land policy lauded by Secretary Acheson is generally summed up in the phrase "the family farm." Jefferson's dictum that "the small landholders are the most precious part of a state" has been called "the classic American statement of the political theory of the family farm."[19] A critical examination of the theory by President Griswold of Yale leads to a conclusion at variance with the classical statement.

The cycle of [farm] policy thus concluded sets the United States apart from both England and France. It shows a national concern for agriculture as a state of society, for private property in land, and for family farming as their mainstay, that has simply not existed in England—a concern that played little part in the development of British democracy and almost throttled its development in France.[20]

Third, what technical problems arise and how do they influence both democracy and production? The world needs both social justice and greater production: "man does not live by bread alone," but he must have bread or obviously he does not live. Or he lives close to the thin line separating him from starvation. The United Nations' Food and Agriculture Organization recently reported that about 1,300 million people—over half the world's population—do not get enough bread, or rice, daily. And the world is losing ground: "though total world production (of food) is now some nine per cent greater than the average in the five year period 1934-38, the number of people is twelve per cent greater."[21]

Prime Minister Nehru graphically summed up the position of the world's peasants when he said, "We are talking about the atomic age while we live in the cow-dung era."[22]

THE PURPOSE OF THIS STUDY

Objectives. — The aim of this study is to examine the three major questions just stated as they apply to a specific large-scale agrarian experiment—that which is found in the important cotton-growing Laguna region of Mexico. There, on October 6, 1936, some 30,000 peasants were granted land expropriated from huge estates in one of the major moves of the twenty-six-year-old Mexican Revolution. The social system of the region closely paralleled that of the southern cotton plantations of the United States where "King Cotton" once had reigned.

The peasants were organized into about three hundred ejidos, farm groups in which the land was communally-owned and cooperatively worked. An earnest attempt was made to replace one fairly well-integrated social system by another based on fundamentally different principles. The move was looked upon as one of the crowning events of the agrarian phase of the revolution. Land distribution had begun twenty-one years earlier, in 1915, after almost four years of civil war. Nowhere previously had Mexican agrarianism undertaken to apply its precepts to an area of commercialized agriculture. Up to that point land redistribution was confined almost entirely to corn and bean subsistence plots.

The reorganization of the Laguna region was widely hailed as an "experiment." It will be treated as such in this study, but in the relatively restricted sense in which it has been used by social scientists. Dewey, for example, pleaded for experimentation in human relationships but admitted that

> what purports to be experiment in the social field is very different from experiment in natural science; it is rather a process of trial and error accompanied with some degree of hope and a great deal of talk.[23]

It is the hope of the author that this analysis of the Laguna experience will help peasants, publicists, politicians, and technicians to profit from the mistakes made, and thus to avoid some of the waste of time, effort, and money which is all but inherent in "natural social experiments by trial and error." And the Laguna experience is meaningful not alone for those who think about or participate in agrarian action, but also for all those who deal with other aspects of the development of "underdeveloped areas" and attempts to create more democratic societies; in fact, for all those who hope for intelligently directed social change.

Democracy Viewed Scientifically. — The term "democracy" is, of course, not self-explanatory, but it is clear that no longer can it be looked upon merely as a political form. Increasingly, both modern social science and the dynamics which inhere in popular participation have been broadening and deepening the concept of democracy. Merriam, a political scientist, says: "The voting process *per se* has no validity unless it is reinforced by a democratic way of life and a democratic practice of choice."[24]

Lawrence K. Frank, writing as a psychologist, defines democracy as

> an aspiration that goes beyond universal suffrage, free speech, economic enterprise and representative government; it is a continuous assay of our culture and our organized society in terms of human values that can not be achieved so long as the personalities of men and women are warped and corroded by fear, anxiety, guilt and hostility.[25]

Robert Lynd, sociologist, adds that "the characteristic thing about democracy is its diffusion of power among the people."[26] He broadens his sights in another treatment:

Democracy, as a frame of reference encouraging recognition of the dignity and worth of the individual and implementing this recognition for political action, is an institutional invention of major importance.[27]

The purpose of this study is to lay the basis for an understanding of the principal problems of agrarianism, insofar as its advocates hope to build a new social system in which democratic values and practices are basic. Thus the study hopes to contribute something to discussions of policy and to the forging of agrarian methods consonant with democracy.

Which of the above ideas about democracy can we accept as a starting point? Here we have the advantage of over two decades of work on the problem by a social scientist who has specialized in this field. Harold Lasswell has recently codified the components of the democratic complex. He contends that widespread sharing of the following elements is characteristic of democratic societies:

1. Power (decision making)
2. Wealth (economic goods and services)
3. Well-being (physical and psychic health)
4. Skill (opportunity to acquire and exercise latent talent)
5. Enlightenment (access to information and comment on which rational choices depend)
6. Affection (congenial human relations)
7. Rectitude (common standards of responsibility in theory and fact)
8. Respect (absence of discrimination on grounds other than merit).[28]

A social system approaches democracy to the degree in which the above eight "goal values" are widely shared; it recedes from democracy as these values acquire a narrower base in the total population.[29]

Chapter 2

THE MEXICAN REVOLUTION:
DESTRUCTION AND RECONSTRUCTION

*T*HE MEXICAN REVOLUTION includes eleven years of
civil war, followed by almost two decades of civil
government intermittently menaced by revivals of domestic militar-
ism and foreign intervention. The major fact of this whole social
movement, for a sociologist, would seem to be the organization of
large numbers of the people themselves into peasant and labor
unions, and their determination to struggle for ideas and ideals
such as expressed in the slogan *tierra y libertad.* But it will be seen
that the Mexican answer to our first question, how to secure power,
was violent and costly in men, money, and energy.

DÍAZ PROSPERITY

Mexico was at the height of a "wave of prosperity" when the
revolution came. Manufacturing and mining had expanded; the
national income had risen from 20 million pesos to 100 million
during the 34 years of the dictatorship of Porfirio Díaz; the budget
had been balanced; Mexico "could borrow all the money it wanted
at a little more than 4%."[1]* Members of the ruling groups were living
in luxury, but the masses had suffered a 75 per cent reduction in
their already low levels of living during the first decade of the
century, according to one calculation.[2]

*Notes to this chapter begin on page 215.

13

CONTRADICTIONS IN THE SOCIAL SYSTEM

"Mexico" was prosperous; but a large majority of the Mexicans were not. This was only one of the components of a situation which was explosive in "strain, tension, contradiction . . . discrepancy," to repeat Merton's phrase. The major institutions were being undermined, often by their very success in carrying out the wishes of those in the upper reaches of the hierarchy in politics, property, or preaching. The "rules of the game" were challenged increasingly by individuals and groups who found them no longer consonant with their values.

A stable social system is achieved when there is a moving equilibrium between two sets of factors: beliefs, value systems, and goals on one side and the institutions out of which they grow and upon which they in turn react on the other. Merton has pointed out that the social structure itself tends to produce rebels under circumstances such as those of Mexico in 1910.[3]

The key to the Mexican change lies in the aspirations of important social groups as blocked by rigid institutional structures. The aspirations could either be old or newly acquired, of course. Both were involved in the social movement called The Mexican Revolution. It is important to note that not until the persons and groups with blocked aspirations were organized did they begin to cause trouble for the personnel of the major institutions.[4] It is also important to note that the Mexican experience justifies caution about accepting any such particularistic economic "cause" as that generally given to explain the revolution. The Weyls, for instance, in a book which does not rigidly follow their economistic dictum, write: "The revolution which transformed Mexico was made inevitable by the steady deterioration in·the living standards of some 10,000,000 agricultural workers and their families, who constituted three-fifths of the population."[5]

THE SOCIAL INSTITUTIONS OF THE OLD ORDER

The 34-year rule of Porfirio Díaz has been referred to as a "military Diazpotism,"[6] but that enormously oversimplifies matters. Actually, Díaz stood at the apex of several interlocking hierarchical social institutions. Their characteristics can be summed up in the sociologists' phrase "a closed class system."[7]

THE "HAVES" AND THE "HAVE-NOTS"

Economic power, political power, and the power exercised by those who spoke in the name of supernatural beings was concentrated socially and geographically. Mexico City was the undisputed metropolis. The small "upper-upper" class came close to being a caste which was tied together by family, personal, political, and ideological bonds and fear of the wrath of the masses whom some of them abused.

On the basis of the 1895 census (since the revolution interfered with the full analysis and publication of the 1910 census) one may get an idea of the over-all situation in Mexico.[8] The upper class represented 1.4 per cent of the people; the middle class, 7.8 per cent; and the lower class 90.8 per cent, according to Iturriaga. Ownership of property was concentrated nationally in the hands of 49,542 upper-class urban dwellers and 133,464 rural people out of a total population of 12,698,330.

THE MONOPOLY OF LAND

The vast majority of the people lived in the rural areas. It was the 1 per cent of the population which owned most of the land that, to the landless peasants, represented the upper class.

The impact of Mexico's highly concentrated power structure fell most heavily on the four-fifths of the population which lived in rural areas or small villages. Land ownership, obviously the basis of life in an agricultural society, was highly concentrated. "More than 95 per cent of the heads of rural families in all but five states were property-less and in all but one state the proportion of rural families owning no rural property whatsoever was greater than 92 per cent."[9]

The relation between man and master was generally one of complete dependence. Physically, the typical hacienda was organized around the *casa grande,* the "big house," where sometimes dwelt the *hacendado.* Nearby were the houses of the workers, an hacienda store, a church or chapel, a jail, a cemetery, and, sometimes, a school. Often the core of settlement was surrounded by a wall with turrets and gun slits at each corner. Many such walls still stand, although they no longer serve their original function.[10]

The hacienda store used the same methods of "short-pencil"

bookkeeping which marked so many of the cotton plantations of the southern United States during the reign of "King Cotton."[11] The result was a system of debt-slavery; debts were bought and sold when rural properties changed hands.

The owner was, typically, a resident of one of the larger provincial cities or of the metropolis. His *mayordomo*, or field-boss, generally rode his territory with a gun or whip to spur recalcitrant workers or to protect himself from possible attack.

Attempts to resist the encroachment of the hacienda on land still in the hands of the Indian villages were drowned in the blood of those who were presumptuous enough to challenge the *hacendado*.[12] Fifteen major outbreaks occurred during the Díaz dictatorship, according to one author.[13]

The resemblance between mediéval Europe and Mexico was capped by the widespread resort of the *hacendado* or his *mayordomo* to the *droit du seigneur*.

A social system marked by the amount of repression which characterized the period of Porfirian "law and order" would, it seems clear on the basis of our sociological frame of reference, finally explode into the "elemental, programless, objectiveless" violence which seems to have puzzled Sorokin and Zimmerman."[14]

There were other institutions which helped structure the Mexican social system of the early years of the twentieth century. Working with the big landowners was a direct, simple state apparatus.

THE MONOPOLY OF POLITICAL POWER

"Authority," writes Lynd, "is a continuous two-way process, or it is tyranny."[15] Under this definition, Mexico lived under tyranny during the Díaz regime, and Díaz was the tyrant.

The Constitution of 1857 was almost a replica of the Constitution of the United States, and provided for a federal structure with the same three branches of government.[16] But the federal political structure was radically at variance with the social structure of the country. Therefore it did not function. Instead, the realities of the social, economic, and even geographic situation in Mexico hampered federalism and bred centralization of political power.

The semicolonial nature of Mexico's economy and the tax system arising out of it was one of the major factors contributing to centralization. An enormous share of the country's income flowed from exports. Export and import taxes provided the largest single share of the federal government's revenues, and federal revenues far exceeded those of state and local governments. Even in the late 1930's, federal taxes accounted for 70 per cent of all governmental income; state and local for 30 per cent. Tannenbaum believes that the "political disequilibrium in Mexico lies in part in the nature of the tax system."[17]

The political genius of Díaz was expressed in his organizing into one vast machine those who had been exercising local and district power and, usually, lining their own pockets. As one historian put it: "Bands of wolves, instead of fighting each other as they had been doing since Independence, were now invited to join each other in an attack on the sheepfolds."[18] Díaz distributed wealth, or opportunities to acquire wealth, to bribe enemies and to reward friends and relatives.[19]

The political system which evolved closely parallels the similar reign of "law and order" which marked Spain from the Bourbon restoration in 1876 to the Republic of 1931, and which was revived in its most essential features after the Republic was suppressed by Franco.[20]

THE MONOPOLY OF FORCE

The *hacendado*, the Díaz politician, the businessman—sometimes the same man, or at least close relatives—also commanded a monopoly of force. The *hacendado* could with impunity flog or even kill the recalcitrant peon. If matters got out of hand on the hacienda, the *rurales* (the rural mounted police) could be called. The army backed up both *hacendado* and the *rurales*, if necessary.

The army in itself constituted a partial social system within the entire Mexican social system. It accurately reflected social class divisions, although it came closer to being an open class structure than the Mexican society as a whole. The "common soldier" was of the "common people." His destiny was to be used and abused by those whom God and the local or state *jefe político* placed over him.

Díaz forged the first national army out of what had been local and regional armed bands. Such groups had previously coalesced only occasionally behind strong leaders since Mexico's independence had been achieved during eleven years of civil war beginning in 1810.

The officers came from among the younger sons of the large landowners, the small middle class, or the children of the professional soldier clique. They were trained in the Military College in the capital, wore resplendent uniforms, attended the balls and parties of "high society," and moved in the "correct" circles. They were the true heirs of a powerful tradition which stemmed back to the Spain of preconquest days. Several centuries of struggle against the Moors had built up a dependence on military men which served the crown well in conquering the New World. The military heritage, complete with *fueros* (privileges, including the right to be tried by military instead of civil courts), has hung heavy over Mexico until only the past few years.

THE MONOPOLY OF SALVATION

Those who can offer paradise or threaten inferno usually exercise enormous authority in a society abounding in ignorance and poverty. If their doctrine is authoritarian, they are likely to be found intellectually on the side of the secular "powers that be." If, in addition, they are organized into a tight hierarchy with those at the top closely linked to the top personnel of other institutions, their value in the maintenance of any social system is tremendous.

The Mexican church not only has displayed these characteristics throughout most of its history; it also has been the country's largest single landowner and largest single banker. Part of its riches were acquired through the confiscation of the properties of persons burned to death by the Inquisition, which served as an arm of the church and the Spanish crown from 1524 to 1820.[21] Land was also secured by grants from the Spanish monarchs and much was acquired as a result of mortgage activities.[22]

The hierarchy bitterly opposed the movement for independence from Spain; the Inquisition excommunicated Hidalgo, Morelos, and other leaders. "The military and clerical oligarchies" were the chief contributors to the constant disorder which characterized Mexico following the achievement of independence, according to Dr. José María Luis Mora, one of the country's greatest political thinkers.[23]

THE DÍAZ REGIME AND THE VALUES OF DEMOCRACY

Mexico in 1910 seemed to many to have achieved "stable systems of social interaction," that is, a stable social structure. True, the

International Bank report of 1948-1949 might have been referring to the Mexico of Díaz in mentioning "underdeveloped nations where there are wide extremes of wealth and poverty," and where "inefficient and oppressive systems of land tenure militate against increase in agricultural output and improvement in the general standard of living." The summary description given in this section of some of the major social institutions indicates that in respect to none of Lasswell's eight elements of the democratic complex could Mexico have been rated as satisfactory. The denial of democratic values was justified by the intellectual retainers of the dictatorship on various grounds: that the "racially inferior" Indians were lazy and indolent; that the masses of the people were ignorant and superstitious; that the people had been oppressed for so long that "they cannot acquire between dark and daylight the aptitudes and necessary virtues in order to govern themselves democratically."[24]

The church, with exceptions few and far between, preached submission not only to the civil authorities but also to the *hacendado*, the factory owner, the mine superintendent. Typical of the general attitude is the pastoral letter of Archbishop Francisco Orózco y Jiménez of Guadalajara:

As all authority is derived from God, the Christian workman should sanctify and make sublime his obedience by serving God in the person of his bosses. In this way obedience is neither humiliating nor difficult. We do not serve man; we serve God, and he who serves God will not remain unrewarded. . . . Poor, love your humble state and your work; turn your gaze towards Heaven; there is the true wealth.[25]

Representatives of the church seemed to be intent on illustrating the thesis of the Marxists that "religion i the opiate of the people." The "opiate" did not work; Díaz resigned on May 25, 1911, and fled from the revolutionaries. What had seemed to many to be a tightly integrated and stable social system underwent profound and violent changes in the succeeding ten years of civil war.

NEW MEN FOR OLD INSTITUTIONS

Who were those who undertook to challenge the rulers of Mexico, and what did they want? Here we must distinguish between those who wanted to change the *personnel* of the institutions and

modify some of the rules (in Merton's terms, the innovators) and those who wanted to change the rules fundamentally and thus remake or replace the institutions (the revolutionaries). The innovators initiated the change; the revolutionaries fell heir to the original impetus and carried it on.

Díaz had been in command for 34 years; he and his coterie of retainers were old, even waning in their physical powers. The dictator himself was 82; "of twenty state governors, two were past 80, six past 70, seventeen past 60 and the youngest was 46."[26]

New men were able and willing; they felt they should be given a chance. The forms of democracy contained in the Constitution of 1857 should be respected; free elections should be held. Democracy cannot succeed without schools, so education should be made available to the people. Freedom of the press should become a reality. This was the substance of the appeal of Francisco I. Madero, an ardent idealist who spoke feelingly about the "restoration" of liberties which had never existed in Mexico. His principal slogan was: "Effective suffrage; no re-election." Madero supplied the inspiration, the charismatic leadership which Max Weber found so essential to important social movements.[27] The merciless bandit-killer, Pancho Villa, left an audience with Madero saying, "I have great visions engraved on my heart."

Madero's ideology was compounded out of his experiences in a secondary school in the United States, five years as a student in France, his studies of the Baghavad-Gita, and the "messages" he received through spiritualist mediums and ouija boards.

His family background helped supply another set of ideas and ideals; they were prosperous owners of lands, breweries, and smelting plants. They had, along with others of a small but rising group of Mexican industrialists, suffered from the competition of United States financial and industrial interests encouraged by Díaz. The slogans of the French bourgeois revolutionists struck a responsive chord in Francisco.

His attitude toward his first job was also influenced by a year's study of "scientific agriculture" in the United States. Fresh from abroad, filled with humane ideas, he was given the management of some of the family properties—in the Laguna region. At first his energies were channeled into the importation of the best United States and Egyptian cottonseed. Then he introduced the first

modern machinery into the region and published a book advocating an irrigation dam.[28]

Next he attracted unfavorable attention from the other *hacendados* by paying higher wages than his neighbors, helping the peasants with their personal troubles, sending his private physician to treat sick workers, and establishing public dining rooms during drought periods. Schools were founded on each of his farms, and he organized and helped support a commercial school in the town of San Pedro.

By 1905 he had begun to run afoul of the political machine of the large landowners. He founded a political club, a weekly political paper, *El Demócrata,* and a magazine of political satire, *El Mosco* (literally "The Fly," but better translated "The Gadfly"). In the municipal elections of 1905 and the state elections of 1909, he organized campaigns against the candidates of the dictator. Attacks on his supporters, stuffed ballot boxes, and threats of arrest increased in 1909.[29]

Díaz himself encouraged others to join Madero by a dramatic announcement to a North American correspondent in March, 1908, that he did not expect to be a candidate in 1910.[30] Madero's book, *The Presidential Succession in 1910,* has been compared with Thomas Paine's *Common Sense;* it became a "best seller," and helped organize an unorganized citizenry. Madero's followers and assorted enemies of the regime organized "anti-re-electionist" clubs all over the country when it became evident that the dictator was going to run again. The Partido Democrático was formed, nominated Madero for president, and gathered strength so rapidly that Díaz had Madero jailed.

Díaz was declared re-elected on October 4, 1910. The following day Madero, who had escaped to the United States, issued a call for armed revolt to begin November 20. Rebellions in various parts of the country indicated that individual and group grievances were widespread. The conscript soldiers sent to suppress rebellion often went over to the rebels. Díaz finally resigned on May 25, 1911, and went into exile.

Madero then found himself facing, in all their naked intensity, the stresses and strains of major institutions in collapse, aggravated by a dogfight of personal ambitions, group rivalries, and treachery in high places. His backers had included many groups with antagonistic motives. There were the Catholic church party, which wanted less restraint than even Díaz had applied; and the Masons and other groups, which wanted the anticlerical Reform laws of 1859 enforced more rigorously.[31] There were businessmen, who wanted protection from foreign competition; and both intellectuals and workers from the shops, who wanted protection for labor against exploitation, whether domestic or foreign. There were land-seekers, who wanted the breakup of church lands to continue because they hadn't been able to acquire any in previous forced sales; and agrarian leaders, who wanted land for those who worked it. There were local leaders of armed bands throughout the country, who were enrolled because of their hopes to better the conditions of their people; and there were bandits, who saw a chance to benefit from spreading disorder.

The Madero movement was, above all, a struggle of the "outs" against the "ins." The "apostle of The Revolution" served as a detonator; the chain reaction which followed brought changes which he at no time envisioned.

New Institutions for Old

Reforms are brought about by the "outs" ousting the "ins" and taking over existing statuses and roles in the political structure. "Outs" vary from "near-outs" to "far-outs" along a social distance scale measured from the sources of power, however. Social revolutions, which change the social structure, are brought about by those who are farther "out" than the political reformers.

The majority of the "far-outs" of Mexico in 1910 were the peasants. Sporadic local revolts plus thousands of cases of individual rebellion expressed in banditry and murder of *mayordomos* had kept the famous *rurales* busy. Generally the peasants were under the influence of fatalistic attitudes, both from their Indian heritage and from the preaching of resignation to earthly superiors. "What is, must be."

Madero's anomalous and contradictory coalition broke the spell for many of the peasants. It had challenged the dictatorship and it had won. But Madero had little interest in the peasants' ideas of fundamental reform; his eyes were fixed upon an abstract ideal. A competent observer reports that during a whistle-stop discussion in 1910 Madero exclaimed, "The people do not demand bread; they demand liberty."[32]

The platform of the party which ran him for president contained no reference to land distribution.[33] There was a passing reference to agrarian injustices in Madero's "Plan of San Luis Potosí" urging rebellion, which the historian Hackett characterized as "molasses to catch flies."[34] But land distribution was started by some localities under the pressure of armed peasant bands. The federal government under Madero issued two circulars (January 8 and February 17, 1912) urging town councils to divide up communal lands. Unused public lands were also divided and distributed.[35]

Madero's conception of the situation was far from adequate to the circumstances. The peasants wanted *both* land and liberty. The roadblock to liberty was the *hacendado* who had large areas of land. Madero, faced with peasant demands and action, strove to assure his conservative supporters that he wasn't responsible. He wrote the editor of a leading Mexico City daily that in none of his speeches or manifestos had he favored "despoiling any landholder of his properties."[36]

The Mexican Revolution as a social movement had begun to move.[37] Madero and his supporters were now dealing with emergent institutions, not with men who wanted to share the spoils of office. Emiliano Zapata is the prototype of the men who took the leadership in organizing the agrarian struggle on a programmatic basis. He was not an hacienda day laborer (peon) but a sharecropper, one step up the status ladder. He was struck by the contrast between the housing and loving care given horses in the stables of the *hacendados* and the neglect and abuse of the peons. This led him to embrace agrarian ideas, according to his own account.[38]

Zapata interpreted Madero's temporizing on the fundamental issues of land as "betrayal of the revolution." His "Plan de Ayala" attacked Madero as "unable to realize the promises of the revolution of which he was the author" and announced that "today we begin a continuation of that revolution." The plan called for immediate expropriation of one-third of the large estates, with indemnification. However, those *hacendados* who "oppose this plan, directly or indirectly, shall have their lands nationalized as war indemnities, the funds to be used for the benefit of the widows and orphans of the victims of the struggle for land."[39]

Zapata's followers knew for what they were fighting. They were usually considerate and well behaved.[40] Residents of Mexico City still speak of their exemplary conduct when the Zapatistas occupied the capital. The followers of other regional chieftains often knew much less of their aims. One eyewitness reports the following colloquy as "the apostle" passed before a throng shouting "Viva Madero! Viva la democracia!":

"And what, amigo, is this *democracia* for which all are shouting?" inquired a pyjamad peasant of another.

"Why, it must be the lady who accompanies him," was the reply, pointing to Madero's wife.[41]

Men of various qualifications and ambitions rose in most regions of the geographically divided country. No matter what their personal ambitions, the surge of the peasant movement made land distribution their dominant motif. The social movement provided the drive; what happened in each region and in detail depended to a high degree on the characteristics of the individual who organized and guided the drive. Often the peasants themselves gained stature by genuine participation; often they were manipulated by the "leader."[42]

Fuel was added to local revolutionary activities by thousands of friends, and especially members of families of persons who had suffered some injustice at the hands of the *hacendado*, the local or state *jefe político*, army officers, tax collectors, or other agents of the Díaz regime. But the major drive behind the upheaval was the demand for land. The agrarian movement continued to push local, regional, and national leadership into action. Carranza, a conservative "revolutionary," fighting to regain the presidency against challenges by Zapata, Villa, and other agrarians, issued the first national land distribution decree on January 6, 1915.

AGRARIAN INSTITUTIONS

Three distinct ideologies illumined and guided the struggle for new agrarian institutions:

1. The first had its roots deep in the Mexican soil. Its organizational form was the ejido, a type of land tenure stemming from the Roman *ager publicus* via medieval Spain. It had features parallel to Aztec communal land ownership, still prevalent when Cortés conquered Mexico.[43]

Zapata was the chief fighter for the ejido and other Indian-based institutions. He was joined by others who were the intellectual descendants of Hidalgo, who roused the Indians and poor mestizos in 1810 by the appeal to recover from "the hated Spaniards the lands stolen from your forefathers three hundred years ago."

2. The "men of the North"—Villa, Orozco, Carranza, Obregón, and Calles—had lived on the periphery of Indian Mexico, in Coahuila, Chihuahua, and Sonora. They were closer intellectually, as well as geographically, to the United States. "Land and liberty" to them meant the right of each man to own, in fee simple, a plot of ground. The manifesto issued by representatives of Zapatista and Villista forces, in its agrarian reference, shows the attempt to encompass both viewpoints.[44]

3. The third program was similar to the subsistence homesteads approach of the early depression years in the United States. It provided that the ejidos be reconstituted, but as supplementary to existing haciendas. The authors were the urban intellectuals Andrés Molina Enríquez and Luis Cabrera. They recognized that the hacienda peon worked only part of the year under the owner's orders and on his land; the remainder of the year he had leisure, but no land to work.[45]

Obviously the three differing concepts of the meaning of *tierra y libertad* would lead to radically divergent programs of agrarian action. These differing concepts were never reconciled; the social backgrounds of their promulgators were widely different and exerted a deep influence on their "definition of the situation" which they were trying to solve. It was more than a theoretical discussion to Villa and Zapata, whose ideas grew out of their personal experiences, but the Mexico City intellectuals were the ones who wrote the laws. One result was an attempt by the agrarian movement to incorporate and act upon *all three* ideologies. The hampering effect will be seen in discussing the Laguna experiment.

These viewpoints are reflected in the various agrarian decrees and laws. *Restitution* dates from the days the peasants seized land forcibly and then sought legal justification. Their contention usually was that the land had been stolen from them or their ancestors, and that the action they expected from the government was simply one of restitution. One Mexican publicist has contended that the gentlemanly nature of the revolution is proved by the fact that no compensation for the use of the land was demanded![46]

While restitution was the earliest of the techniques of land distribution, another came into use as the revolution developed. The second method, *dotación* (endowment or grant), has been the most commonly used. It is applied when a village, or other center of peasant population, petitions for land on the basis of its need to work its own land rather than that of someone else. In using this method the government offers to pay for the land in agrarian bonds.

Ownership of the land is held by the group in all cases, and not by the state as in Russia, or by individuals as in most Western countries.

Land was secured only by nibbling at the edges of the large estates, up to the Cárdenas administration. The ejidos formed were cut up into strips or parcels. Each family worked a plot and sold any surplus produce. Essentially it was a subsistence farm with the peasant barely able to keep body and soul together if the neighboring hacienda did not give him day labor. But generally the Indian peasant was satisfied. His hunger for land had been allayed.

Most of the area distributed by the revolutionary governments from 1915 to 1934 was poor land, badly located from the standpoint of either selling products or procuring supplies. Insufficient credit was available and no adequate attempt was made to educate the peasants in better agricultural practices. After fifteen years of land distribution, the 1930 census showed the agrarians in possession of only 9.9 per cent of the actual or potential farming land of the country.

Land distribution was speeded up during the administration of President Lázaro Cárdenas (1934-1940). More than twice as much land was distributed during his six-year term as in all of the previous years since 1915. The number of ejidos created was almost twice that of the previous eighteen years, and the number of rural workers receiving land was slightly over twice that of the former period. Groups which had formerly been excluded were given permission to apply for land. A banking system geared to the specific needs of the ejidos was created. More money was spent by the national government on rural schools, medical services, sanitation, provision of safe drinking water, and additional irrigation.

Cárdenas tackled the question of the expropriation of large-scale producing units for the first time. The ejido, which had played a purely supplementary role in the national economy, was to become one of the pillars of farm production. It was given a more adequate organization. Cooperative working of the farms was added to group ownership. The first application of these new ideas and techniques was made in the Laguna region.

Other areas in which the new approach was applied include: Yucatán; the Yaqui Valley of Sonora; Nueva Italia and Nueva Lombardía, Michoacán; the Mexicali region of Baja California; and Los Mochis, Sinaloa. Some of these have shifted from their original cooperative organization to the working of family plots.[47]

Land distribution has slowed down since 1938. The administration of President Manuel Avila Camacho, who followed Cárdenas, distributed only 6,648,400 *hectáreas*, contrasted with 16,753,730 during the preceding administration. It should be noted, however, that this total compares favorably with the 7,099,880 *hectáreas* distributed in the entire pre-Cárdenas period of the revolution, as does the distribution of 5,360,000 *hectáreas* during the presidency of Miguel Alemán (1946-1952).[48]

One of the factors accounting for the decline in land distribution is the scarcity of acceptable land. Only 10 per cent of Mexico's land is arable, as compared with over half the land in the United States. Of this 10 per cent, "only in 7 per cent can the farmer work without irrigation, and even then he needs drainage work, ditches and the regulation of streams, all of which we have only recently been able to begin."[49] Various governments in recent years have spent increasingly large sums on attempts to wrest farming land out of the hands of the desert.[50] Geography here, as in the mountainous nature of most of the Mexican nation, has presented man with serious obstacles, and has added enormously to the costs of economic progress.

DISTRIBUTION OF LAND OWNERSHIP — 1950

Land is much more widely distributed today than it was in 1910, on the eve of the revolution. The 1950 census found that farm properties had increased 2,855 per cent over the last pre-revolutionary census. The 1910 census had showed an increase of only 302 per cent over 1854. The figures for number of farms in the five censuses of the past century are:[51]

1854	15,085
1910	47,939
1930	858,209
1940	1,233,609
1950	1,370,625

The postrevolutionary figures are more revealing when analyzed further. Each ejido is counted as one farm property in the census. Out of 1,370,625 farm properties in 1950, 18,027 were ejidos. Those ejidos, however, contained some 1,884,116 members, each of which is legally a landowner. Therefore, the total number of landowners might well be reported as 3,236,714. This would give the astronomical increase of 6,750 per cent between 1910 and 1950! Land distributed and the number of ejidos and *ejidatarios* by year since the beginning of the land distribution program are shown in Table 23, Appendix.

" . . . AND A MULE"

The old homesteaders' slogan, "Forty Acres and a Mule," holds the lesson that manpower alone is not sufficient for adequate farm management. Animals and more modern equipment must be added. Many parts of Mexico still know only the archaic wooden plow; in some there is still the type of resistance expressed in the phrase, "Steel is 'cold' and poisons the earth."

The government has spent much time, energy, and money educating the peasants to the need for modern machinery and supplying credit for both animals and equipment. The once property-less peasants have now become substantial owners of animals and the tools of farming. Those *ejidatarios* alone who receive credit from the *ejidal* bank (about 26 per cent of the total, partly because of the severe limitations on agricultural credit) show the following, and only partial, capital goods increase in the fifteen years between 1936 and 1950:[52]

	1936	1950	Per Cent Change
ANIMALS			
Oxen	186,195	195,015	105
Mules	57,062	193,996	340
Horses, draft	91,650	194,338	212
Horses, other	7,762	120,203	1548
Burros	118,833	159,469	134
Cattle	259,008	522,820	202

	1936	1950	Per Cent Change
Goats	326,530	632,123	193
Sheep	55,968	330,778	591
Pigs	67,477	415,170	615
MACHINERY			
Plows	149,606	347,352	232
Trucks	257	2,042	794
Cultivators	664	43,826	6600
Pumps	234	2,563	1095
Tractors	109	3,072	2818
Threshers	126	538	427

The same *ejidatarios* owned 224 irrigation units in 1950, with an investment of 21,968,000 pesos and an annual production valued at 42,179,000 pesos.

Credit made available to both *ejidatarios* and small private owners by official banks in 1950 amounted to about 30 per cent of all agricultural credit. It is available at from 6 to 8 per cent interest annually. Private banks, which charge 12 per cent, account for around 15 per cent of all farm credit, leaving the lion's share (55 per cent) to private lenders at rates which run from 120 to 240 per cent per year.[53] This is a measure of the distance still to be covered by governmental and reasonable private credit sources.

The "land" part of the demand, *tierra y libertad*, seems to have been fulfilled in fair measure, given the shortage of arable land. The "liberty" part will be examined in detail later.

URBAN WORKERS MOVE FOR LIBERTY

The peasants were not alone in their antagonism to existing institutions. Small but growing groups of urban workers saw in the downfall of Díaz an opportunity to make gains for themselves; they contributed both ideas and additional power to the nascent social movement. They were organized, even though in a loose manner. They had ideas, although poorly formulated. The crucial facts were (1) that their ideas were radically at variance with those of the dictatorship, and (2) their organizations were usually a direct challenge to the existence of the feudal type of industrialism. The very existence of workers organized autonomously was a threat to both agrarian and business institutions as then constituted, as was recognized in federal and state penal laws.

The Creelman interview of March, 1908, led to the mushrooming of spontaneous labor political organizations, since labor economic action was illegal. All shades of radical political ideology were represented; they were unanimous on one subject: "Díaz must go!" Madero received an overwhelming reception by organized labor groups when he entered Mexico City after the Díaz capitulation, in spite of the fact that the labor problem had not been mentioned in the Plan of San Luis Potosí.

Unions evolved from political clubs; from workers' secret societies; from artisans' guilds; from fraternal and insurance groups—all within a matter of weeks.[54] Nationwide organization was not achieved until July 15, 1912, when a "united front" of several unions was formed under the glorious title of Casa del Obrero Mundial (figuratively, House of the Workers of the World, a name showing the influence of the then-important Industrial Workers of the World in the United States). The Casa, under the leadership of anarchists, syndicalists, and socialists, launched a broad-scale program which included legislative as well as economic demands. It created a "Rationalist" school and established a newspaper. It organized a demonstration for the eight-hour day and a Sunday holiday on May 1, 1913.[55] The dictatorship of Huerta, who had deposed Madero, soon discovered that the existence of a free labor movement was incompatible with its prerogatives. The Casa was suppressed.

Carranza was persuaded by his more progressive followers to woo the labor movement as he was wooing the agrarian movement. An agreement was signed under which the Constitutionalist chief agreed to give attention to the "just claims of the workers in any conflicts which may arise between them and employers" and to give workers "all possible aid in the formation of new unions."[56]

"Red Battalions" were organized to support Carranza's forces. The workers, enrolled by unions into six battalions, elected their own officers. Conquest of a town was followed by the "organization" of all the shops and factories; strikes were always won, since the workers were also the armed forces.[57]

While succeeding revolutionary governments varied from open hostility to cordial support, the labor movement from that day to this has been a factor with which one must reckon. It has sometimes expressed its wishes through its own political party, it achieved in the 1917 Constitution the most advanced labor code in the world of that day, it later forced the expropriation of the crucial oil industry, and at one time it managed the nationalized railroad system.

Labor opinion carries great weight in public discussion of foreign as well as domestic policy, as well as in more strictly labor fields. It is protected by minimum wage laws and by an elaborate system of courts and commissions, in all of which it has participation.

LABOR ORGANIZATION TODAY

The main ideologies in the background of the Mexican working class were anarchism, anarcho-syndicalism, socialism in various forms, communism, followed by corporativism, cooperativism, "pure and simple" unionism, fraternalism, fascism, and most recently, Peronism. The major tendencies have been expressed in various organizations since the revolution. Often, the same organization will shift its position and express a different theory one year from its stand the previous year.

One constant factor has been government influence. The labor movement was given a great deal of government help in organizing the workers in the early days, but it was also made dependent on the government in many respects. This dependence was the subject of a stern warning by President Lázaro Cárdenas in 1936. He told unionists, in Monterrey, Mexico's greatest center of heavy industry, that "the workers will not have at their command real, authentic, indestructible power while they depend on official aid."[58]

The history of labor organization in Mexico bears out this warning. When the government supports one labor organization, it prospers and local unions flock to its banner. Mexico's first important major trade union organization, commonly known by the initials CROM (Confederación Regional Obrera Mexicana) rose very rapidly to power under the protection of presidents Calles and Obregón but lost membership rapidly when Portes Gil became president. The most important national organization at the present time is the CTM (Confederación de Trabajadores de México). It rose to great power during the Cárdenas regime but was weakened considerably under the administration of his immediate successor. It seems to have recouped much of its power under Ruiz Cortines. It probably had around 400,000 members in 1955 and had undisputed leadership in electric power, railroading, mining, oil, and telephones.

Government workers make up the second largest federation

with perhaps a quarter of a million members, in twenty-eight affiliates. They were "requested" not to join the CTM by President Cárdenas.[59]

The CROC (Confederación Revolucionaria de Obreros y Campesinos) probably held third place in 1957 with a membership variously estimated at 40,000 to 70,000. The once-powerful CROM now ranks fourth, with perhaps 30,000 to 40,000 members.

There are three more federations, none of great importance. One, the UGOCM (Unión General de Obreros y Campesinos Mexicanos), was founded in 1949 when the Communists abandoned their attempts to "bore from within" the CTM. It is affiliated with the Communists' World Federation of Trade Unions through its Latin American branch, CTAL (Confederación de Trabajadores de América Latina).

A number of independents are unaffiliated with central bodies because of ideological or personal reasons, which also are among the causes of the existence of such a large number of central federations.[60] There are also state-wide unions unaffiliated nationally. They are often nothing more than tools for the political clique in control of the state government.

Liberty for the workers and peasants of Mexico has become a fact, at least insofar as legal expression can make it so.[61] But one is reminded of the comment of a great Mexican scholar years ago:

The common people are the most docile in the world and the most subject to their leaders and *caciques*, so that if a *cacique* says to a village of a thousand or two thousand inhabitants "let us go tonight" in the morning there will certainly be no one in the village, for all will follow their leader. . . .[62]

Workers and peasants fought the long civil war and weakened or destroyed much of the formal feudal and semifeudal social structure. Reconstruction of the informal, attitudinal aspects of the Mexican social system will take many years. An idea of what Mexico suffered is essential to an understanding of the country's social institutions and difficulties today.

Civil War Damages

Widespread and violent social change usually not only wrecks the institutions challenged, but also damages the productive machinery of the society involved. The Mexican Revolution was no exception.

Only one estimate has been found of monetary costs in connection with the civil war, and that only for about the first two years. Bulnes figured that, to March, 1913, the cost had been 3,412 million pesos, or $1,706 million at the 1910 rate of exchange.[63] The following nine years were certainly more thoroughly destructive. Mining, which in 1910 had given employment to 96,000 men, all but completely ceased and the mines were flooded. Guanajuato, one of the oldest and most prosperous mining centers, fell from 40,000 inhabitants to 15,000 and they were almost entirely unemployed. The Monterrey smelters, steel works, and related industries closed, leaving 90,000 persons without an income. So with textile mills, sugar and oil refineries, food processing, and on down through the list of Mexico's few industries. Manufacturing, mining, agriculture —none operated more than sporadically during eleven years.[64] Destruction of capital equipment was all but universal in many parts of the country.

Another idea of the amount of damage which occurred is found in demographic data. The national population grew by 1,553,097 between 1900 and 1910, or 11.4 per cent; during the civil war it fell by 825,589, or 5.5 per cent. If the birth and death rates for the previous decade had remained in effect, and if there had been no net in- or out-migration, the population would have been 17,061,479 in 1921. This means a net population loss of 2,726,699 during the civil war period. Over 200,000 Mexicans migrated to the United States during the period, since labor shortages had arisen during World War I, thus supplementing civil war "push" with the "pull" of employment opportunities.[65]

The obliteration of populated centers gives another indication of the extent of the damage. The census of 1910 reported 70,830 clusters; eleven years later the number had been reduced by 7,951, the big majority being rural villages. The states of the north, Pacific northwest, and central regions suffered the most dislocation, thus measured.[66]

Famine was widespread during 1915 and the American Red Cross sent thousands of carloads of relief food and clothing. Currency depreciated faster than presses could print new bills; prices soared to the fabulous heights usually seen during runaway inflation, and especially during civil wars.[67] One reason why there was not more suffering than actually occurred is found in the loose-knit character of the society of the time. Transportation and communication were poor, and a large percentage of the population lived outside the monetary economy.[68]

ECONOMIC ADVANCES

Mexico has travelled a long distance since the civil war. National income data are available only for recent years; they show the following totals, in millions of pesos:[69]

1929	2,042
1939	5,737
1944	15,551
1949	31,263
1950	37,816
1951	46,800
1952	52,000
1953	50,200
1954	59,180

This does not mean, of course, that the Mexicans were some twenty-nine times as well off in 1954 as they were 25 years earlier. Two factors have interfered: inflation and population growth. For example, the working class cost of living index in Mexico City had risen four and one-third times between 1939 and 1953.[70] The population of Mexico had increased from 16,295,918 in 1929 to 28,052,513 in 1953, or by 11,756,595, that is, 72 per cent.

Per capita income, in 1950, expressed in United States dollars still reached the figure of $180, which put Mexico in the group which includes Brazil ($200), Colombia ($235), and Cuba ($310) and ahead of Guatemala and Turkey (each $130). The average for the underdeveloped areas of the world was around $100. The figure for the United States, on the other hand, was $1,500.[71]

Consumption of goods is a more reliable index than income per capita. The total volume of consumption rose 105 per cent between 1939 and 1950, but the per capita rise was only 55 per cent. In other words, population increase took away over half of the rise in available consumer goods.[72]

The same phenomena are found in the case of food consumption, as might be expected. Food available for consumption increased by 72.2 per cent from 1939 to 1950, but per capita consumption of food rose by only 30.2 per cent.

The distance yet to be travelled by Mexico in feeding her population is indicated by the recent statement of Dr. Federico Gómez, director of the Children's Hospital in Mexico City, that malnutrition was responsible for from 40 to 60 per cent of deaths of children aged one to four.[73]

Agriculture, fishing, and forestry still gave employment to 57.8 per cent of the labor force in 1950 as compared with 66 per cent in 1910, but manufacturing employment had risen to 972,542 (11.6 per cent) over 137,000 (2.5 per cent) in 1910. Transportation workers had increased from 52,000 to 210,592, an indication of the strides which had been made in cutting down geographic isolation.

Geographic barriers might well be an advantage for isolated groups during such catastrophes as the civil war, but obviously a nation could not be built without overcoming them. More adequate transportation was one of the factors essential to diversification as well as to increase of production. Agriculture shifted away from older subsistence crops to a greater reliance on commercial production. Exports were also diversified, in a swing away from concentration on metals.

The proportion of minerals to total exports (by value) fell from 65.3 per cent in 1939 to 33.0 per cent in 1950, while agricultural exports rose from 28.2 per cent to 55.4 per cent, and exports of manufactured goods increased from 5.6 per cent to 10.2 per cent. Foreign investments also were found in a wider variety of enterprises, and external payments on investment account amounted to only 1.5 per cent of the national income.

Mexico is beginning to see possibilities of a better balanced economy, one not so dependent on the vicissitudes of the international market for exports, imports, or investment. The country has experienced thirty years of almost complete internal peace—only the second sustained period of tranquility since 1810.

POPULATION TRENDS

Domestic peace and increasing welfare have brought with them one of the highest rates of population increase in the world today. The 1950 census found 25,791,017 inhabitants; the 1910 had shown

15,160,369, an increase of 70 per cent in spite of the population loss during the civil war. The 1921 and succeeding censuses show how population increase has gained momentum:

Year	Number	Increase or Decrease
1921	14,334,780	−5.4%
1930	16,552,722	15.5
1940	19,653,552	18.7
1950	25,791,017	31.2

Net migration into Mexico between 1940 and 1950 was insignificant (203,170 persons) and accounted for only 3.3 per cent of the intercensal population rise. Therefore, it may be assumed that the rate of natural increase was about 3 per cent. Continuation of this rate would result in the doubling of the population in a little less than 25 years.[74]

Mexico is recapitulating the experience of many other areas in the first stages of the "demographic revolution." Death rates are dropping, birth rates remain high. Officially reported birth rates showed the following annual averages for the periods given:

1895-1900	33.7 per 1000
1901-1910	33.5
1922-1930	34.4
1931-1940	43.5
1941-1950	44.9
1955	46.2

It is doubtful that there has been any actual increase in birth rates during this time, however. The apparent increase almost certainly came about through better registration of births.[75]

Official death rates, generally more reliable than birth rates, have shown a consistent downward trend since the 1890's (except for the civil war period). The following are annual averages for the periods cited:

1895-1900	33.9
1901-1910	32.9
1922-1930	25.5
1931-1940	24.1
1941-1950	19.4
1955	13.3

This places Mexico in the upper middle range of the countries of the world—between the group including Argentina, Australia, Canada, Denmark, New Zealand, Puerto Rico, and the United States, all of which have death rates lower than 10; and the lesser developed areas such as Egypt, Guatemala, Rumania, and others with death rates in the 20's.[76]

Infant mortality is an even more significant figure indicating advancing welfare than is the crude death rate. Mexico has reduced its deaths during the first year of life from 286 per 1,000 live births in the first decade of this century to 131.6 in 1930, 125.7 in 1940, 96 in 1950, and 80.5 in 1954.[77]

Mexico's progress in this respect has taken it out of the class with Rumania (181 in 1950), Chile (161 in 1950), India (134 in 1949), and Hungary (106 in 1948). It is still above such lower mortality countries in 1950 as Finland (52), United States (32), and Sweden (24).

Life expectancy in Mexico in 1940 was 39 years at birth; ten years earlier it had been 36.3 years.[78] The continued fall in the death rate indicates that a further improvement will be registered when the next life table is calculated. Data for other Latin American areas show that Mexico does not differ much from them. The industrialized countries have life expectancies in the middle and upper 60's, however. Life expectancy is possibly the most meaningful index to the over-all welfare of a people, especially for comparative purposes.[79]

One of the lessons the "demographic revolution" would seem to hold for Mexico is that unless steps are taken to encourage the lowering of the birth rate, the increase in population will continue to absorb a large proportion of the economic advances being made. Urban parents have already begun to plan the number of their children, as is indicated by the median of four in villages of under 10,000 inhabitants and three in larger urban areas (1940 census data). The 1950 census showed the same trend.[80]

One of the chief economic disadvantages of the kind of population growth now occurring in Mexico is the skewed age distribution. The 1950 census showed that 41.7 per cent of the people were younger than 15 years of age. Thus two-fifths of the population is eliminated from possible labor force participation and must be supported and educated by those who do produce. This is a far heavier burden, proportionately, than is carried by the producers of the more highly developed nations. The percentage under 15 in European countries is 24.6; in the United States 27.1. England, France, and Belgium show those under 15 as only 21 per cent of their population.[81] A lower proportion is found in the most productive ages (15 to 59) in Mexico (52.6 per cent) than in the United States (60.7 per cent).

These and other more definitely social differences (for example, attitudes antagonistic to women working) account for a lower proportion of the total population being economically active than is found in the countries with longer histories of industrialization and urbanization. Mexico's censuses during this century have consistently shown a little less than one-third of its people in the productive categories.

Provision of educational facilities is extremely difficult with Mexico's heavy concentration of children in the population. President Ruiz Cortines in June, 1957, created a "National Technical Council on Education" in order to intensify efforts to cope with over 3 million children denied schooling because of classroom shortages estimated at 24,000 and a deficit of 70,000 teachers.[82]

The urbanization process has been speeding up in the recent past. Three census results tell the story in short:

1910	28.7 per cent urban of total population
1940	35.0
1950	42.6

The urban population grew 7.6 per cent between 1940 and 1950, whereas the rural population increased only 1.6 per cent. The big cities have grown at a more rapid rate than most of the smaller and medium-sized cities. Mexico City and Monterrey are now six times their size in 1900; Guadalajara has increased four times. The big cities display many of the pathological symptoms recorded in the Industrial Revolution in England: for example, both infant mortality and general death rates in the 1940's were appreciably higher in urban than rural areas. The capital has a poor record, especially in infant deaths.[83]

SHIFTS IN STRATIFICATION

Two conceptually distinct but overlapping systems of social stratification have marked Mexico since the conquest: "racial" and economic. The descendants of the handful of conquistadors who became the ruling class early in the sixteenth century have, on the whole, maintained that position. Their rule has been shared increasingly with the mestizo. Some Indians have climbed up the ladder of economic and political wealth and power in recent years. Mexico today is much further toward ethnic democracy than it was at the beginning of its struggle for independence from Spain. There were then four castes: *gachupines* or *peninsulares* (Spanish in origin), creoles (born in New Spain of Spanish parents), the mixed-blood mestizos, and Indians. The mestizos were subdivided into sixteen groups representing "various combinations and permutations of Spanish, Indian and Negro descent."[84]

The population in 1805 divided along "racial" lines as follows:

Whites	1,000,000	18 per cent
Mestizos	2,000,000	36
Indians	2,500,000	46

The proportions had shifted by 1910 to:

Whites	1,150,000	7.5 per cent
Mestizos	8,000,000	53.5
Indians	6,000,000	39.0

The 1940 census showed a drop in the Indian proportion to 14.9 per cent and the 1950 preliminary figures indicate 9.6 per cent.[85] Possibly the most significant fact connected with such census data is the definition of Indian adopted in the 1930 and succeeding decennial enumerations, and the attitude behind it. "Indian is as Indian does" might summarize the approach. Instead of trying to judge the degree of "blood" represented in any given citizen, the census classifies as Indian those who speak an Indian language (there are fifty still in use in the country) and who wear traditional clothing and eat *tortillas*. This gives considerable latitude to the interpretation of census data on ethnic groups. Moore points out that a few years ago "estimates of the Indian population in Mexico ranged from 25 per cent to 55 per cent."[86]

The new census definition is part of what has sometimes been referred to as "the reconquest of Mexico" by the Indian.[87] It started with the rebellion against Spain and has continued intermittently ever since. The revolutionaries have always considered the "redemption of the Indian" as an essential ingredient in their programs. There are no statues to Cortés, the conqueror, in the country, but there are prominent monuments to Cuauhtémoc, who resisted him. It was not until 1943 that there was a street in all of Mexico bearing the name Cortés. Then one appeared in an ostentatiously *nouveau riche* suburban real estate development. The remains of the old ruling class and some of the urban upper middle class still do not identify themselves with the Indians, except as objects of occasional charity. One Mexico City store owner, referring to Diego Rivera, said to the writer, "Isn't it a pity he looks so much like an Indian?"

The "incorporation of the Indian" into Mexican life is proceeding at an increased pace because of the revolution, but it would take us too far afield to examine the situation in any detail.[88] There is still a long way to go. Loyo estimates that 24 per cent of the Indian population lives in extreme misery.[89] The Indian increasingly is becoming part of an undifferentiated Mexican proletariat. The differentials between Indians and the rest of the Mexicans are now becoming those of rural versus urban, illiterate versus literate, and subsistence versus cash economy.

The class structure of Mexico has changed since the revolution, but extremes of riches and poverty are still great. The following distribution by average monthly income is shown by an analysis of the 1950 census data on the labor force:[90]

Receiving under 100 pesos	($11.60)	40.67 per cent
Receiving 101-300	($11.72-34.80)	45.33
Receiving 301-1000	($34.92-116.00)	12.57
Receiving over 1000	(over $116.00)	1.43
		100.00

Income to labor (wages, salaries, and supplements) ran from 21.5 per cent to 27.9 per cent of the national income in the 1941-1950 decade, according to the International Bank study. Most of the years found it closer to the lower figure. Profits, on the other hand, rose from 30.7 per cent in 1941 to 41.4 per cent in 1950. The proportion of income going to labor is low even for an under-developed country. Even Kenya, with a proportion of 34.8 per cent (1949) is considerably higher, as are Northern Rhodesia (37.7 per cent), Chile (46 per cent), Peru (42.2 per cent), and Japan (45.8 per cent). The more highly developed countries range from the 59.4 per cent of Switzerland to the 65.1 per cent of the United States and the 67.2 per cent of the United Kingdom.[91]

Economic extremes are seen on every hand in most parts of the country. Enormous new expensive real estate subdivisions lie within sight and sound (and smell) of one-room adobe huts containing seven or eight persons plus the family pig and several dogs. Less dramatic is the spreading of apartment houses and other multiple dwellings which house increasing numbers of groups lumped together under the rubric "middle class."

Occupationally defined, the middle class groups about doubled as a proportion of the total population between 1895 and 1940. (This comparison seriously underestimates the growth of such groups between 1921 and 1940, since much of the middle class was wiped out during the civil war.) Iturriaga compares the 1895 and 1940 census data, with the results shown in Table 2.

TABLE 2

MEXICO: CHANGES IN CLASS STRUCTURE

1895-1940

Social Class	1895		1940		Proportional Change
	Number	Per Cent	Number	Per Cent	
Total Population	12,698,330	100.0	19,653,552	100.0	
Upper	183,006	1.44	205,572	1.05	− 27.1
Urban	49,542	0.39	110,868	0.57	+ 46.2
Rural	133,464	1.05	94,704	0.48	− 54.3
Middle	989,783	7.78	3,118,958	15.87	+ 104.0
Urban	776,439	6.12	2,382,464	12.12	+ 98.0
Rural	213,344	1.66	736,494	3.75	+ 125.9
Lower	11,525,541	90.78	16,329,022	83.08	− 8.5
Urban	1,799,898	14.17	4,403,337	22.40	+ 58.1
Rural	9,725,643	76.61	11,925,685	60.68	− 20.8

Source: José E. Iturriaga, La Estructura Social y Cultural de México, pp. 28-30.

The significance of the changes can be more easily grasped if the rates of increase of the various groups are compared. When the rate for the upper class is taken as 1, the urban middle class rate is seen as 17.5, the rural middle class as 19.9, the urban lower class as 11.8, and the rural lower class as 1.8. The 1950 census results would undoubtedly show a continuation of the same trends.[92]

Component groups in the middle class are quite varied in their composition.[93]

1. The historical nucleus is found in the government bureaucracy, which has always been comparatively large in the Spanish countries. The increased functioning of the government following the revolution increased the number of "bureaucrats" (in Mexico not an opprobrious expression). Government employees in 1921 numbered 63,074; by 1950 they had increased to 250,000. The bureauc-

racy increased almost five times as fast as the population in that period.

2. The educational system born out of revolution has greatly increased the production of professional people. Licenses to practice the recognized professions granted between 1938 and 1948 totalled 50,761 compared with 51,117 in the 1901-1937 period. Professionals practicing in 1940 numbered 42,719; a decade later there were 60,442. These included professions such as doctors, dentists, lawyers, engineers, agronomists, teachers, and nurses. One interesting shift is that away from legal training and toward engineering and medicine. The rate of increase of professionals during the decade mentioned (41.4 per cent) unfortunately was not greatly above that of the increase of population (31.2 per cent).

3. The number of small privately-owned farms has also increased, as was seen above.[94] Whetten and other students have pointed out that the revolution is also responsible for the middle class receiving recruits from above.

4. Growing industrialization and the increases in commerce and trade which have come with it are also important contributors to the middle groups.

THE COURSE OF THE REVOLUTION

No group had the influence and the disciplined organization to do in Mexico what the Bolsheviki did in Russia seven years later. The Mexican Revolution was the result of a volatile mixture of repressed wishes, new hope on the part of large numbers of the "outs," plus increasing debility and indecisiveness of the "ins."

Seventeen years passed before a group crystallized which has since "managed" the revolution. The present Party of Revolutionary Institutions (PRI) was formed in 1929 as the National Revolutionary Party and for a few years in between was named the Party of the Mexican Revolution. It is a loose-knit organization, largely dependent for its sustenance on deductions from the paychecks of government employees. Other parties are allowed to function, run candidates, maintain newspapers, use the radio, and hold meetings, but the official party wins just as regularly as the Republicans in Vermont or the Democrats in Mississippi.

Just as there has been some change in the "Solid South," there are indications of changes in Mexico. The basis of the revolutionary victories seems to be the same as that of the Democrats, in spite of fraud, violence, and antiquated voting procedures. Violence is decreasing steadily and a new electoral code which may help reduce electoral skulduggery was recently adopted.[95] The 1940, 1946, 1952 and 1958 federal elections were held with little more trouble than Kansas City or Chicago elections of recent memory.

The real struggle takes place in the PRI primaries, just as under similar circumstances in the United States. Even more important is the discussion which takes place in the labor unions, peasant leagues, women's civic groups, and other organizations which express themselves politically through the dominant party. An attempt was consciously made by Plutarco E. Calles, architect of the inclusive revolutionary party, to build a potentially democratic structure as a "caretaker" until more widespread democracy was possible.

Typical of the process as he originally envisaged it is the development of women's suffrage. The revolutionaries have been torn between conflicting attitudes. On one hand there was their imported belief that women should be allowed to participate in the democracy they were trying to build. On the other was their feeling that the women of Mexico were "conservative, uneducated and incredibly superstitious."[96]

The first step was to organize a women's department in the revolutionary party. It had officials assigned to unions, peasant groups, the army, and other institutions. Housewives were organized to help in literacy, infant welfare, and other campaigns. Women who belonged to unions, union feminine auxiliaries, peasant leagues, or the party's own women's groups were given the right to participate in its primaries. Next, they were allowed to vote in municipal elections and hold local offices. The final step in enfranchisement came in 1953 with ratification of constitutional amendments to grant full suffrage.

Increased participation in all aspects of civic life, plus improvement in levels of living, literacy, transportation, and communication, are all helping broaden the political base of the Mexican democracy. The masses are no longer impotent, therefore the few are no longer all-powerful. The monopoly of political power has been broken, and a substantial start has been made in replacing it with a formal structure which shows signs of achieving a democratic function.[97]

Monopolies in other fields have been destroyed or severely damaged. The army has been brought under civilian control. There have been no armed revolts since 1938, and the last previous attempt of the military to return to the "good old days" was in 1929. The economic power of the landlords and the church has been broken. The struggle between the latter and the revolution continues, but on the same plane as the struggle between the civil power and the church in France since the revolution there.

The monopoly of learning has given way to widespread systems of rural and urban primary schools, cultural missions, community organization, literacy campaigns, and other formal and informal educational movements.

Producers and consumers cooperatives, quasi-governmental economic organizations with civic participation, have joined with labor unions and peasant leagues to add a measure of democracy to economic life.[98] Measures in the field of health, sanitation, infant mortality, hospitalization, unemployment insurance, old-age pensions, and other aspects of social welfare are spreading. Mexico is going through its industrial revolution attempting to avoid many of the pathological aspects of the early days of industrialism in England and western Europe.

Possibly in the long run the greatest contribution to the building of democracy in Mexico will prove to have been in what are popularly called "cultural" activities. Plastic and graphic artists found inspiration in the people's struggle for justice, and interpreted the struggle to the people in leaflets, pamphlets, textbooks, and more important, on the walls of thousands of government offices, schools, libraries, hospitals, and other public buildings.

Rivera, Orozco, Siqueiros, Charlot, Covarrubias, and dozens of others won world-wide reputations as participants in the first "renaissance" in the plastic arts since Giotto and his colleagues.[99]

Novelists used incidents and themes from the civil war and produced such masterpieces as *The Underdogs*, (*Los de Abajo*) by Mariano Azuela; *The Eagle and the Serpent* and *La Sombra del Caudillo* by Martín Luis Guzman; *Tierra, la Revolución Agraria en México*, and *El Indio* by Gregorio López y Fuentes. These and hundreds of others have helped shape the "living convictions" which are filling out the democratic forms created by the revolution.[100]

Novelists and graphic artists have also been active as critics of the deviations from the early ideals of the social movement (witness the blast at local politicians who betray the peasants in Mauricio Magdaleno's recent novels, and the hoglike caricatures in the murals of Rivera and Siqueiros of Luis Morones and others who became rich as "professional revolutionaries").

The *corrido*, however, may well be the most important mass-educational medium to come out of the revolution. Sir Andrew Fletcher's aphorism is highly relevant even if not completely accurate. His statement, "Give me the making of the songs of a nation and I care not who makes its laws" came closer to the concept of "living convictions" more than four centuries before its formulation by contemporary sociologists.

The *corrido*, based on an Andalusian folk-song form, has been the "voice of the people" since Mexico's colonial days. It has expressed fears and hopes, has celebrated success, and has bewailed defeat. Often it is sharp-tongued, sarcastic, and occasionally witty; more often it is sentimental. It served as the equivalent of the news commentator and editorial writer for millions of Mexicans before newspapers, magazines, and radio spread across the nation.[101] It played an important role in heightening the political consciousness of a people trying to shake off centuries of misery and oppression, of a people trying to achieve the dignity of human existence in a world where many of them had been treated as so many animals.

Peasants, workers, Indians, women, intellectuals, and some of the urban middle class have been striving since 1910 to find ways to reach the goals they have come to value. They listen first to one group, then another; first to a *líder*, then to an "apostle." The revolution swings to the right, then to the left. It yields to pressure from the United States; it reacts against "foreign interference." It speeds up land distribution; it slows down to consolidate. Anticlericalism flares up and dies down. Mexico does not seem, on the whole, to have had more swings of the pendulum than has Russia during almost the same period of attempting to solve many similar troublesome and complex problems.

There is a tremendous difference in the treatment of human beings in the two revolutions, however. Mexico never accepted "the dictatorship of the proletariat," the theory of the "master race," or any of the other slogans under which democracy has in recent years been denied in the name of "clearing away the wreckage so that the foundations of democracy can be laid." Neither infallible "big brother," nor party, nor sect speaking in the name of divine or secular "revelation" has been able to bend the Mexicans to its will. There have been no "brain-washings," no tyranny over the free play of intellectual forces and ideas.

The Mexican Revolution has welcomed ideas. It is still seeking answers to many of the questions which have puzzled mankind for centuries, as well as to some new ones. Basically, the idea behind the development of the revolution is a new idea, especially new in a semimedieval environment such as Mexico has known until recently. It is the idea that man can remake his social institutions.

How this idea was applied in a specific region of Mexico, beginning a quarter of a century after the revolution itself began, is the subject of the remainder of this book.

Chapter 3

THE REVOLUTION REACHES LA LAGUNA

THE PEASANTS of the Laguna region waited twenty-one years before they could secure an application of the agrarian laws to their situation. During most of the eleven years of the Mexican civil war, the region had been in turmoil. The landowners and most of the businessmen in the cities supported Díaz and later Victoriano Huerta, after he had Madero assassinated. The hacienda and urban workers supported the revolution. "Pancho" Villa swept through the region three times, capturing and recapturing Torreón, with attendant bloodshed, property destruction, and pillage.

When order was restored to the region in 1921, the workers and peasants found that the revolution in which they fought had left political and economic power in the hands of the same group which had wielded it before 1910. A few concessions were made to the social welfare clauses of the 1917 Constitution. A few more schools made their appearance. But labor organization and strikes met with bitter resistance. Organizers were jailed, exiled, or shot. "Land to the landless" remained a mere slogan.

La Laguna, Mexico's most important commercial agricultural area, supplied almost half of the country's cotton, and was the third most important wheat zone in the middle 1930's. Its metropolis, Torreón, had been the nation's fastest growing city for over fifty years. Application of agrarian laws in the region was delayed for several reasons.

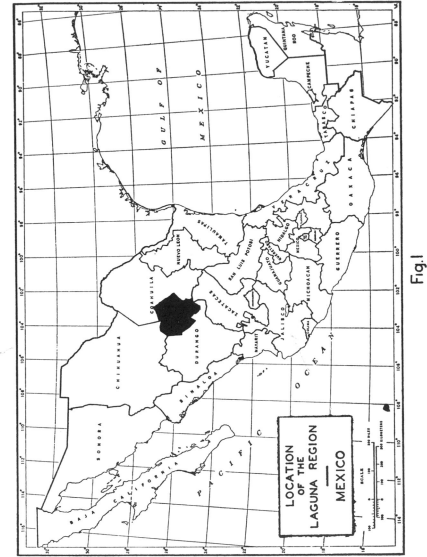

REASONS FOR THE DELAY

First, the area was comparatively isolated and lacked rapid communication with the more densely settled sections of the country. Peasant representatives could not easily travel from the earlier agrarian centers to the distant region.

The Laguna region is located in north-central Mexico on the arid plateau between the Sierra Madre Oriental and the Sierra Madre Occidental. Foothills of the latter dot its alluvial plain. The size of the region depends on the definition adopted. Geologically, it occupies most of the estimated 11,000 square miles of the Bolsón de Mayrán. Politically, it is defined as nine *municipios* (comparable to United States counties) in the states of Coahuila and Durango: Francisco I. Madero, Matamoros, San Pedro, Viesca, and Torreón in the former; Gómez Palacio, Lerdo, Mapimí, and Tlahualilo de Zaragoza in the latter. The area, thus defined, contains 3,299,200 *hectáreas* (12,738 sq. mi.). Socially and economically, the region is the hinterland of Torreón, since no other city within 200 miles competes seriously with it as the center of services and supplies. Torreón is 230 miles almost due west of Monterrey, 300 miles southeast of Ciudad Chihuahua, and 200 miles northeast of the city of Durango. It contained, by the 1940 census, 75,796 inhabitants, of the 290,000 in the region. The 1950 census showed an increase to 128,971 in the metropolis out of 429,832 in the region. Chief satellite towns are Lerdo (1950 pop. 13,390), Gómez Palacio (pop. 45,842), and Mapimí (pop. 12,974), in Durango; San Pedro (pop. 19,258), Matamoros (pop. 10,154), and Viesca (pop. 3,047), in Coahuila.

The demographic data available are based on *municipios;* therefore the political definition is adopted. It coincides quite closely with all relevant aspects of the economic and social life of the region.

FOREIGN INFLUENCE

The second reason for the delay lies in the fact that six of the largest landholders in the region were foreigners or foreign-owned corporations. Diplomatic officials could be relied upon to "make representations" to the government when disputes arose over water rights or over agrarian laws. An example of the activities of a foreign group is afforded by the Compañía Agrícola, Industrial, Colonizadora, Limitada del Tlahualilo, S. A., formed by British capital, later supplemented by money from the United States. It held in 1927 a total of 46,630 *hectáreas* (115,176 a.), of which 18,030 *hectáreas* (44,534 a.) were irrigable lands, 325 *hectáreas* (803 a.) of "temporal" (usable if rain is sufficient), and 28,275 *hectáreas* (69,839 a.) of pasture. The fiscal value was set by the company at 4,098,025 pesos ($2,049,013).

Disregard of agreements reached between the Federal government and the Tlahualilo Company led to a lawsuit that became one of the issues which exacerbated diplomatic relations between Mexico and the United States. The Mexican historian Francisco Bulnes lists this dispute as one of the ten reasons for the downfall of the Díaz regime.

The experience of the Tlahualilo Company furnishes a case history in the organization and conduct of a corporation in Mexico which is not an isolated phenomenon. In 1887 a colonization contract was granted to a relative of Porfirio Díaz. He was to bring colonists to the former bed of the Laguna de Tlahualilo, which had been dry for over fifty years. Mexico at that time was attempting to attract settlers from abroad and gave generous concessions to those who promised to bring them. The former lake bed provided rich soil but it was some distance from the Nazas River. On the ground that "There is plenty of water for all" he was granted the right to one-half of all the water from the Nazas, and was to be allowed to build a dam slanted upstream three-fourths of the way across the river.

The following year an English group incorporated themselves as the Tlahualilo Land and Colonization Company, taking over the previous concession. The company was allowed the use of the law of eminent domain in the construction of its canal, and was given several varieties of tax exemption. Colonists were to be settled on the land in the proportion of twenty-five foreigners to seventy-five Mexicans, and each colonist was to get three *hectáreas* (7.4 a.) of land plus tools and equipment for the working of the land.

The attempt of one of the upstream users to take half of the region's total water supply gave rise to protests from the downstream people. These protests were particularly vigorous when the company continued building the dam and closed the river entirely, utilizing an obscure equivocal point in the contract.

The company floated a loan of 350,000 pesos in London and

New York in 1896. A pamphlet issued at the time claimed that "except in years of extraordinary scarcity the company has more water than actually necessary to irrigate its entire area." The government later alleged that at the time the pamphlet was issued, less than half of the area mentioned as irrigated was actually cultivable.

The company secured injunctions against the government's 1895 attempt at regulation of the water supply in the general interest and fought the case through the courts until the Supreme Court ruled against it in 1909. At that time the company claimed monetary damages of $11,348,743 plus other unspecified damages resulting from the enforcement of the regulations. The fight against the Supreme Court's decision was taken to the British and United States governments and attempts were made to secure diplomatic intervention. Bulnes charged that the case was one of the reasons for the withdrawal of support of the Díaz dictatorship by the Taft administration. Even conservatives in Torreón do not hesitate to say that the only persons who made any money out of the Tlahualilo Company were its promoters. Thousands of investors in both Great Britain and the United States, according to local observers, were embittered toward Mexico by the maneuvers of the personnel which, first, kept them from knowing the actual state of the properties and, second, raised money for extensive legal fights to maintain themselves in their jobs.[1]*

INFLUENCE OF THE HACENDADO

La Laguna was one of the areas in which capitalism imported from abroad had been mated with rural feudalism to produce a hybrid set of economic and social institutions different from those of most of Mexico. Agricultural production was organized on a large-scale basis and almost exclusively for the market, instead of on the subsistence or semicommercial basis characteristic of much of the rest of the country. Machinery was extensively used; the wooden plow so ubiquitous in most of rural Mexico had practically never been used in the region. Agriculture had resulted from the comparatively recent installation of irrigation systems in a desert area and did not have its roots in pre-Columbian cultures.[2]

*Notes to this chapter begin on page 223.

Neither the ideology of the "men of the North" nor that of the "Indianists" seemed to supply feasible guides to action under the peculiar conditions of the region. Probably equally important was the often reported financial relationship between the big landowners of La Laguna and federal officials. Sizable contributions to campaign funds helped keep the Laguna region outside the range of consideration. The Laguna *hacendados* collected a purse of 100,000 pesos ($50,000) as a gift to President-elect Calles in 1924. Obviously, his acceptance of the money gave them fairly good assurance that the agrarian laws would not be applied during his administration. Similarly, a purse was offered President-elect Cárdenas in 1934. His refusal of the money caused the more intelligent landowners to start subdividing their haciendas.[3]

The Laguna peasants had kept up a constant agitation for land distribution. Fourteen petitions for land are on record between 1928 and 1934. Nothing came of these efforts until the federal government was under the control of a president who would listen sympathetically and who would dare to grapple with the new kinds of problems the region presented to the agrarian movement.

THE EVOLUTION OF LAGUNA LAND TENURE PATTERNS

Land tenure patterns differed from those in Indian Mexico for reasons involving geography and demography. The arid and semiarid plateaus of north-central Mexico were inhospitable to dense settlements of Indians. There were scattered, seminomadic groups living on the margins of rivers and lakes when the Spaniards came.[4] They died of smallpox, were killed in battles, or were driven into the mountains. Smallpox, introduced by the Spaniards, increased as the result of the conquistadors' practice of gathering Indians into towns. Beginning with the first epidemic in 1608, smallpox caused thousands of deaths.[5] Thousands of Indians also died during abortive revolts. Some of the uprisings, such as that of 1690, were settled by the restoration of lands, but gradually the Indians lost out. Even the Tlaxcalan Indians, who were brought to the region in 1598 as buffers against the natives, lost their water rights to Spaniards and as a result were almost entirely wiped out by hunger and disease.[6] Though a few Indians have migrated into the region in recent times, scarcely a trace of indigenous culture is found today. The extensive Laguna region was once known as "Shepherd's Corner" of an estate of more than 19 million acres. The area owned by Francisco de Urdiñola in the province of Extremadura was remarkable even among the enormous landholdings of early colonial times. As a favorite of the Spanish king, he held about 3 million *hectáreas* (7,410,000 a.) within twenty years of his arrival in the New World in the middle 1600's. The Marqués de Aguayo, by marrying Urdiñola's granddaughter (and her 3 million *hectáreas*), became lord of the vast domain.

A later Marqués de Aguayo resigned as governor of Coahuila y Texas, in 1722, to devote himself to enlarging his possessions. For 250 pesos and "half one year's income" the Marqués purchased most of the present Laguna region from the crown of Spain in 1731. He then owned more than 8 million *hectáreas*.[7]

For the next century little development took place. Cattle and sheep grazed on the lands and a few squatters worked strips along the river banks. The disturbances of the War of Independence (1811-1821) forced the then Marqués de Aguayo to sell his property. His descendants in Spain, the Sánchez Navarro family, owners in 1848, had to sell some of their holdings in that year to pay pressing debts.[8] Grazing then began to give way to agriculture.

Settlers had begun to move into the region following the War of Independence. As disturbances continued during the internal struggles between various factions, more uprooted families escaped into the semidesert region. They settled along the banks of rivers —traditionally central government property—or purchased land as economic pressures forced the sale of some of the largest properties.

Commercial crops, outside finance, improved transportation, industries, and demands for land propelled the region toward commercialism. Land values rose and with them rose the pressure to divide the latifundia. How far the region had been forced from the traditional landholding pattern is shown in Table 3. Capitalist organization of large-scale agriculture became the dominant system, although it adapted itself to the feudal heritage. The civil war swept through the region repeatedly, but the owners were able to retain control of the state and local governments and to name one of themselves or one of their retainers as commander of the federal army post located at Torreón.

Only a halfhearted attempt to apply the agrarian laws of the

1917 Constitution had been made before 1936. Corporate and individual ownership was dominant and was expressed in haciendas, *ranchos*, and *fraccionamientos* (in descending order of size, although no formal limits were recognized). The last named generally were worked by their owners, who had purchased them, often on time, from an *hacendado*. A few small plots were held communally by groups called *congregaciones* (villages of co-owners) or ejidos.

TABLE 3
ACQUISITION OF TITLE, BY METHODS
LA LAGUNA

	1 Coahuila (except Col. 3)	2 Durango	3 Cuadro de Matamoros
By inheritance	56.5%	52.1%	20.8%
By sale or foreclosure	43.5%	47.9%	79.2%

Source: 1932 survey by Ing. Heriberto Allera.

The Laguna region is one of the few areas in Mexico in which corporation farming became dominant. It had been one of the regional characteristics for over fifty years prior to 1936. Foreign corporations owned large tracts of land before the expropriations. The Tlahualilo Company has already been mentioned.

Another corporation was the British Guillermo Purcell y Cía., which owned twenty haciendas in the *municipio* of San Pedro. Santiago Lavín, a Spaniard, owned the Cía. Algodonera e Industrial de La Laguna, S. A., which held the 48,866 *hectáreas* (120,699 a.) called the Perímetro Lavín, valued at 2,027,254 pesos ($1,013,627).[9]

The three properties mentioned, plus three others, also foreign-owned, in 1927 were valued for tax purposes by their owners at 21,290,211 pesos ($10,645,105). The value of all farm property in the region in that year was 55,609,744 pesos ($27,804,872). There were 222 owners. In other words, less than 3 per cent of the owners, all foreigners, possessed 38.3 per cent of the property by value. The distribution of ownership by sizes is shown in Table 24, Appendix.

Leasing, renting, and cropping on shares were quite general. It should be noted that the percentage of the value of farms worked on such arrangements, 63.6, is almost three times as great as the percentage of the area, 22.9 (Table 25, Appendix).

The data just cited do not include those properties managed by superintendents working for absentee owners, either personal or corporate. Neither does Table 26, Appendix, which lists as owner-managed such properties as those of the Tlahualilo Company. It was one of the two listed in Mapimí. The other was an ejido. The twenty Purcell properties were included in San Pedro.

ECONOMIC HISTORY

The economic history of the Laguna region was marked by little change from colonial times until the second half of the nineteenth century. The breaking up of large scale landholdings did not begin until the 1850's, when grazing began to yield to agriculture. Settlement along stream banks, irrigation, the coming of railroads, industry, in-migration, and the development of towns marked the next fifty years.

Unfortunately for the new settlements, their downstream location was highly vulnerable. The first diversion dam was built in 1849 near the entrance of the Río Nazas into the Laguna basin. Other irrigation dams followed in increasing tempo. The first of a long series of armed clashes between downstream colonists and upstream *hacendados* began in 1862.[10] An 1880 battle had a thousand armed men on each side. The battle for adequate irrigation and control of water facilities continues to the present.

Torreón, which developed into the metropolis of the region, was the latest settlement. The name was derived from a tower built in 1850 as part of the dam and irrigation works of one of the haciendas. In the subdivisions which took place in the next decades, the Torreón ranch made its appearance, and a small settlement grew up around the tower.

The owner persuaded the Mexican Central Railway to make Torreón a stop on the El Paso-Mexico City route by the offer of free land for a station. The rails reached the tower on September 23, 1883. The Mexican International was next persuaded to cross the Central lines at Torreón, giving the farmers a connection with Durango on the west and Saltillo, Monterrey, and Piedras Negras on the east and northeast.

The rails crossed on March 1, 1888. The foundations of Torreón's coming prosperity were laid. In 1887 the owner had hired an architect to lay out the streets of the future city. Lots were sold with difficulty until the railroads joined. Then a boom began. Each train brought new groups looking for land. Tents were set up for stores. Wooden shacks and adobe huts were thrown together for living quarters.[11]

By 1895 the ten-year-old town of Torreón had a population of 3,969, a soap factory, a textile mill, and a brewery and ice plant. It had replaced the town of Viesca (founded in 1731) as the county seat.[12] The 1900 census showed 13,845 inhabitants, an increase of almost 10,000 in five years.

The first years of the town were marked by crises arising from lack of water in the Río Nazas. In 1888, 1889, 1891, 1893, and 1895 water was either absent or came in insignificant amounts. Crisis conditions in 1894 led to a riot of the unemployed. In 1896, a smallpox epidemic killed hundreds. The town continued to grow and to attract new industries in spite of these troubles.

The region possesses a much more adequate network of transportation and communication than do most areas of Mexico as a result of the major differences between its economic history and that of most of the rest of Mexico (Fig. 2).

SOCIAL INSTITUTIONS OF CAPITALISTIC FEUDALISM

Feudalism in its classical, European phase was characterized by the supremacy of the lord of the land. This was tempered by a system of mutual rights and obligations of lord and vassal. The serf was bound to the land but had a certain degree of security against the dangers of medieval society.[13]

The existence of rural feudalism in Mexico prior to the revolution has been established. The social system of the Laguna region prior to the application of the agrarian laws might aptly be called capitalistic feudalism. It partook of the nature of feudalism as a type, insofar as the entire social relationship revolved around landownership and the power which such ownership gave over the welfare and even the lives of the landless land-workers. It assumed a capitalistic character in that production was for the market and that the "cash nexus," instead of fealty to the lord, bound men together.

The masters of the land were to a considerable extent foreigners who disdained the "hands" both because they were peasants and

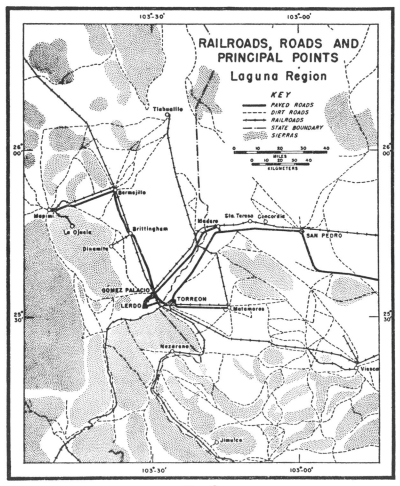

Fig.2

The Laguna region is a nearly level area almost entirely enclosed by sierras. The area is served by a network of highways and by three railroad systems. Torreón and two satellite towns, which compose the commercial and industrial center of the region, are located near the point where the Río Nazas enters the plain.

because they were Mexicans. Land and its products gave them the economic basis upon which they built political power. This enabled them to maintain their own police force and to depend upon the federal army if necessary.

The *casa grande* and its environs epitomized the feudal structure. Typically it was surrounded by high walls, with gun turrets at strategic intervals. The walls enclosed the church or the chapel, jail, warehouse, machinery storage sheds, possibly a cotton gin, and in some instances a school. The residence was often used only for part of the year; the owner spent much time in Mexico City or abroad. The hired manager was in residence all year. Sometimes he had a house in Torreón in addition to his rural residence.

No adequate survey of the social system of the Laguna hacienda was ever made. Conditions varied from one property to another. Some owners and managers were harsh, others benevolent. On some haciendas the schools required by Article 123 of the 1917 Constitution had been erected and teachers hired. The Madero family had supplied hospitals on several of its properties, but on the vast majority there was a complete absence of medical care for the peasants. Company stores, saloons, and gambling houses characterized many haciendas. Many of the riding bosses who supervised work in the fields carried whips and wore revolvers.[14]

In general, the Laguna region had its share of the practices prohibited by the 1917 Constitution and the labor code based on it. The more important of these provisions were: payment in cash instead of company script or in kind; wages not to be paid inside any store or saloon; employers forbidden to maintain stores on their properties or to prohibit the creation of free markets; peonage for debt is outlawed; and sons may not be made subject to debts contracted by their fathers.

A commission investigating the region in 1927 and 1928 recommended that some of the bitterness found between owners and their peons could be lessened by abolition of blacklists, building of schools required by the constitution, provision of more adequate housing and of small garden plots near homes of the workers. The commission suggested that the many days of idleness a year could be used to raise small animals or fowl or cultivate a garden.[15]

The housing of the people varied from one hacienda to another, depending largely upon the humanitarian feelings of the *hacendado*.

Sometimes adobe row-houses were built by the owner and furnished to the peasant rent-free, as long as he "behaved himself." Often the peasants were allowed to erect their own huts on hacienda land, subject to the same warning. Danger of petition by their peasants for application of the agrarian laws was sometimes met by expulsion of the workers and destruction of their homes, so that they could not prove the legal residence required to become eligible for a grant of land.[16]

A consistent pattern of clusters of peasant houses isolated from roads which might have public transportation facilities was dominant. Only the *hacendado* and his agents thus had access to transportation. The same was true of communication media on most of the haciendas. Post offices were few and far removed from most peasants. Even if the peasant could have read, newspapers and other contacts with the world outside were usually effectively denied him.

Education and organized recreation were almost exclusively the prerogatives of the land owner and his family. They were obtainable in the urban centers; reachable only by those with cars. Baseball in the peasant villages provided one of the few exceptions. It had been brought back from the United States by some of the civil war refugees and by those who had heeded the call from north of the border for farm hands.

Spaniards, Germans, British, and Americans had exclusive clubs in Torreón. The Casino maintained dancing, gambling, and other club facilities for the *hacendados* and the "properly introduced" businessman. A country club, with golf, tennis, and swimming, was guarded to see that the only poorly-dressed persons admitted were the servants. Even the rich and well-dressed Syrian retail store owners of the city were not admitted, although they had "contributed" a sizable sum to build the club. The "contributions" were solicited by the chairman of the finance committee who was the commander of the regional garrison.

The Laguna region lies in a section of Mexico where the church was never as strong as it was on the southern part of the Central Plateau. However, the churches which did exist were found on the side of the landowners before and during the revolution. In this region, as in other parts of Mexico, the church suffered because, as a Roman Catholic source has declared, "Church institutions had tied their external position to the politicians of the old regime and to the aristocratic land system."[17]

One of the first actions of the peasants when the revolution broke out was to shoot the bells out of church steeples. Their hatred was poured out upon the bells because these had been tolled in the mornings to awaken them and send them to the fields for the day's work from which they could not return until the bells again tolled in the evening. In some cases a checkoff system had been worked out by the *hacendado* and the priest so that tithes were taken from the peon's wages and turned over to the priest by the landowner.

In the Laguna region and immediate vicinity priests carried on an intense propaganda against agrarianism. A peasant union (Sindicato de Campesinos de Durango) in 1922 sent to the archbishop of the state a detailed complaint of the political activities of his priests, among which the following specific cases are found:

Fr. Reyes of Gómez Palacio is so violently anti-agrarian that he refused to administer the last rites to Eulalio Martínez merely because in life he had been an agrarian.

Fr. Santiago Zamora of Mapimí sustains on every occasion that taking possession of idle lands is theft, and that the government which authorizes it as well as the *campesinos* and their families who benefit by it, are bandits.

Juan Sarmiento, parish priest of El Oro, is openly engaged in politics. We have seen him take part in every election. He carries on his propaganda undisguisedly and recommends his candidates. He attacks agrarianism harshly and takes every opportunity to asperse the Constitution of 1917.

The priest of Nazas, Manuel Gallegos, is an avowed protector of the *hacendados* of that region, whom he serves unreservedly, attacking article 27 of the Constitution within and without the church.

The priest of Tlahualilo . . . affirms that the government is a thief because it robs the *hacendados* of lands which in his view it has no right to touch.[19]

During the rebellion of 1927 the commander of the military garrison at Torreón reported rebel activity organized by the Catholics in that area.[20] According to another student of Mexican affairs, "The Archbishop of Durango endorsed this sanguinary civil war" in a pastoral letter issued from Rome, which stated in part:

To our Catholic sons risen in arms for the defense of their social and religious rights, after having thought at great length before God and having consulted the sagest theologians of the city of Rome, we say to you: Be tranquil in your conscience and receive our benedictions.[21]

Credit arrangements, both private and governmental, strengthened the hold of the larger owners.[22] Farming in the Laguna region has always been a gamble. Large sums of money invested in the planting of cotton have been lost when the Nazas failed to deliver enough water. The periodic crises arising from water shortages led to the loss of parts of the properties held by the large landowners.

Money was borrowed by the early Laguna owners either from private individuals or companies dealing in cotton. The result was a tendency toward carving up the region into a few large properties, the owners of which could take the risks of bad years. A new tendency developed early in this century; that of "sharing the risk" by renting, leasing, or sharecropping land. The outcome of this tendency already has been noted. The risk was also shared by the majority of the peasants who worked on a day-labor arrangement and who spent many days of the year in idleness and without income.

The federal government has operated a rediscount agency in the Laguna region since 1916 through one organization or another. The first was the Comisión Monetaria. Within a few years the local office was in such poor condition that it had to close with 27 million pesos ($13,500,000) worth of bad paper. One person alone, a lessee of several large haciendas, had been lent 20 million pesos without the legally required collateral. Of this, 9 million ($4,500,000) was a total loss.[23]

CONFLICTS OVER WATER RIGHTS

The "dog-eat-dog" competition characteristic of the frontier days of railroad building, prospecting for precious metals, buying range lands, and assuring water sources, in the United States, also characterized the building of irrigation dams and canals in the Laguna region. The case of the Tlahualilo Company has already been mentioned, as have the armed clashes between retainers of large upstream owners and the smaller "downstreamers."

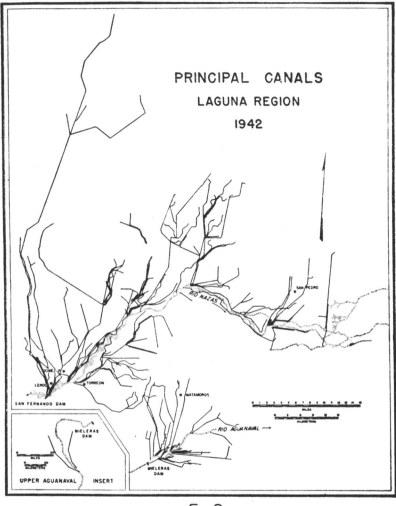

Fig.3

The canal system of the Laguna region is like Topsy—it just grew. Millions of dollars have been spent in building duplicating facilities with canals running mile after mile a few yards apart. Many canals crisscross, one running over another in a concrete trough. It is obvious from the map how much more important in supplying water for the region is the Río Nazas than the Río Aguanaval.

Favorable locations fell to the first comers; their canals were then closely followed by others until the entire irrigable surface was a topsy-turvy network attempting to get something from an undependable source of water (Fig. 3). Ten dams and twenty-eight principal canals have been built in the Río Nazas system, and four dams and four principal canals on the Río Aguanaval. Dams were located close to each other and canals only a few feet apart were run parallel for miles. There are many instances of one canal crossing others. While this system has often been attacked, it should be noted that it was not illogical under the circumstances of land tenure at the time. It is, however, completely illogical and uneconomic in terms of an attempt to plan for the region as a whole.

The struggle for water turned from armed force to political action when regulation of the Nazas' flow was attempted first by a federal law passed in 1891 (reformed in 1895 and again in 1909), which continued in effect until the expropriations in 1936.[24] These regulations were enforced intermittently.

The regulations of the federal government set up a Comisión Inspectora del Río Nazas, which was responsible for the operation of the dams and the equitable distribution of water, but the uneven flow of the river plus political interference made its work exceedingly difficult. (Fig. 4.) Each of the principal canals was controlled by its users, in most instances one or two men or a company. Regulation of the water of the Aguanaval was not put into effect until 1926.[25]

Regularization of the Nazas water flow through the construction of a storage dam had been discussed for more than fifty years. Francisco I. Madero wrote a book on the problem in 1907.[26] The region has been split on the desirability of a dam. Large owners generally opposed it, small owners favored it.

ATTEMPTS AT AMELIORATION

Obviously the stage was set for trouble if and when the national and state governments decided that the labor, agrarian, and social welfare provisions of the 1917 Constitution were seriously to be applied to the Laguna region.

Successful small-scale attacks on the dominant system had occurred between 1917 and 1930. The peasants of eleven com-

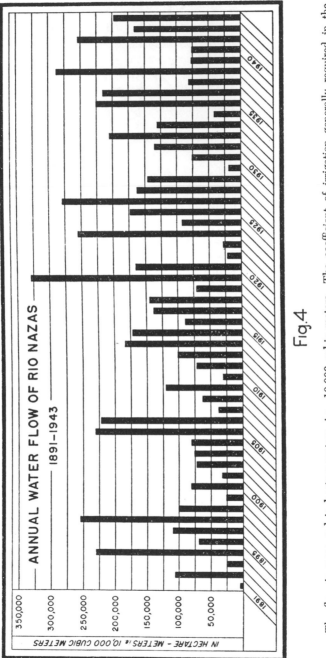

Fig. 4

The flow is measured in hectare-meters, i.e., 10,000 cubic meters. The coefficient of irrigation generally required in the Laguna region is water to the depth of 1 meter over each *hectárea* of cultivated land. The yearly flow is extremely irregular. In addition it is generally badly timed from the standpoint of efficient irrigation.

64

munities had been able to secure land grants benefitting 2,318 heads of families and totalling 5,600 *hectáreas* (13,832 a.).[27]

All these ejidos, with one exception, were on the periphery of the region. The lands were of little value, water was scarce or completely lacking, and the distance to commercial centers was great. But these small concessions to the laws of the country were virtually the only indications between 1917 and 1930 that the constitution of Mexico applied to the Laguna region. The world-wide depression of the latter year led to widespread misery among the peons and stimulated demands for social change. By 1934 agitation for applications of the agrarian legislation in the region had reached a serious stage. The Chamber of Agriculture, hoping to head off any drastic moves, in that year offered to purchase land on the outskirts of the region and give it to the peasants who wanted land. In exchange they asked for perpetual immunity from application of the laws. President Abelardo Rodríguez agreed to this arrangement and on October 15, 1934, decreed the creation of two ejido districts. One in Durango contained six properties totalling 1,460 *hectáreas* (3,606 a.) of allegedly irrigable land. The other in Coahuila covered four with 2,843 *hectáreas* (7,022 a.). Altogether, 1,025 heads of families were settled in the two districts.[28] This device succeeded for a time in removing from the haciendas small groups of "agitators," but more serious trouble was to come the following year.

The peasants had attempted from time to time to organize unions and demand the application of the federal labor law. It was not until 1935, however, that they felt the possibility of support from the president of the Republic. Lázaro Cárdenas had been elected the previous year; his campaign speeches were not so much promises of what he would do as exhortations to the people to do something for themselves. He advocated labor and peasant unions, cooperatives, and women's civic and educational groups.

Peasants on the Hacienda de Manila struck in September, 1935. Their demands included the signing of a collective bargaining contract, increases in wages to 1.50 pesos (42 cents) a day, reduction of hours to eight per day, and the right to name a checker when cotton delivered by the peasants was being weighed.

The strike was partially successful and was followed by others. One important strike was called by a union which had been formed by an *hacendado* as a guarantee against labor trouble! Strikes were answered by discharges, evictions, and arrests, which 'in turn led to greater bitterness and more strikes. A general strike was called for May 26, 1936, as a protest against wholesale discharges of those active in organizing peasant unions. At the request of President Cárdenas the strike was postponed and a commission of experts, with members agreed upon by both employers and workers, was appointed. After three months the commission presented a report favoring the workers. When the employers refused to accept the report, a general strike call was again issued for August 18. The state labor services of both Coahuila and Durango immediately declared the strike illegal and the military zone commander supplied soldiers to protect strikebreakers.

President Cárdenas, feeling that a stalemate had been reached in the region, called the strike leaders to Mexico City and asked them to end the strike in exchange for his promise that the agrarian law would be applied in the region as soon as possible. With this promise the leaders returned to Torreón and called off the strike. A local office of the Agrarian Department was set up in Torreón and engineers began to study the region with a view to the expropriation of lands to satisfy the peasant demands.[29]

On October 6, 1936, Cárdenas decreed the expropriation of about three-fourths of the irrigated land and one-fourth of the nonirrigated usable land in the region. This land was turned over to approximately 30,000 peasants organized into about 300 ejidos, or communal farms. A new stage in the economic history of the Laguna began. "King Cotton" had been toppled from his throne.

The answer to our first question, "How are peasants to achieve the power to carry out land reform" is seen to have involved eleven years of civil war, some decades of the spread of new ideas and the nation-wide organization of those who wanted social change. It was not until the land-workers of La Laguna organized and acted for themselves that they were able to secure application of national laws to the region.

Overnight the majority of the peasants found themselves plunged into attempts to solve problems which had not been solved by generations of the pioneers of La Laguna, with a voice where they had been silent, with responsibility for decisions the terms of which they scarcely knew. Their world expanded from the limits of their village to the circumference of the earth. It became a world in which decisions by Tokyo textile tycoons or at Washington Cotton Crop Conferences directly affected their chances of success or failure in their new role of owners of the land.

They found that many of their problems were intimately connected with the geography of the region—with the natural resources, the rain, the river flows, the subterranean water level, the hail and the frosts—and with the patterns man had already woven in the use of those resources. It is to the geographic stage which is La Laguna we now turn and to the economic forces which have "set the stage."

Chapter 4

GEOGRAPHIC AND ECONOMIC FACTORS
IN REGIONAL DEVELOPMENT

*E*CONOMIC DEVELOPMENT is deeply influenced by geographic factors, particularly if the economy is largely based on agriculture. An understanding of the agrarian experiment of La Laguna depends on an understanding of some of the elements of the geography of the region. Climate, soil, topography, natural vegetation, water resources, and occurrence of minerals all have their role to play in setting the stage for success or failure. The ejido which is located on good soil with adequate water obviously has an initial advantage over others located on alkaline or rocky soil with no dependable water supply.

BASIC NATURAL RESOURCES

The region is technically classified as "desert steppe"—flat, arid, with scanty undependable rainfall. Annual mean temperature is around 70° F., but December and January are often marked by frosts and by destructive hailstorms. Highly developed agriculture would be impossible without irrigation.

A successful growing season in the Laguna region requires adequate floods from the rivers at the proper time, rain also properly timed, frosts no later than February, and absence of hail. However, the major and minor rivers have always been highly undependable as sources of irrigation water, both in quantity and timing, and late frosts and hail are frequent.

68

Soil fertility varies greatly from one part of the region to another, depending partly on the nature of the drainage. Irrigation with wells has brought problems of excess alkalinity as well as lowered water levels.

KING COTTON IN LA LAGUNA

Cotton was king in the region and its environs for over a century. The region was the chief cotton producer of Mexico for many decades. Both situations have changed.

The earliest notice of cotton in the state of Durango mentions sizable crops on the banks of the Río Nazas from 1811 to 1827. From 70,000 to 80,000 arrobas (875 to 1,000 metric tons) were cropped near the town of Cinco Señores (now Nazas) about 46 miles west of the Laguna region. Other areas along the Nazas brought the state total up to 250,000 arrobas. Only an insignificant portion of this came from the region as here defined. After irrigation works were built, the natural advantages of the climate caused a shift to the region. Cotton is ready to pick in the region in about five months instead of the seven required upstream.

Competing with Durango in the early days were tropical and subtropical regions of the Gulf Coast of Mexico. Cotton was grown in middle colonial times in Oaxaca and Veracruz.[1*] As late as 1906, a Mexican economist wrote: "The best lands of the world for cotton are the coastal lands of Veracruz. The soil is rich, the salt breeze helps make a stronger fiber, and humidity makes the plants extraordinarily productive."[2] Cotton was once one of the main crops of the state of Yucatán, which for the past seventy-five years has dedicated its land almost exclusively to raising henequén.[3]

The great textile center of Mexico, the Río Blanco-Orizaba-Atlixco district of the states of Puebla and Veracruz, was originally built on the water power of the region plus its nearness to the Gulf Coast cotton-producing centers. That center has maintained its lead in spite of the major shift of cotton production to the desert and semidesert regions of the north. Figures for the nation's cotton production for 1945 and 1950 show the Laguna region as first in area, yield, and production (Table 27, Appendix) in the former year. By 1950 the newly developed Matamoros region was out-

*Notes to this chapter begin on page 225.

stripping the Laguna region in acreage and production, although not in yield. Mexico is in the midst of a cotton "boom." The years between 1925 and 1954 saw an increase of 435 per cent in area planted to cotton, and a ninefold rise in production. Only 171,929 *hectáreas* had been cropped in the former year as compared with 919,128 in the latter (Table 4). The rate of increase has risen sharply since World War II.

TABLE 4

MEXICAN COTTON PRODUCTION, AREA, YIELD
1925-1926 TO 1954-1955
(crop years)

Crop Years	Area Hectáreas	Production Metric Tons	Yield Kilograms per Hectárea
1925-1926	171,929	43,467	253
1926-1927	248,184	78,016	314
1927-1928	132,041	38,862	294
1928-1929	203,243	60,376	297
1929-1930	198,938	53,344	268
1930-1931	157,944	38,487	244
1931-1932	129,114	45,581	353
1932-1933	77,854	22,015	283
1933-1934	171,696	56,465	329
1934-1935	169,123	48,345	286
1935-1936	266,062	68,256	257
1936-1937	342,967	86,127	251
1937-1938	335,991	73,591	219
1938-1939	259,782	66,494	256
1939-1940	262,308	67,645	258
1940-1941	253,657	65,495	258
1941-1942	316,097	81,209	257
1942-1943	362,216	102,952	284
1943-1944	408,893	115,873	283
1944-1945	389,614	106,120	272
1945-1946	365,816	97,586	267
1946-1947	327,443	91,137	278
1947-1948	332,832	95,927	288
1948-1949	404,678	119,668	296
1949-1950	548,786	207,690	378
1950-1951	760,534	260,019	342
1951-1952	883,504	287,612	326
1952-1953	784,047	264,542	337
1953-1954	753,484	273,699	363
1954-1955	919,128	389,734	424

Source: Dirección de Economía Rural, Secretaría de Agricultura.

La Laguna has contributed substantially to national production during this time (Table 5). It still in 1954 maintained the lead in yield and had increased its production about 650 per cent in the past two decades. It has fallen behind other regions in volume because it has not been able to expand its crop area as Matamoros and Mexicali have.

TABLE 5

COTTON: TOTAL AREA CULTIVATED, PRODUCTION, AND YIELD
LAGUNA REGION
1930-1931 TO 1953-1954
(crop years)

Crop Year	Area Hectáreas	Production Bales of 507 Lbs.	Yield Kilograms per Hectárea
1930-1931	68,870	141,446	472
1931-1932	43,231	59,340	316
1932-1933	78,800	175,853	513
1933-1934	60,751	132,350	502
1934-1935	66,468	146,412	507
1935-1936	133,100	173,000	299
1936-1937	120,000	140,000	268
1937-1938	89,670	147,000	377
1938-1939	85,300	133,000	359
1939-1940	73,908	105,016	327
1940-1941	105,984	120,846	262
1941-1942	120,000	203,931	391
1942-1943	151,328	262,298	398
1943-1944	143,316	191,266	307
1944-1945	134,103	187,411	321
1945-1946	108,410	144,704	307
1946-1947	100,518	160,025	366
1947-1948	76,968	159,952	478
1948-1949	84,700	210,000	570
1949-1950	121,930	245,223	443
1950-1951	121,144	215,563	410
1951-1952	139,102	227,655	377
1952-1953	134,324	230,272	395
1953-1954	140,170	232,385	382

Source: Dirección de Economía Rural, Secretaría de Agricultura.

COTTON IN THE WORLD ECONOMY

Cotton is a good cash crop for the Laguna but it is also a risky one. Cotton was left standing in the fields along the banks of the Nazas in 1825 because the importation of cheap foreign cloth depressed the price. Corn and wheat were planted in place of cotton. Demands for protection from foreign competition were sent to the central government. The world has been influencing La Laguna ever since. Its chief product is the second most valuable raw material in international trade, surpassed solely by petroleum. Only sugar rivals it as the commodity with probably the most uncertain future in the world economy. The past existence and future probability of unmanageable surpluses has led to the creation of the International Cotton Advisory Committee "to observe and keep in close touch with the world cotton situation." The committee, representing both producer and consumer countries, eventually must attempt to stabilize international cotton trade, it is to be hoped on the basis of increased consumption.

The United States, the world's largest producer and exporter, is committed to a price support policy in the field of cotton which is out of line with its general proposals for freer international trade. Its subsidy to exporters places United States cotton in a most favorable competitive position.

Brazil has entered the world picture as an exporter in recent years. Russia has begun to meet eastern European and even British needs. The cotton trade of the world is almost completely governed by import or export controls, or both. The major part of the world's cotton is grown under direct or indirect government price and production schemes. The world outlook is complicated by United States "dumping," as it is referred to in Mexico.[4]

Mexico is deeply concerned about the world cotton market, even though she produces only about 2 per cent of the global total. Her exports now amount to three times the domestic use: 1,350,000 bales sold outside in 1956 compared with 450,000 bales consumed domestically. This, plus high levels of production in the United States and other major growers, indicates why cotton prices have been erratic in recent years.

Mexico is caught in a dilemma in view of her high degree of dependence on exports of cotton cloth. If her export tax is reduced, the Japanese and Indian textile mills will buy her cotton more cheaply and thus compete more advantageously in world markets with Mexican textile exports![5]

Cotton prospects on a world-wide basis seem to be only fair. Flax and synthetic substitutes have both been outstripping it in recent decades. Total world consumption in 1948 was 5,946,000 tons, a decrease from the 6,620,000 tons of a decade before.[6] On the other hand, world rayon production increased from 1,016,000 tons in 1939 to 1,226,000 tons in 1949, in spite of serious war damages in Japan, Germany, and Italy. They were the world's largest producers before the war but were surpassed during the fighting by the United States, which now produces well over one-half of all rayon.

TEXTILES IN THE MEXICAN ECONOMY

Home manufacture of clothing and serapes is found throughout Indian Mexico. It is almost exclusively based on wool, however. Near the Laguna region this was early supplemented by machine spinning, weaving, and the making of cloth from both wool and cotton. The industry developed near the city of Durango where water power was available. Then it moved to the periphery of the region and finally the most important factories shifted to Torreón and Gómez Palacio.

A cotton goods factory in Durango city ran from 1811 to 1822. Fifteen years after its failure a German and a Mexican started a factory on the Río Tunal, near Durango. Machinery was shipped from Germany and New England to Matamoros, Tamaulipas, by sailboat and carried the thousand miles overland by oxcart and muleback. Operations began in January, 1841. Forewomen had been recruited from the mills near Boston and were "models of cleanliness and hard work." Some trouble was encountered in getting the Mexican women to remove their *rebozos* (shawls), which caught in the machinery. The owners reported very little other trouble with the two hundred workers, three-fourths of whom were women and children.

Most significantly, they list as one of their chief troubles "a division of property so vicious that almost all the Mexicans can say with the Romans 'we have only enough land to build a hut and dig a grave for ourselves.'" The result of "rural feudalism," they reported, "is a society in perpetual anarchy."[7]

The mill was reported still running in 1885. Durango had seven textile mills in that year. La Constancia, in Mapimí, was one of them. The owners decided in 1888 to move it to Torreón. Better transportation for both raw material and finished goods, plus tax exemption granted by the Coahuila legislature, dictated the move.[8]

La Constancia and La Fé, the latter founded in 1898, became the backbone of the regional textile industry. Smaller plants, such as one with 350 looms maintained on the Hacienda "El Rosario" up to 1897, had to give way. La Estrella, a mill started in Parras by the Madero family in 1870, is now one of the largest in the northern states. La Constancia mill was completely destroyed when the Villa forces occupied the city in 1914. La Fé is now the region's only important cotton textile producer. It hires nearly six hundred men and women.

Textiles are Mexico's oldest industry, so competition with the regional factories is widespread. The cotton branch is the most important, with 80 per cent of total textile production. Most of the looms are old, if not obsolete. Except for its favorable position near raw materials, the Torreón cotton mill is typical of the national industry.

A study by the United Nations Economic Commission for Latin America in 1951 found 85 per cent of Mexican spindles and 95 per cent of the looms out of date. The number of man-hours-per-kilogram of production was estimated to be 269 per cent higher in Mexican cotton mills than in standard modern textile plants.[9] A 1957 publication of the textile unions' international trade secretariat reported 20 modern plants out of a total of 313.[10]

Several commissions have been appointed by the government, by the industry, and by the textile workers' unions to investigate the conditions of the factories. While it is admitted that the mills generally are inefficient, high-cost producers, both owners and workers have expressed their opposition to modernization. Many of the owners are content to drift along behind high tariff walls. Workers fear the introduction of speed-up systems which caused so much trouble in United States mills in the late twenties.

The Bank of Mexico and Nacional Financiera estimated that modernization of the industry would require an astronomical invest-ment of close to two billion pesos ($231,213,872) in 1951 prices, and suggested a twenty-year period for the drastic changes such a program would involve. The ECLA report recommended that rudimentary improvements in plant organization and management practices could increase productivity measurably without substantial investment.

The war cut down exports of raw cotton, but caused a sharp

rise in cotton textile exports. They increased from 0.5 per cent of all production in 1939 to 34 per cent in 1946. Central American and northern South American countries raised their imports to replace goods the United States could no longer supply. Increased export demand plus more effective consumer demand in Mexico during the war led many factories to put on second and third shifts, and pushed up the price of textiles to heights unknown in recent years. In November, 1943, a bolt of coarse cotton cloth (*manta*, the only factory-woven cloth known to most rural people) cost 95 pesos ($19) compared with 54 pesos ($10.80) one year earlier.[11] Exports of cotton goods were prohibited for a short time in August, 1943, in an attempt to hold down domestic prices, and were resumed under licensing restrictions and export taxes.[12]

The end of the war brought a drop in cotton textile exports and a slackening in the increases in production which marked the war and immediate postwar period. Exports made up only 10.7 per cent of total production by 1950 and average annual increases in production dropped to 2.6 per cent for the 1946-1950 period compared with 8.6 per cent during the previous five years.[13]

Mexico is close to the world average in per capita consumption of cotton (Mexico = 5.8 lbs.; world = 6.25 lbs.) but still has a long way to travel to bring its average up to that of the United States, which is 25 pounds.

The industrialization of Mexico was speeded up by the war. Since increased consumption of cotton goods is highly correlated with industrial activity, it would seem likely that the domestic market will absorb a greater production than previously.

However, the general price level for textiles was 285.2 in 1950 (over a base of 100 in 1939). This was reflected in only a small increase in domestic consumption (124 in 1946-1950 over 100 in 1939). Population increased faster than consumption during the same period so that per capita textile use decreased to 99.4 per cent of the 1939 figure. One needs only to drive along any rural road or urban slum street in Mexico to realize that the decrease is not a reflection of decreased need but of decreased "effective demand." The International Bank points out that the only reliable market for the textile manufacturers to seek is the domestic market.[14] That can be expanded only by lowering prices.

Rayon-cotton mixtures might lead the way in reducing textile costs and eventually help increase domestic consumption of cotton. Mexico's rayon-making "infant" industry is a result of the war, which cut off imports from Japan and Italy and reduced the ability of the United States to fill orders. Production began June, 1942, and by 1949 amounted to 9,000 tons. Some of the more modern plants are weaving cotton-rayon cloth.

All of this points to an era of stiff competition in which cotton will have to struggle to hold a significant part of its once dominant position. The wolf is just outside the door, unless the consumption of soft fibers is increased greatly, as it would be if all persons who need clothing had the money to purchase it. The rate of increase in the use of cotton and rayon shows no evidence of approaching the potential increase in production, however.

Mexican cotton must be prepared to cope with these conditions —but there are few signs that it is or will be.

COTTON DISEASES AND PESTS

La Laguna suffers from the same kinds of biological handicaps found in all major cotton areas of the world.

Among other notable events in the Laguna region is the first appearance of the pink boll worm in the Western Hemisphere in 1915. It seems to have been imported from Egypt in some seeds for an experimental plot of the Chamber of Agriculture. An investigating commission from Mexico City in 1917 met with such lack of cooperation from the growers that it returned home defeated. In the same year, a representative of the United States Department of Agriculture made a study of the new danger to North American cotton. As a result, an International Commission was formed in that year. Later a regional commission was organized.[15] Since that time there has been continuous cooperation between Mexican and United States authorities in the fight against this and other cotton pests.

Losses of a fourth of the total crop were reported as common in a study made in 1928, and loss of as much as one half of the crop was not infrequent.[16] The Secretary of Agriculture estimated that the loss from pests and diseases in 1940 was 20,000 bales, or almost a fifth of the total production.[17] An unofficial but reliable source has estimated that the losses per season are as given in Table 6. This would make a total of 61,420,755 pesos for five years.

The principal pests are: Pink bollworm (*Pectinophora gossypiella*); Boll weevil (*Anthonomus gradis Boh*); Cotton leafworm (*Aletia argillacea Hbn.*); Corn worm (*Claridea absoluta*); Conchuela del Algodón (*Cholorochroa ligata*); Cotton aphid (*Aphis gossypii*); Grasshoppers (*Melanoplus differentialis*); and Lubber grasshoppers (*Brachystola magna*). The chief diseases are Wilt (*Neocosmopora vasinfecta*) and Root rot (*Phimatrotichum onivorum*).

TABLE 6
VALUE OF COTTON DESTROYED BY DISEASE AND PESTS
LA LAGUNA
1936-1937 TO 1940-1941

Date	Loss in Pesos
1936-1937	17,232,209
1937-1938	12,916,072
1938-1939	12,382,625
1939-1940	11,048,949
1940-1941	7,840,900

Source: Secretaría de Agricultura, Torreón office.

Occasionally a swarm of locusts bred in the Durango mountains devastates a portion of the region's cotton fields. A cloud approximately four miles long and three wide swept the northern edge of the *municipios* of Mapimí and Tlahualilo in July, 1943.[18]

Two weeds have also caused tremendous damage; Johnson grass (*Andropgon halepensis*) and Zacate Chico or Grama grass (*Hilaria genchorides*). Only in the past few years since collective action has become an accepted technique has any real progress been made in coping with these and similar handicaps to higher productivity in the region.[19]

REGIONAL RIVALS OF KING COTTON

Laguna agriculturalists generally have demonstrated a belief in putting their eggs in one basket, or at most two. Wheat was a relatively late development, as an auxiliary crop to cotton. Corn, beans, and squash—subsistence crops—were the first cultivated in the region when settled agriculture started about a century ago.[20] Later, small numbers of fruit trees were planted near the river banks. As cotton gained in importance, these crops were all but abandoned and the region imported foodstuffs which formerly it had grown.

Alfalfa became an important crop as the number of mules increased. Some *hacendados* saw its value as a soil-builder and as protection against a drop in the prices of cotton and wheat. It was also valuable for the dairy herds of the Laguna and nearby regions. Beans, corn, melons, tomatoes, grapes, figs, and peaches are the only vegetables or fruits of any present importance; grapes are the leaders by far. The Laguna is part of a larger region which holds first place in Mexican grape production.[21]

Wheat, the second most important crop in the Laguna region, has been increasing in importance in recent years. The region held third place as a source of the nation's wheat from 1926 to 1937. During this period, it planted 5.6 per cent of the total wheat area and supplied 8.3 per cent of the production. It has moved up into first place as a producer several years since the expropriations. By 1944-1945 it planted 16.3 per cent of the total area, supplied 21.8 per cent of the production, and 21.6 per cent of the total value.[22] Recently other irrigated regions have surpassed it.

Lack of, or badly-timed, irrigation water, and frosts, wind, and hail storms have already been mentioned as handicaps to greater productivity in the region. Occasionally damage is caused by high humidity, which encourages fungus growths. The three wheat "plagues" known in the region are called locally *pulgón,* or plant lice (*Toxoptera graminum*); *chapote,* or pill bug (*Porcellio scaber*); and *hongo,* or rust (*Puccinia graminis*). In 1939 the first caused damage of a quarter million pesos.[23] However, most other wheat-growing regions have greater handicaps. Recent data show La Laguna with the second highest yield of seventeen wheat growing regions; 29 per cent above the national average.

Soft and semihard winter wheat of red and white varieties predominate. The two most important red wheats are Colorado Manzano Torreón and Colorado Torreón, the two whites are Blanco Torreón and Blanco Norte semiduro.[24]

The region is highly mechanized as compared with most other parts of Mexico. This is expressed in the high percentage of use of tractors, seeders, and combines. Seven types of cultivation are found, depending on the nature of the soil and the availability of water. They are given in Table 28, Appendix, with the average cost of production (including interest and taxes), yield, and profit per *hectárea*; and cost and profit per metric ton at a price of two hundred pesos ($41.24) per ton. Breakdowns for the highest and lowest cost types are given in Tables 29 and 30, Appendix. The average cost per *hectárea* was 193 pesos ($38.97) per acre in the 1926-1937 period. The average cost per metric ton was 137 pesos ($28.24).[25]

The region's experience with wheat is shown in Table 7. Total production can be compared for the six years before and ten years after the expropriations. From 1931 to 1936, a total of 228,484 metric tons was raised in the region. From 1937 to 1946 the total was 579,005. Averages were 38,080 for the first period and 57,900 for the second, or an increase of 52 per cent. The annual average

TABLE 7

WHEAT: TOTAL AREA CULTIVATED, PRODUCTION, AND YIELD
LAGUNA REGION
1930-1931 TO 1953-1954
(*crop years*)

Crop Year	Area *Hectáreas*	Production Metric Tons	Yield Metric Tons per *Hectárea*
1930-1931	33,333	38,591	1.29
1931-1932	27,629	32,784	1.19
1932-1933	45,073	50,007	1.11
1933-1934	30,016	33,000	1.10
1934-1935	18,295	22,202	1.21
1935-1936	37,000	51,900	1.40
1936-1937	26,500	29,451	1.11
1937-1938	52,353	66,939	1.27
1938-1939	69,500	85,000	1.22
1939-1940	59,021	90,000	1.52
1940-1941	57,778	63,957	1.11
1941-1942	70,420	56,479	0.80
1942-1943	40,485	46,126	1.14
1943-1944	33,664	35,094	1.04
1944-1945	57,042	79,954	1.40
1945-1946	31,916	26,005	0.81
1946-1947	57,228	62,405	1.09
1947-1948	69,679	80,151	1.15
1948-1949	56,991	63,777	1.12
1949-1950	91,405	88,705	0.97
1950-1951	66,783	47,215	0.71
1951-1952	31,934	27,644	0.88
1952-1953	27,114	23,513	1.00
1953-1954	26,500	30,807	1.11

Source: Compiled from raw data sheets in the Dirección de Economía Rural.

for the fifteen years following the change (1937-1951) reached 61,417 metric tons. Thus, in wheat as in cotton, total production increased, although much more sharply. However, the drought years have hit wheat production hard since expensive well water is applied with more profit per hectare to cotton than to wheat. Thus, there has been a steep drop in wheat production in the past few years. The tonnage for 1952-1953, for example, was almost as low as in the great drought year 1934-1935.

The region shows the highest profit per ton, that of 80.53 pesos ($16.60), for the wheat resulting from the seventh type of operation described in Table 28, Appendix. The lowest profit per ton in Mexico is found in the State of Oaxaca, 14.64 pesos ($3.02). With few exceptions, the higher profit regions are in the northern and northwestern parts of the country.[26] ·

Proper timing of water flow and other factors being equal, it is more profitable to raise cotton than wheat. The area of wheat which gave a profit equivalent to one *hectárea* of cotton in 1939 was as follows for each of three types of mechanization: light, 1.98 *hectáreas;* medium 1.96; heavy, 1.87.

Until 1941 no sustained experimentation on seed had been carried on in the region. Usually Canadian seed was imported and planted each year. A few years ago a large consignment of Kansas red was planted without previous tests. It failed completely.[27]

When it is considered what great strides have been made in the United States and Russia in obtaining better yields from improved strains, it would seem that the Laguna agriculturalists have failed signally in planning to expand profit possibilities in wheat. One of the peasant demands in recent years has been the establishment of "a real experiment station."

The demand for wheat and other foodstuffs has risen markedly in the recent past as a response to increased incomes, nutrition education, and increased urbanization, but Mexican wheat production lagged behind the demand until 1955-1956. That crop year Mexico met its domestic needs for the first time, with a record production of 1.2 million tons.[28]

COMMERCIAL DEVELOPMENT

Mexican commercial census data draw a distinction between "economic" and "backward" *municipios*. Only 5,529,000 persons of the total population of 19,450,000 lived in "economic" *municipios,* according to the 1939 census. Such *municipios* are defined as those in which there is at least one factory with an annual production of 10,000 pesos ($2,062) or more.

Only 112 of the country's 2,325 *municipios,* or about 5 per cent of the total, met this test in the 1939 Industrial Census. Within this twentieth of the political subdivisions of the nation live 28 per cent of the population. This fraction of the people carries on 82 per cent of the commerce of the country.[29]

Coahuila included only six "economic" *municipios,* of which three were in the Laguna region. Saltillo, the capital of the state, was listed among the thirty-two "backward" entities. Durango contains thirty-seven *municipios,* of which three were classed as "economic." Two were in the region; the other was the capital of the state. The region's five "economic" entities are Torreón, Gómez Palacio, San Pedro, Lerdo, and Matamoros, in order of importance commercially.

Torreón stands out as having larger stores, selling more expensive goods, and paying higher wages and salaries than any other entity in the region. Torreón's sales averaged 525 pesos per capita in 1938, compared with 120 for Mexico as a whole, 130 for Gómez Palacio, 70 for San Pedro, 44 for Lerdo, and 36 for Matamoros.

Authorities agree that retail sales have increased significantly since the expropriations, but the only indices available do not take us back beyond 1938, which surpassed most previous years. An index is available for six groups of consumer goods by which 1946 experience in the region may be compared with a 1938-1939 base. The index for December, 1946, stood: clothing and notions, 597; yard goods, 88; work clothes, 257; groceries, 110; drugs, 105; shoes, 256.[30]

The upward trend of clothing and shoe sales should be noted especially. If furniture stores were included they would undoubtedly show an even greater increase, since thousands of peasants and their families now sleep in beds instead of on straw *petates* laid on the earth floor.

The leading local daily, *El Siglo de Torreón,* in its review of 1937 wrote:

The acquisitive power of the peasant population rose considerably, and on a much greater scale than the city workers, notwithstanding the fact that the latter also obtained advantages in the social struggle.

The following year's review was more specific:

1938 was in general a good year; the level of sales rose considerably above previous years and held up to the end. . . .
Especially in clothing, shoes, hats, hardware, drugs, etc., there was considerable movement with consequent profit. . . . The increase in business was due to various causes, among others being the better distribution of money as a result of ejido work. The distributions of profits by the Banco Ejidal, even when not great, always start waves of buying which become noticeable immediately after the distribution. . . . With the increased purchase of shoes in place of old *huaraches;* hats of better quality for *huicholes;* better clothing for women and children; beds and other furniture; tableware and kitchen utensils, the desire of the peasant for material improvement has been demonstrated.

Since the fall of 1937 there has been an almost uninterrupted construction boom in Torreón. All the principal retail stores have been remodeled. New chromium, glass, and marble fronts have been added to old buildings, and many new modernistic stores and homes have been built. The erection of 2,000 new buildings in the three-year period, 1937-1939, was matched by 2,134 built in the next three years. In the latter period, 5,289 permits for major repairs or remodeling also were issued.[31]

Comparison of the 1939 and 1952 telephone directories show these changes: Drug stores, increased from 26 to 67 listings; doctors, 50 to 110; dentists, 8 to 18; and hotels, 13 to 25.

Torreón's position as a commercial center as early as 1899 is indicated by the seven hotels it had at that time. Its population was about four thousand.[32] Early founders of retail stores and services such as laundries and restaurants were Chinese. They had achieved enough wealth by 1906 to found a bank. For many years their orchards and truck gardens supplied the region as well as their chain of railroad restaurants. Their colony was almost wholly wiped out during the civil war.

Their place was taken by Syro-Lebanese, now the largest group of owners of small establishments. Several have become money lenders to small farmers and one runs a small mattress factory. Occasionally one finds competitors resorting to the same kind of anti-Semitic agitation used against Jewish retailers in the United States.

The larger businesses, including the hotels, are predominantly in Spanish hands. German activity has always been important in hardware, stationery, photo supplies, and farm and other machinery. In recent years a number of sons of former hacendados have established local outlets for United States products, for example, automobiles, radios, and tractors. Repair shops, garages, and filling stations have become increasingly important. Many of the mechanics formerly worked in Detroit or picked up automotive experience as migratory workers in beet, cotton, and fruit picking.

INDUSTRY

Metallurgy, vegetable oils and soap, textiles, and guayule rubber are the principal industries.

As in most of Mexico, the oldest industry is mining. Mapimí in the last half of the past century and the first decade of this was a thriving mine and mill center. Mineral production from its seventy-seven mines in 1886 was valued at 672,978 pesos ($336,489). There were a smelter and six foundries. Gold, silver, lead, copper, sulphur, and salt were mined.

Viesca was another important mining district in the past century. Velasco lists sixteen copper-lead-silver mines there in 1897, and notes that dozens of abandoned mines, homes, furnaces, wells, and holes testified to previous activity.

Seven British and United States concerns of importance were listed in the 1914 *Mexican Yearbook* as running mines in the region. All but two of these have passed from the scene. Mining was revived in parts of Mapimí by the high prices of copper and lead during World War II. No figures are available on the number now employed, but it probably does not reach much more than two hundred. There are also a few mines on the western edge of the *municipio* of Lerdo, and salt is still produced in Viesca.

While mining proper is peripheral, both economically and geographically, the largest plant in the region lives from mineral production. The Cía. Metalúrgica de Torreón has a 1,350-ton smelter with an arsenic department and eight 1,000-ton furnaces. It is owned by the Cía. Metalúrgica Peñoles, S.A., which is controlled by the Cía. Minera de Peñoles, in turn controlled by the American Metal Co., Ltd., of New York. The latter is one of the two United

States concerns which produce all the smelted and refined lead in Mexico. Cía. Minera de Peñoles owns the leading Mapimí silver-lead mine and claims on copper land in Viesca.[33]

The metallurgical and mining companies were both originally Mexican firms, the first being headed by Ernesto Madero. The Peñoles company owned 3,545 *hectáreas* of mining properties, smelting works, an electric power plant, the railroad from Mapimí to Bermejillo, and three other mining properties. Both were absorbed in the 1920's by American Metal Co., which also owns silver, lead, and zinc mines, a lead smelter, an arsenic plant, and a flotation plant in the other parts of Mexico as well as mines and plants in the United States.[34] The Torreón plant is among the largest of the 127 in Mexico.

Low grade bauxite has been reported many times in the vicinity of Mapimí. Two large United States firms, American Smelting and Refining Co. and American Metal Co., have considered development possibilities. Further work depends locally on the availability of water power and coal for concentration and reduction.

Processing of agricultural products is also important to the economy of the Laguna region. The chief industries are cotton-ginning, wheat milling, vegetable oils and soap manufacture, and the elaboration of rubber and wax from two desert shrubs, guayule and candelilla.

One of the obstacles holding back further industrial development is a serious power shortage. Mexico has suffered from such shortages for many years, although big strides ahead have been made in the recent past. The power production index rose to 179.7 in 1950 (1929 = 100). While the Laguna region was ahead of most other sections of the country until recently, the capacity of local plants was reached several years ago.

A combination of restricted generating facilities and a "thin" market in the rural districts had led to a distribution system inadequate for pumping units, rural industries, or lighting. Only about half the pumps in the region use the system. The others use Diesel or other internal combustion engines at the well. Four small Diesel plants generate power enough for a dozen to twenty *ejidal* wells each. Many private properties have small plants for their houses and barns. The San Pedro and Matamoros town plants are obsolete and break down practically on schedule.

Plans for Lázaro Cárdenas dam called for the erection of a supplementary dam downstream which would store 180 million cubic meters of water. The combined hydro-thermo plant to be built will produce 116 million K.W.H. per year. A fifteen-year study showed that 79 per cent would come from water power and 21 per cent from the steam plant. In the most unfavorable year of the study period, 42.4 per cent would have had to come from steam.

Regional cooperation to build the power dam and plant has been discussed for years. A mixed company would be formed by the Central Union of Collective Credit Societies, the Chambers of Commerce and of Industry, the small property owners' association, and the federal government. The *ejidatarios* and the government would invest 3 million pesos each, the small farmers 2 million and the business men and industrialists 2 million, to raise the 10 million pesos ($2,016,000) required. The prolonged drought has stilled such discussion in recent years.

It is hoped that the dam, plus modernization of some of the plants in the smaller towns, will enable the rural districts to be electrified.

Industrial fuels used locally are oil and coal. Direct railroad connections with the northern Coahuila coal fields and the Tampico oil fields have kept costs in the region below those of less favorably located zones. Monterrey uses natural gas, however, and there is competition between several regional industries and those of "the Pittsburgh of Mexico." A move to bring natural gas to Torreón from near Tampico has been under study since the summer of 1943. The same meeting which launched the plan for the mixed electricity company voted 10,000 pesos ($2,016) for a survey of pipe-line possibilities. Unsatisfactory rail deliveries are a factor as well as lower cost fuel. Homes generally rely on wood and charcoal for cooking and occasional heating. The widespread use of gas would help the campaign against ruinous deforestation in Mexico.[35]

TRANSPORTATION AND COMMUNICATION

Colonial road building in Mexico was largely confined to arteries for the movement of precious metals from the country. The main north-south highway connected Mexico City with Querétaro, Guanajuato, Zacatecas, Durango, Chihuahua, and Santa Fé in the province of Nuevo México. It passed some two hundred miles west of the Laguna region.[36] Durango remained the center of the roads and mule trails for this section of the country during most of the colonial and Independence periods. The nearest metropolis to the east was Monterrey.[37]

Generally, railroad builders followed the same plan as colonial road builders. Many and bitter have been the criticisms of the manner in which foreigners built the Mexican lines without regard to the internal economy of the country.[38] However, geography, which placed so many handicaps in the paths of transportation and communication in Mexico, helped Torreón become a railway center. It was much easier to run the rails down the central plateau than to follow the old stagecoach route along the Sierra Madre Occidental. Tannenbaum mentions the Laguna region as one of the few areas in the country where railroads influenced agricultural organization.[39]

Within the larger haciendas are narrow-gauge tramways on which mule-drawn flat cars transport cotton, wheat, and supplies. At the time of the expropriations there were about eight hundred kilometers (496 mi.) of these *vías de Decauville* (named for the Belgian town in which the equipment is manufactured) in use. They were acquired by groups of ejidos at a cost of around 600,000 pesos ($166,677).[40]

Both railroads and tramways have given way in many instances to bus and truck transportation as highways and local roads opened up parts of the region which could formerly be reached only by rail or by horse. The Laguna region is now undoubtedly the best served in Mexico, after the Federal District. Buses run on regular schedules from Torreón to San Pedro, Matamoros, Bermejillo, Mapimí, and El Palmito, as well as to Durango. Connections across the desert to Saltillo and Monterrey are available nine times daily, each way.

Most of the regional bus lines are owned and operated by cooperatives of the workers who borrowed money for the purchase of equipment from the government bank for cooperative promotion. Demands on all the lines have increased sharply since the expropriations. The peasants now have much greater mobility than they had before. Some of the needs are met by the trucks and buses they now own, but the public carrier system is straining under the new load.

Trains and buses are supplemented for long distance travel by daily plane connections with Mexico City, Ciudad Juárez, Monterrey, Durango, Mazatlán, and La Paz, B.C.

Adequate postal service is available in the towns, but there is an increasing and unfulfilled demand in the rural districts. Outside the urban zone of Torreón there are only fifty post offices in the entire region. Prior to the change of systems there was not much mail to and from the rural regions. Since 1936 there has been a great increase in both first- and second-class mail. The lack of official postal service is partly filled by school inspectors who travel throughout the region by motorcycle, car, or horse and who collect and distribute mail in addition to their regular duties.

There are three local radio stations, of 100, 200, and 500 watts. Two have connections with national chains. Weekly they transmit "The National Hour," which is a government report to the nation through all the stations in the country.[41] They also carry public speeches, educational material, and civic announcements. Many ejidos have purchased community radios, and groups listen in to ball games and other important events.

Cultural factors working on its peculiar geography have combined to bring the Laguna region much closer to the "outside" world than are many other Mexican regions—this in spite of its physical location in the middle of a desert some five hundred miles from the boundary with the United States.

Provision of more adequate transportation within the region and with the outside world is no accident. The Automobile Club of Torreón, the Chamber of Commerce, service clubs, and, since the expropriations, the *ejidatarios* have formulated programs and pressed them before local, state, and national governments as well as with private transportation firms.[42]

This type of civic action is so rare in Mexico as to merit special mention. It is an indication of a significant difference in outlook of the Laguna local leadership as compared with that of other regions. It is part of what people have in mind when they say "Torreón is the most Americanized town in Mexico."

The contrast between the "Americanized" metropolis and the rural feudalism of the hinterland was often mentioned to the author as one of the factors in producing widespread discontent. The old social system had made a more or less satisfactory adjustment to the geographic and economic hazards of the desert environment and the one-crop economy. It was the small landowner, the tenant farmer, and the peasant who suffered most when drought, hail, frost, or locusts plagued the region or when prices fell precipitously. What was the new system which would attempt to cope with these and other problems?

Chapter 5

THE FRAMEWORK FOR AGRARIAN DEMOCRACY

*N*EW SOCIAL AND ECONOMIC INSTITUTIONS were created for the region almost overnight following the expropriations. The decree of October 6 cut through many of the legal and political difficulties which had deferred the coming of agrarian reform. It could not, in the nature of the case, eliminate the social results of years of feudalism nor many factors in the Mexican heritage which have interfered with building democracy.

CREATION OF NEW INSTITUTIONS

An ambitious attempt was made to create democratic forms which could then be filled in with democratic meanings by the development of the people themselves. The first of our major questions, "How do the peasants get the power to bring about agrarian reform?" had been answered. Now came the second, "How is democracy to be achieved?" Neglect or refusal to separate the two questions has been one of the important factors in limiting the extension of democracy. The Mexican revolutionaries, as many others throughout the world, confuse the achievement of power with the achievement of the revolution.

The Laguna experiment was launched as a result of peasant pressures plus a friendly hand at the helm of the federal government. It started suddenly, just as did the revolution of 1910; it was planned at the last second, not forecast and thought through.

It had no firm body of policy and doctrine to guide it; it was experimental, just as the revolution had been. It did have one great advantage; the people involved were brought into participation. This was confined, on the whole, to regional matters, however. But many of the decisions were outside the reach of the people of the region, both temporally and spatially. The problems and solutions of other times and other places still influenced what happened in La Laguna.

APPLICATION OF THE AGRARIAN LAWS

However, the Cárdenas program broke with past agrarian practices in important respects. In his message of explanation to the Mexican people he said:

Groups of peasants were in the past given worthless bits of land, and lacked farming implements, equipment, credit and organization; this was meagre fruit indeed after the great sacrifices made to attain it. The ejido so conceived would have ended not only in disappointment but also in giving large land owners one more excuse for cutting down to a still viler level wages that were already vile enough, alleging that farm hands now had an additional means of livelihood.[1]*

The expropriation decree of October 6, 1936, was based on the agrarian code of 1934. Among other things, this code provided that no fewer than twenty persons must join in applying for land. If their petition was favorably acted upon by local, state, and national authorities, land was to be granted to them at the rate of four *hectáreas* (9.88 a.) per person. Eligibility of the peasants was determined in several ways. The chief criteria were residence within seven kilometers of the property to be affected, and at least six months of work in the region.

The decree affected 114,814 *hectáreas* (283,590 a.) of irrigable land in the region and 127,272 *hectáreas* (314,362 a.) of the 1,314,224 *hectáreas* (3,246,133 a.) of land classified as nonirrigable but usable for pasture and other purposes.

The principal points of the decree were as follows:

A minimum of 150 *hectáreas* (370.5 a.) of private property used for farming was to be respected as inalienable.

*Notes to this chapter begin on page 227.

The location of this area would be chosen by the owner. If a proprietor were left with land beyond that legally requested under the agrarian law by the peasants and beyond his 150 *hectáreas*, he might divide this land into areas of not more than 150 *hectáreas* and sell these areas with the security that they would be inalienable.

If the lands in the region were found to be insufficient to meet the needs of all the peasants legally entitled to land, the government would provide land in other parts of the country and move those families who wished to move.

Owners who contributed toward the cost of creating the ejido districts (mentioned above) were to be reimbursed for their actual outlay.

New regulations for the use of the waters of the Nazas and the Aguanaval were to be drafted.

The Banco Nacional de Crédito Ejidal was given responsibility for organizing ejido credit societies, for supplying them with funds, and for the direction and control of agricultural work on the ejidos.

The Banco Nacional de Crédito Agrícola was given responsibility for supplying credit to small property owners in the region.

The nature of the large-scale agriculture which had developed in La Laguna made it obvious that much previous practice in land distribution was not applicable. Cotton and wheat grown on irrigated land require exploitation on a fairly large scale and with expensive machinery to bring economic success. The answer was the cooperative ejido, an adaptation of the Zapatista ideology with its legacy from both Aztec and Spanish land tenure, plus some of the aspects of the Russian *kholhoz* and of the experience of the Farm Security Administration in the United States.

The Cárdenas program broke with previous theory, but it did not escape the effect of the habits developed among the personnel who were to carry out the redistribution of land in the region; neither could it escape the limitations of a legal code based on the idea that the ejido should be purely a supplement to the hacienda system. These handicaps led naturally to a series of moves which profoundly influenced the development of the new system.

A land tenure map of the Laguna region shows a "crazy quilt" pattern. Some ejidos have plots of land separated from each other by several intervening private properties (Fig. 5). Some have almost 100 per cent of their area in first-class lands; others have almost their total area in lands practically worthless agriculturally. Some

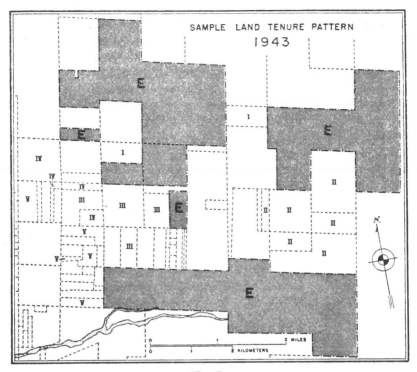

Fig. 5

The area represented by this map is located near the eastern end of the usable waters of the Río Aguanaval, shown by stipple in the lower left-hand corner of the map. In this section one ejido (E) contains 876 *hectáreas* of irrigable land and 1,346 *hectáreas* of nonirrigable land in five noncontiguous plots. The ejido membership embraces 82 families. Roman numerals I to V represent private properties of different individuals or families. While legally each plot shown with a separate number is a separate property, the contiguous properties shown with the same roman numerals are worked as a unit, e.g., roman numeral II.

The area included in the property of family II is 465 *hectáreas*. In the upper left-hand corner of the map note the U-shaped area cut into the ejido property. The property owner to the north chose to retain this area because it contained one of his wells.

All the owners but family II hold other property outside the section shown. The small strips not numbered or lettered belong to other small owners.

ejidos were cut off from irrigation ditches and roads. In one case known to the writer a well which was planned to supply supplementary irrigation for an ejido was discovered to be considerably lower than the land it was to irrigate. In computing the total area of irrigable land serious errors were made, and lands which had been irrigated only during seasons of exceptional river flow were classified as irrigable. In some cases the boundaries of ejidos overlapped each other. In other cases, ejido boundaries encroached on private property and vice versa. The Tlahualilo hacienda was divided into thirteen ejidos and around one hundred fifty small properties, thus crippling the unity of one of the most important large-scale enterprises in the region.

Possibly the most serious move of all was the inclusion in the agrarian census of most of the seasonal migratory workers who were in the region at the time of the expropriations. This meant, first, that in the ejidos were included thousands of persons who were not full-time farmers and who had none of the stable habits of persons who for years had worked the land the year around, and second that the *ejidal* system was burdened with a much larger number of persons per unit of workable land than had been true in the past or was to be true of the private properties in the region.

When to the lack of previous preparation is added the fact that the reorganization of the region was brought about in forty-five days, the possibility of errors in judgment, political and personal influence, and hasty surveying and map-making are seen to be overwhelming. Not a single soil, land-use, or adequate topographic map of the region was available to guide the engineers, for example.[2]

When accounts were cast, it was found that 6,918, or almost one-fifth, of the peasants legally qualified to receive land had not been able to secure a place in the new system. This has proved to be an irritating factor throughout succeeding years. Coupled with it is the fact that Article 51 of the 1934 agrarian code provided that in cases in which there was a scarcity of land the inalienable area could be reduced to 100 *hectáreas* (247 a.). Peasant leaders have never ceased to ask why this provision has not been implemented.[3]

Payment to the owners for improvements on the land expropriated, for example, wells and warehouses, was made by the federal government in ten annual installments and totalled 10,566,000 pesos ($2,893,150). Agrarian bonds, issued in payment for the land itself, were not applied for by many of the owners. Their position was that they would weaken possible court actions against the government by applying for or accepting the bonds. No figures have been made public on either the total land values or the bonds accepted. The basis of valuation was assessed value plus 10 per cent.

TENURE SINCE THE EXPROPRIATIONS

The region in 1943 displayed the following forms of land ownership:

"Collectivized" ejidos, owned and worked cooperatively, which totalled 140,616 *hectáreas* of "irrigable" land occupied by 28,388 members of 262 ejidos.

"Parcelized" ejidos, owned cooperatively but worked individually; 12,443 *hectáreas* for 3,164 peasants in 47 ejidos.

Private property owners numbered 1,539 and held 57,118 *hectáreas*.

Agricultural colonies, in which individual ownership is supplemented by a certain degree of community cooperation, which numbered 23, with 829 members and 17,655 *hectáreas*.[4]

To these groups should be added a small but undetermined number of persons who have permission from the federal government to take advantage of strips of unoccupied arable land along the banks of the two main rivers.

Ejidos, both cooperative and parcelized, have certain common characteristics. The land in both is owned by the group as a whole, not by individuals. This is not a foreign idea to the Mexicans. The Aztecs had the same law.[5] The group and its members have a "use title" to the land. They can not sell, lease, rent, mortgage, or alienate the land in any way. Nonuse for two years is the only method by which one may lose title. The plot or the membership in the cooperative ejido reverts to the group if a family moves away or dies out. Aztec and early Spanish legal usage contained the same provisions.

Most of the 28,388 members of cooperative ejidos in 1943 were heads of families. Their ejidos owned lands totalling 322,227 *hectáreas* (795,901 a.). The "urban zone" of the cooperative ejido villages covered 1,361 *hectáreas* (3,362 a.). The rest of their land, or 180,250 *hectáreas* (445,217 a.), was usable only if extraordinary amounts of river water were available, or if rains should happen to be heavier and better timed than usual. Theoretically, each *ejidatario* was entitled to four *hectáreas* of irrigable land, but a study made of the amount of land cultivated in the 1937-1938 season showed that a relatively small proportion of the *ejidatarios* were able to work that much in that year, because of water shortages (Table 31, Appendix).

The urban zone of the parcelized ejidos contained 165 *hectáreas* (407 a.) and the remainder of their 203,197 *hectáreas* (501,896 a.) was arable only under the conditions mentioned for the nonirrigable land of the cooperative ejidos.

Each colonist in the twenty-three colonies owned land varying in area from ten to fifty *hectáreas*. There were also pasture lands used in common by members of the colonies.

Some of the changes in the first fourteen years can be seen by statistics, presumably for 1950, contained in the detailed agronomic study published in 1951.[6]

Unfortunately, no distinction is made between cooperative and parcelized ejidos. Ejidos are shown with the following land:

Irrigable	149,139 *hectáreas*
Dependent on rainfall	7,752
Pasture and waste	248,139
	405,030 *hectáreas*

Ejidatarios numbered 30,337 in 1950. Assuming the figures on area and membership to be correct for both dates, there was a reduction in irrigable *ejidal* lands from 153,059 *hectáreas* in 1943 to 149,139 *hectáreas* seven years later—a drop of 2.6 per cent. The number of members dropped from 31,552 to 30,337 in the same period, or by 4 per cent.

This may well reflect two phenomena: desertion of lands which proved to be completely unproductive, which would reduce the *ejidal* population, coupled with natural increase in the ejidos which remained organized and in possession of their lands, which would offset the population decrease from out-migration.[7]

Private properties increased from 1,539 in 1943 to 2,394 in 1950, a rise of 55 per cent. Their area rose from 57,118 *hectáreas* of irrigable land to 61,591 *hectáreas*, or 8 per cent. They also held 31,537 *hectáreas* of pasture and waste.

The area of irrigated land per capita in 1950 of the two major land-tenure systems was, therefore:

Ejidos	4.4 *hectáreas*
Private properties	25.7

The average for the private properties does not show two phenomena of importance: (a) the fact that 5 per cent of the owners held 26 per cent of the private land and 14 per cent owned 55 per cent, and (b) that even these data underestimate the amount of concentration because they do not reflect the simulated sales which took place widely on the eve of and immediately following the expropriations.[8]

Furthermore, it should be noted that 66 per cent of the land possessed by the private owners was irrigable land while only 37 per cent of that of the ejidos was so rated.

ORGANIZATION OF THE COOPERATIVE EJIDO

The structure of the cooperative ejido was worked out in many days of discussion among the peasants and between them and Cárdenas and his advisors. The president stressed their link with the country's Indian past in his message to the nation explaining the government's moves in La Laguna.

Following is a short summary of the structure and main functions of an ejido which works with the Banco Ejidal through a Society of Collective Ejidal Credit, a legal entity usually coinciding in membership with the membership of the group owning the land.

The members in general assemblies elect an administrative committee of three members and three alternates as the executive body of the ejido. From among the members one is chosen to be the executive officer in certain matters.

Supervising the work of the administrative committee and of the individual members in their appointed tasks is an elected vigilance committee. It is particularly charged with seeing that the land is used in the best possible manner, and that ejido investments (such as in machinery, mules, and goods for the cooperative store) are well made. Its president, acting jointly with the executive officer of the administrative committee, signs the legal papers of the society. If two "tickets" are presented at the election, and the minority obtains more than 30 per cent of the votes, it elects the entire vigilance committee.[9] Twenty to 30 per cent entitles it to name two members and 10 to 20 per cent, one. Members of both committees serve for three years.

General assemblies also elect a work-chief, or foreman, and his assistants. They also elect a warehouseman, a herdsman, a manager for the cooperative store, if one exists, and other important officers in charge of community undertakings. The key man is the work-chief. Each week he meets with the administrative committee, the vigilance committee, and a representative of the Banco Ejidal to map out the work program. He makes a detailed distribution of work to each member, keeping track of what is assigned and what is accomplished. Each member carries a work card, which at the end of the week shows what he has done and to what weekly compensation he is entitled. A duplicate card is kept by the ejido office as a check and in case the original card should be lost. The work-chief also keeps a detailed daily record of the use of the society's machinery, animals, feed, fuels, and other resources. Weekly, the Banco Ejidal representative sends a summary of the work to the bank headquarters, where records are compared with past performance and with those of other ejidos.

Obviously, few of the *ejidatarios* were prepared for such fundamental measures of democratic control over their economic activities. The Banco Ejidal had been charged by the president with furnishing the technical guidance they would need, as well as credit. The cry was raised immediately that the bank was to be a dictator over the *ejidatarios*. A common expression heard by the writer during a visit to the region six months after the expropriation was, "The peasants will soon learn they have exchanged their old bosses for a single new one. And the new one will be impersonal and heartless. The personal bond between the owner and his people will no longer protect them." Two business men in Torreón and one in Saltillo made the same prophecy to the author, "Give them two years and they'll crawl on their hands and knees begging to be put back to work for their old employers."

The record of the Banco Ejidal is by no means spotlessly white. However, during the first four years of its existence (1936-1940) it consistently endeavored to train the *ejidatarios* to be able to accept more responsibility. Since then it has wavered according to political pressures dealt with later. Its organization and its efforts in this direction will be described in the sections on credit, peasant organization, health, irrigation, and education.

"FREE" EJIDOS

There are cooperative ejidos which do not work with the Banco Ejidal. Such ejidos are colloquially called *ejidos libres*. They may have ceased operating with the bank for any of the following reasons:

Bank refusal to continue advancing credit. (The bank may suspend or liquidate the credit society but it may not take the land from the group.)

Private credit arrangements made with some individual or firm.

Enticement of the group or its leaders by a local or state politician who offers credit on easier terms than those of the bank in exchange for political support within the powerful Confederación Nacional Campesina (National Peasant Federation) to which all *ejidatarios* belong.

The society has saved enough from its profits so that it can finance its own crops.

An analysis of a 1943 list of "free" ejidos showed a total of 49. The number had risen to 101 by March, 1946, and to 121 by August, 1948. The largest group, 29, was found in the Gómez Palacio area where political interference by the governor of the state has been the most persistent. Adverse economic factors would seem to govern in the majority of cases, however, since the "free" ejidos uniformly have smaller area, lower yields, fewer members, and fewer tractors, mules, and wells, and more back debts.

PARCELIZED EJIDOS

The administrative machinery of the parcelized ejidos is less complex. The principal committee is called the Comisariado Ejidal. It is composed of the same number of persons and elected in the same manner as the administrative committee in the collective credit societies. A vigilance committee of three members and three alternates is also elected and serves the same general functions as in the other type.

Parcels are laid out by the agrarian authorities and are assigned by drawing of lots among the *ejidatarios*. The lots are then worked as a family plot and are handed down to the heir of the *ejidatario.* The holder has a "use title." The Avila Camacho administration pledged itself to supply each parcel user a certificate of title, showing the boundaries of his plot, and the Alemán and Ruiz Cortines governments have continued the slow process of surveying to lay the basis for the issuance of such documents.

Lerdo stands alone as an example of the success of the parcelized ejido. It has made only qualified progress in spite of two favorable factors not present in the rest of the same class of ejidos; nearness to markets and an almost certain supply of irrigation water. The members have been wiser than other *ejidatarios* in this group. They have not tried to raise cotton, but have planted fruit trees and grapevines and cultivated vegetables for the urban markets.

Modern machinery is almost entirely absent in the parcelized ejidos and the agricultural technics are in general duplicates of those used in other regions of Mexico which have never had the advantages of mechanization.

CREDIT FACILITIES

One of the most crucial factors of success in the gamble which is farming in La Laguna is credit.[10] It has been seen that the federal government underwrote credit for the *hacendado* of the past and took much of the loss. It still plays the same role, but today with the participation of the peasants who are now landholders.

The Banco Nacional de Crédito Ejidal is now the chief regional banking institution. The Banco Nacional de Crédito Agrícola, an older institution, carries on minor operations. The number of private banks and other credit institutions has increased.

The Banco Ejidal had the bad luck to be called "bank," and therefore it is widely expected to follow orthodox banking procedures. It is striving to do so now but in the early days of the new regime it was forced to be a combination of banker, agricultural expert, family doctor, school teacher, lawyer, athletic director, cooperative store organizer, seed selector, machinery salesman, and wet nurse.

The bank was created in December, 1935, as part of the Cárdenas program to take the agrarian movement out of the hands of its enemies and attempt to carry out the original revolutionary slogans.

The first agrarian bank had been organized in 1926. Although, theoretically, it was to help the peasants who had secured plots of land, actually a large percentage of its resources was spent in loans to large landowners, most of which were never repaid. Another portion of its capital was used to lend money to the village usurers who then lent it at the usual exorbitant rates to the local *ejidatarios!*

The Banco Ejidal, it was hoped, would break with these practices. It was forbidden to lend money to individuals, and in addition to its lending functions, it was charged with the task of bringing modern techniques to the peasants and supervising their organization into groups through which they were to be educated in the use of these techniques.

Legally, the bank is an autonomous corporation. Ownership is held in three classes of stock: Class A, subscribed by the federal government; Class B, open to subscription by state and local governments, and Class C, salable only to local credit societies. Local credit societies had to purchase fixed percentages of Class C stock as they borrowed money under the original plan. It was hoped that in time Class C would outvote the government stock and thus the peasants would have achieved control of their credit institution. Although this hope is a vain one under present conditions or those of the foreseeable future, it does mean that the peasants have a voice and a vote in the annual stockholders meetings of the bank. They have representation on the board of directors, which consists of nine full members and five alternates. Four of the regular members and two alternates are chosen by the federal government; two and one respectively, by Series B stockholders; and three and two by the *ejidatarios.*

The bank makes two classes of loans and helps the credit societies arrange for a third. They are called *avío, refaccionario,* and *inmobiliario.*

Avío loans run for not longer than eighteen months and are made to keep a local credit society going during land preparation, cultivation, and harvesting operations. The loan may be made up to 70 per cent of the expected value of the forthcoming crop and must be repaid from the proceeds of that crop.

Refaccionario loans may run from one to five years and are used to finance the preparation of new land for cultivation, the purchase of farm machinery, work animals, fertilizers, or other goods or equipment which will last more than one season. Generally, the loan must be repaid in equal annual installments.

Inmobiliario loans are made for longer range purposes, such as permanent improvements, and may last as long as thirty years.

Interest rates are high compared with those charged for loans in the United States. The credit societies pay the bank 8 per cent and they charge their members an additional 1 per cent for administrative and operating expenses. Private agricultural credit in Mexico brings interest of 12 per cent at the least. Generally it runs between 18 and 25 per cent and in the less developed communities may exceed 100 per cent.

Originally bank stock had to be purchased to the extent of 1 per cent of the *avío* loans, 3 per cent of the *refaccionario*, and 5 per cent of the *inmobiliario*. A revision of the law provided that the societies which do not wish to subscribe to bank stock are obligated to place in a "collective guaranty fund" of their own the above-named amounts. This fund was to be used to carry the share of the debt left by members who have died or who have become incapacitated for work or other losses to the group which arise from causes outside of the will of the members. In addition, each society was required during the first few years to maintain a social fund which in no case could be less than 5 per cent of the gross proceeds of the season's crops. It could be used only for community purposes, such as schools.

The social fund was made voluntary in 1942. The move was followed by widespread charges that the bank took this step in order for some of its officers to sell farm machinery to the ejidos which had accumulated substantial reserves.[11]

An example of the financial transactions of the Ejido Barcelona is given in Table 8. The sale of wheat raised by the *ejidatarios* of Barcelona at 200 pesos per ton brought a return of 96,770 pesos ($19,354). After both business and community deductions were made, 77 members of the ejido divided 53,676.75 pesos ($10,735.55) among themselves.

The bank is divided into the following eight departments; credit, trust, technical, commercial, legal, organization, administrative services, and bookkeeping, and operates through thirty-five agencies located in the most important agricultural zones of the country.

Working with the Banco Ejidal nationally in 1955 were 27 unions of *ejidal* credit societies, 48 collective credit societies formed for special purposes (such as joint ownership of a generating plant by a number of ejidos), 7,998 local credit societies, and 460,040 members representing a peasant population of 2,600,000. This is an increase of 2,792 societies and 53,289 members above the 1936-1946 annual average. The bank still served only 26 per cent of the peasants who have received land under the agrarian program.[12] Many ejidos are now self-financing or receive credit from other governmental institutions such as the Bank for Foreign Commerce,

TABLE 8

EXAMPLE OF EJIDAL FINANCIAL TRANSACTIONS
EJIDO BARCELONA, STATE OF DURANGO
1939

(in pesos)

Repayment of one-fifth of loan for machinery, implements, and semipermanent improvements (*refaccionario*)	6,116.31
Interest	600.77
3% for purchase of Class C stock in Banco Ejidal	170.32
Repayment of Bank's loans which were used for the daily advances to its members, forage for work animals, oil and gasoline for machinery (*avío*)	26,644.53
Interest	732.58
1% for purchase of Class C stock	269.14
Taxes (3% of value of crop)	2,903.10
Social fund for local community betterment (5% of crop value)	4,838.50
Medical service contribution	593.00
Irrigation fee (5 p. per hectárea)	225.00
(a) Total disbursements	43,093.25
(b) Distributed as dividends to 77 members	53,676.75
Realized on sale of wheat (a plus b)	96,770.00

Source: Banco Nacional de Crédito Ejidal.

Henequeneros de Yucatán, the Forestry Federation, state governments, and others. Most of them are still dependent on private sources, often the local usurer.

The Torreón agency divides the Laguna region into thirteen zones. In each zone a representative of the bank holds the title of zone-chief and represents the agency in its dealings with the peasants. An assistant zone chief is located in each ejido where there is an *ejidal* credit society operating with the bank. He is now usually a local *ejidatario*.

Purely banking functions are carried out through the credit department. The trust department was set up to manage properties such as gins, light and power generating plants, and the *vías de Decauville*. It also manages central repair shops for farm machinery. Its technical department provides advice and the plans needed for such projects as the drilling of wells, building of houses, laying out of streets, providing drinking water, setting up local plants for the industrialization of regional products, or building local meeting houses or schools. The commercial department takes over the crops of the ejidos and attempt to sell them on the best possible market. This may require storage until prices rise or the negotiation of sales to foreign companies or governments is completed. This department works in close cooperation with national agencies for the control of prices and with the Banco Nacional del Comercio Exterior, a semigovernmental export-import institution.

The sale of the *ejidal* cotton crop is the region's biggest single transaction. The Banco Ejidal has used several systems. The first year it bought the cotton outright and held it for sale. The result was a loss of 8 million pesos, caused by a sudden price drop. Next, the cotton was sold for the peasants and their return was made dependent on the sale of each lot. Both systems followed past practices to some extent, since there was never much of a "free market" for cotton in the region. Credit institutions were generally the only possible purchasers under the terms of the loans.

The bank introduced the auction system in December, 1943. Bidding was spirited and carried the price above previous years. The successful bidder topped his nearest competitor by 1 million pesos.[13] This system has since been followed each year.

The credit department supervises the creation of new *ejidal* credit societies and the functioning of those which already exist. It also makes studies of ways in which community organization may be improved. It has the responsibility for the promotion of consumers' cooperative stores. The functions of the legal, bookkeeping, and administrative services departments are self-evident.

The Torreón agency of the Banco Ejidal is the most important in Mexico. It lent 34,394,000 pesos ($7,091,546) in 1946 out of a national total of 108,768,000 pesos ($22,426,391). This represents 31.6 per cent of the total sum available to organized *ejidatarios* in that year.

Other regions rose in economic importance in the following eight years. The Laguna agency in 1954 lent only 175,707,544 pesos out of a national total of 532,619,036 pesos. The credit made available to the Laguna *ejidatarios* rose five times, but their share of the national total remained about the same, 33 per cent.

Private credit institutions have. been lending the bank money since 1938. Thirty-eight per cent of its national operations were conducted with such funds in that year. The proportion had risen to 77 per cent in 1945, fell to 19 per cent in 1950, and rose again to 87 per cent in 1953.

The total amount of private capital handled by the bank in the eight-year period, 1938-1945, was 439,733,295 pesos ($90,666,-658). The Torreón agency pioneered in securing private funds. The Houston cotton firm of Anderson, Clayton and Co., operating in the region for many years, was the first important business group to recognize that the ejido organization was probably permanent. It lent the bank money in the second year after the expropriations. The Torreón agency has conducted its entire *avío* operations for the past several years with private funds.[14]

The bank pays 4.5 per cent interest on crop loans to its private capital sources, which leaves it 3.5 per cent for operating expenses. Both sound high by United States standards. Both seem low under the circumstances, particularly when the nonbanking functions must be paid for out of the bank's shares.

The number of societies operating with the bank varies from year to year. The total rose from 22 in 1937 to a high of 423 in 1954. Members of ejidos operating with the bank numbered 23,774 in that year.

Recovery on loans is highly dependent on weather conditions and irrigation water supply.[15] Since published reports do not differentiate types of loans, amounts due on *inmobiliario* and *refaccionario* loans cannot be determined.

1937	81 per cent repaid	1943	79 per cent repaid	1949	90 per cent repaid
1938	86	1944	143	1950	105
1939	100	1945	120	1951	91
1940	100	1946	54	1952	62
1941	91	1947	106	1953	58
1942	93	1948	94	1954	87

Years showing over 100 per cent reflect payments made against loans outstanding from previous years.

The relative success of the Banco Ejidal, *as a bank,* was made possible to a large extent by casting loose those ejidos which were no longer good credit risks. Thus the bank, while more successful financially, tacitly declared itself a failure in some of its other functions, such as educational and organizational services. If there had been a system similar to the rural extension services of various other countries, the bank's default might not have been so serious. The aid to rural advance and reconstruction which is provided when education is linked with credit is an important aspect of land reform which is often neglected.[16] Even with the highly developed extension work in the United States, somewhat similar experience here, that of the rural rehabilitation program, showed a collection rate of 68.5 per cent at the end of the first ten years.[17]

Before the expropriations, there were eleven private banks in the region. In addition, money was lent by the large purchasers of cotton and wheat. Now there are nineteen private banks.[18] The Banco de México so increased its business in the region that it built a modern six-story office building in Torreón.

An example of the relations of the various groups is furnished by the credit record for the 1938-1939 cotton season. The Banco Ejidal lent money for the cultivation of 56,727 *hectáreas* (140,116 a.); Banco Nacional de México, 7,290 (18,006 a.); Banco de la Laguna, 6,754 (16,682 a.); Banco Agrícola, 4,607 (11,379 a.); Banco Mexicano Refaccionario, 550 (1,358 a.). Private sources listed lent money for the following areas: J. Abusaid, 1,500 *hectáreas* (3,705 a.); Russek Bros., 1,450 (3,581 a.); Buchenau y Cía., 750 (1,852 a.). The governor of Coahuila lent money for the cultivation of 585 *hectáreas* (1,445 a.) and owners who were able to finance themselves planted 3,953 *hectáreas* (9,764 a.). Since there was nothing unusual about this season, it may be assumed that the usual credit practices in the Laguna were followed and that self-financing plays an exceedingly minor role in the region.[19]

The question of private agricultural credit in Mexico requires much more extended treatment than can be given here. In recent years, special efforts have been made to offer private banks government guarantees for agricultural loans. Bank deposits in Mexico have increased rapidly and the government has tried to canalize some of this money into agricultural production. For that purpose, the president issued a decree on June 1, 1942, creating a trust fund to be administered by the Banco de México to guarantee agricultural credits by member banks. The federal government placed in the fund an initial 5,000,000 pesos ($1,030,928). Among other risks against which the fund was to insure lenders were damages arising from expropriations of land under the agricultural laws.[20] This move does not seem to have had much influence on private interest rates in La Laguna. The organ of the private owners complained in January, 1947, that credit cost between 12 and 18 per cent.[21]

The structure of credit facilities in the entire country still leaves much to be desired. The National Banking Commission, in a study released during the summer of 1953, found that "credit payments made by commercial and savings banks represent only 11.5 per cent of the production needs of Mexican industry, 5 per cent of livestock, and 6.8 per cent of agricultural financing."[22] "Lending by merchants and other money lenders on usurious terms still accounts for more than half of Mexico's crop credits" according to the International Bank study.

IRRIGATION

Water is another essential key to the success of farming in La Laguna. It has been seen that the struggle for the control of water has involved armed combat as well as domestic politics and international diplomacy. It continues to be a political issue of great complexity.

The Federal Commission organized in 1895 was disbanded after the expropriations, and the regulation of the irrigation system was turned over to the National Irrigation Commission, which created Irrigation District No. 17, covering the region.

New regulations, put into effect by presidential decrees published May 7, 1938, and August 1, 1939, provided for the following order of preference in the distribution of water:

1. Domestic uses and public services in the cities and the villages were given first priority.
2. Ejidos and small properties with areas not exceeding 20 hectáreas (49.4 a.) came second.
3. Lands of small property owners with areas falling between 20 hectáreas and 150 hectáreas (between 49.4 and 370.5 a.) followed; with
4. Other properties entitled to the remainder, if any.

The same decree provided that the National Irrigation Commission might alter the distribution of water from one canal to another in special cases where there was a danger of an important loss of crops so long as they worked within the above four-point order of preference.

Studies of the possibility of supplementing the undependable river waters by wells started in the early 1920's. By 1928, 160 wells had been drilled and by 1932 the number had risen to 360. In 1941, 1,060 wells were in operation; 1,531 were reported in 1948. The seven-year drought forced the drilling of more wells; the total rose to 2,710 in June, 1954, and to 3,000 by October, 1956.[23]

Sinking wells was carried on in the same way in which the canals were dug. No general plan was followed. The result was that wells have been dug which turned out to be too costly to operate. Others tapped supplies of alkaline water which ruined the land. It was found that some wells "pirated" water from nearby wells and put them out of use. Rapid and planless drilling, plus a succession of drought years, has lowered the water level drastically. Many wells have ceased functioning as a result. There is considerable doubt that the water level will ever be restored to former heights, since relocation and lining of canals plus proper timing of water flows from the dam will cut down waste water which formerly contributed to underground water supplies.

The cost of irrigation with wells ranges from 25.15 pesos ($5.03) per *hectárea* (2.47 a.) to 55.29 ($11.06). In general it has been found that cotton yields are raised from 600 to 1,000 kilos per *hectárea* by two auxiliary irrigations with well water. Wheat yields are raised from 800 to 1,200 kilos.[24]

The ejidos in 1948 had about 38 per cent of the wells in the region to water 70 per cent of the land and the private properties, with about 30 per cent of the land, had the other 62 per cent.[25] This has given rise to dissatisfaction on the part of the *ejidatarios*, who have insistently demanded that control of all wells be included in the federally-managed irrigation district. A presidential decree of February 12, 1941, ordered that this step be taken. Thus far (March, 1958) it has not been put into effect. The reasons given for the delay is the desire of the Irrigation Commission to include the wells in the over-all reorganization which supposedly would take place after the Lázaro Cárdenas dam was put into operation.[26]

Naturally, the former owners, in choosing the land they were to keep, selected areas served by wells so far as they could. In some cases the shape of the remaining property was thrown askew by the attempt. While the agrarian law provided compensation for expropriated improvements, some of the owners did not leave the pumping equipment in the wells. Pumps were removed from 156 wells during the preliminaries to the expropriation.[27]

Much of the controversy about water in recent years has revolved around the dam. Plans for building a dam were discussed intermittently until the 1930's, when a general agreement was reached upon El Palmito as a site for the dam.[28] The location is approximately 230 kilometers (143 mi.) west of Torreón, a few miles below the confluence of the Ramos and El Oro rivers, the two principal tributaries of Río Nazas. At this location the rivers carry 55 per cent of the flow from the entire Nazas watershed.

At the time Cárdenas decreed the expropriations, he made arrangements for work to start on the dam. It began early in 1937 and progressed slowly and irregularly, depending in the first few years largely upon the state of the federal treasury. The dam structure was ready in 1941 but the high-grade steel for the gates and valves was not available during World War II. El Palmito (now called Lázaro Cárdenas dam) was formally inaugurated October 6, 1946, on the tenth anniversary of the expropriations. The first regular service thus began with the eleventh crop year of the new regime.

The dam could store 3,200 million cubic meters (4,182 million cubic yds.). It is estimated that it has cost 82 million pesos ($16,907,216). The presence of the uncompleted dam saved the Laguna untold millions of damages in the severe storms of September, 1944. Even though water was pouring out through three unclosed tunnels at the rate of 1,100 cubic meters per second and the dam overflowed, it still held back the flood sufficiently to reduce property damage and loss of life such as occurred farther north on the same watershed in Chihuahua.

Since the closing of the dam gates, many questions which have not been squarely faced have cried out for solution. The National Irrigation Commission, the Department of Agriculture, the Banco Ejidal, the peasants' and the private property owners' groups have all been striving to lay plans for the solution of these problems. During the early years of work on the dam, the extremely unwise prediction was made that over 300,000 *hectáreas* (741,000 a.) could be irrigated after the dam was in operation. This gave rise to completely unfounded hopes in the minds of both *ejidatarios* and private proprietors that there would be more benefits from the dam than could possibly be realized. It is now admitted officially that the dam might provide for the regular irrigation of around 110,000 *hectáreas* (271,700 a.).[29] To this area it is now estimated that another 70,000 *hectáreas* (172,900 a.) can be added as a result of more scientific planning and sinking of wells.

Obviously an area in which the ejidos hold 153,059 *hectáreas*, colonists hold 17,655 *hectáreas*, and private owners 57,118 *hectáreas*, making a total of 227,832 *hectáreas* (562,745 a.) of "irrigable" land, will have to undergo serious readjustments if only 180,000 *hectáreas* (444,600 a.) can be irrigated. There will be 47,832 *hectáreas* (118,145 a.) which will have little chance of ever securing sufficient water.

Overexpansion of the cultivated land in the region was seen in 1909 by the Díaz Minister of Agriculture and Development, Olegario Molina. He warned at that early date that there was more land depending on irrigation than could be covered by the river flows except in occasional years. But there was always a "gambler's chance" that more water would flow and that the good years would more than counterbalance the bad.[30]

The National Irrigation Commission made plans to relocate the principal canals after the completion of the dam. A ten-year program involving the expenditure of about 75,000,000 pesos ($15,463,918) is now being executed. The canals were built to carry large flows of water, since every possible use had to be made of the floods as they came down the river. The result has always been a high percentage of seepage, in addition to a high rate of silt deposit. This has made the cleaning of the canals an expensive process. It is hoped that with the regularization of the water flow and with fewer miles of canals for the water to travel, it will be possible to reduce the seepage loss considerably. There is also discussion of a plan to line some of the canals with concrete.

Some saving of water can be counted on if it can be released at the time it is needed in the fields. An average of 15.7 per cent was wasted during the fifteen-year period 1926-1941, with the wastage as high as 23.3 per cent in some years.[31]

PROPERTY RELOCATION

The organized peasants of the region have discussed these problems for several years. Their demands were set forth at a congress of *ejidatarios* held in May, 1943. First, they insisted on being informed of plans for the management of the irrigation system after the dam was closed. Second, they requested that the plan for the relocation of canals and the area to be irrigated by each canal be drafted and submitted to the peasants for discussion. Third, they wanted the soil studies, which were then being made, to be available so that the *ejidatarios* could participate in making plans for the shifting of ejidos from poor lands to properties containing better soil and with available water. Fourth, they demanded that the authorities make public the basis on which land was to be redistributed in the region.

This latter point is the sorest one of the entire complex of problems. It has been stated by the Secretary of Agriculture that the unit to which each *ejidatario* in the Laguna region should be entitled must be six *hectáreas* (14.8 a.) of irrigated land. A presidential decree backed this opinion. If a program *were* put into effect which increased the unit from four to six *hectáreas* (from 9.8 to 14.8 a.), the present *ejidatarios* alone would require 182,022 *hectáreas*, which is 2,022 more than the area estimated as irrigable when El Palmito dam is in "normal" operation. Obviously the average is deceptive, and the legal rule of six *hectáreas* is just as unscientific as the rule by which the expropriated property was distributed in 1936. Instead of using area alone, location and productivity should be taken into account. However, assuming that each *ejidatario* were to be given six *hectáreas*, that would mean that 829 colonists with an area of 17,655 *hectáreas* (43,608 a.) and all the 2,394 private property owners with an area of 61,591 *hectáreas* would be faced with virtual certainty of insufficient water for their crops.

Legally, the problem is a complicated one. Amendments to the agrarian code have provided that 150 *hectáreas* (370 a.) of land used for the cultivation of cotton are inaffectible and cannot be expropriated for agrarian purposes.[32] The peasants charge that although private properties now seem to be relatively small, in actual fact they are not, since many of the divisions of the large properties have been subterfuges. One example cited by them in 1945 was that of a man who held 900 *hectáreas* near San Pedro and

700 in Durango, a total of 1,600 *hectáreas* (3,952 a.), "in the name of his wife, his sons, his nephews and even some nonmembers of his family."[33] The 1943 peasant congress, referring to the oft-mentioned scheme to move *ejidatarios* to other parts of the country, said "Those who must leave the Laguna region are the large landowners." It also charged that the private owners were working discreetly but assiduously to get advance information on where the canals were to run under the new system so that they might tie up any available land.[34]

The *ejidatarios* have carried their battle for more water to the president of Mexico and to the Supreme Court. President Manuel Avila Camacho increased the amount of water to which ejidos were given preferential rights in 1945 but his ruling was immediately attacked in 450 injunction suits filed by private owners. The Supreme Court overruled the president.[35]

New regulations published for public discussion in October, 1947, again gave the ejidos rights to 995 million cubic meters compared with 229 million for the privately-owned farms. No objections were made by the *ejidatarios* to this distribution. A question of fundamental political importance has been raised, however. This regulation, as have previous ones, treats each ejido as a group which has one vote in the assembly which elects members of the board controlling water distribution on each main canal. Each private farmer has one vote. The *ejidatarios* point out that several thousand members of ejidos may thus be placed in a minority position if they are located on a canal with more individual private farmers than there are ejidos. This and many technical objections were raised in half-page advertisements in the Torreón dailies.[36]

Only the most general announcements have come from government officials on their plans for the reorganization of the region. The Irrigation Commission, the Agrarian Department, and the Banco Ejidal have all been working on the compilation of the necessary maps and data for the carrying out of this vast project. The president, in a decree of February 12, 1941, ordered the Secretary of Agriculture and the Agrarian Department to study the possibility of grouping all the ejidos together in one block and all the private properties in another, but no public announcement of any such move had been made up to May, 1958.

The solution of the key problem of the region would seem to

require the fullest use of modern techniques of democratic discussion among contending groups as one method of securing some consensus on what steps need to be taken.

COMPENSATION AND PROFITS

The region is one of the few in Mexico in which land values have followed the trajectory so familiar in the United States. As has been noted, the original cost for all the land of which the Laguna was just "Shepherd's Corner" was 250 pesos in 1730. A century later the region was valued at 20,000 pesos. In 1848 Zuloaga and Jiménez purchased the Laguna lands for 80,000 pesos. The best estimate of the commercial value of the rural parts of the region in 1936 was 250 million pesos.

Large profits went to a few of the biggest landlords, who did not work their land. The 1928 survey, published by the Chamber of Agriculture, reported 7 million pesos ($3,500,000) profits to those who rented, leased, or sharecropped their land, and did not work it themselves. Over three-sevenths went to four owners in the *municipio* of San Pedro.

Guerra estimates average gross income to Laguna farm owners at 15 million pesos each year from 1877 to 1936, with net income 2.5 million pesos. The average annual cash rent for an *hectárea* was 20 per cent of the value of the property. Shares varied between 20 and 25 per cent for wheat and corn and were 25 per cent for cotton.[37]

Contrasted with these returns to the large owners is the experience of nineteen small farms studied in 1931. The farms were chosen as typical of the region and represented 12 per cent of the area's cotton production. The average cost of production per *hectárea* was listed at 244.47 pesos, broken down as follows: labor costs, 30.6 per cent, animals, 6.4 per cent; materials, including seeds, 16.1 per cent; and "other expenses," 46.9 per cent. Income from cotton and seed totalled 189.60 pesos, leaving a loss of 54.87 pesos for the average farm. Sixteen of the nineteen farms studied reported losses ranging from 3.66 pesos to 181.60 pesos per *hectárea*. The three which showed profits ran 24.17, 60.66, and 139.34 pesos per *hectárea*.[38]

The system of compensation used in the ejidos is complicated. It was worked out in discussions between President Cárdenas and the peasant groups during the forty days the President stayed in the region in the fall of 1936.

There are three principal methods of remuneration for the *ejidatarios*. The first is based on the skill required for the work done in the preparation of the fields, in cultivation, and in harvesting. Each ejido determines, within the limits of its own financial situation, the rates to be paid. Generally, in 1953, the field laborer was getting four or five pesos per day. Tractor mechanics, pump operators, and other semiskilled workers received from six to seven pesos. The work-chief got seven or eight pesos.[39]

During the cotton picking season piece rates are paid. Generally the entire family participates in the field work. A third method is used after the crops have been sold. When the ejido operates with the Banco Ejidal, the Bank sells the crops, deducts the seasonal loan (*avío*), one-fifth of the five-year loan, and any other charges, as illustrated in Table 8 (p. 102). The ejido deducts its social fund or its guarantee fund and then distributes the remainder to its members. The basis is the number of man-hours worked during the season, irrespective of the amount which was received for the work at the time it was done. Each ejido decides on the basis of its own needs and the available funds whether all the money is to be distributed to the members or whether sums above those legally required are to be utilized for some special community project.

A new system made its appearance in the region in 1941. It was worked out in some of the ejidos in which there was a fairly well-defined group of active and energetic members and another group of members who did not take their work so seriously. Under the new system collective work is done as before, up to and including the planting of the cotton. Then the members draw lots for sections of the land. From that time on the sections are cultivated and harvested either individually or by family groups. Day rates are paid during the first period. The individuals or small groups working their allotted divisions are paid on the basis of production on the divisions. The system introduces an additional complication into the internal organization of the ejidos, but its inventors claim that it has resulted in greater production and does not penalize the better workers as the previous system did. It is estimated that almost 90 per cent of the cooperative ejidos in the region have adopted this system in recent years.

The "mixed" system, as it is known in the region, has led to many complications. Several ejidos have been split as a result of groups being formed to attempt to secure rights to a particularly rich area within the *ejidal* lands. The Central Union has denounced officials of the bank for promoting dissension which leads to the formation of several sectors within an ejido. Officially the bank has followed a "hands-off" policy. The individual working of plots has made cotton theft and the illegal traffic in unginned cotton much easier. It has made the bookkeeping of both bank and ejido more involved.

Recently the Central Union has become much more open in its criticism of the new system. It is endeavoring to educate the *ejidatarios* to the dangers of continued division within their ranks. It is able to cite several examples of ejidos which had been making profits until they divided into sectors. The losses then brought the members to their senses and the reunited group was again making money.[40] The technical requirements of successful wheat raising are such that the "mixed" system is feasible only in cotton and in small crop cultivation. This fact alone may hold in check any widespread attempt to wreck the large-scale nature of the agriculture of the region.

No valid generalization about "profits" can be made which would fit every ejido. Some have prospered in every way and have made good use of good land and available water. On the other extreme are the ejidos which have had irrigation water less than half the seasons since the expropriations. Seven villages which were unable to water their lands for four successive years were visited from year to year by the writer from 1937 to 1941. The *ejidatarios* worked on other lands as day laborers or tried to secure employment in the towns or cities. Other ejidos have been partial failures even though they had land and water. Some have failed until a troublemaking minority was eliminated, and then have improved markedly.

The major factor in the success or failure of *ejidal* production as a whole, however, is the infrequent occurrence of the combination of favorable climatic factors outlined in the previous chapter. This is shown, with regard to the cotton crop, by the history of 18 years of the annual profits distributed to the *ejidatarios* working with the bank. It will be noted that the highest annual profit (45,578,423 pesos) is about 66 times as great as the lowest (692,012 pesos).

Year	Profits Distributed (in pesos)
1937	1,163,542.30
1938	1,081,176.54
1939	1,777,276.67
1940	692,011.99
1941	2,532,955.08
1942	7,489,723.59
1943	11,840,120.47
1944	1,580,485.26
1945	3,732,244.96
1946	4,725,306.21
1947	6,049,738.94
1948	10,412,047.78
1949	13,217,459.80
1950	24,276,498.20
1951	6,144,324.60
1952	1,935,344.00
1953	5,932,145.66
1954	45,578,423.38

The bank has divided all the Laguna ejidos working with it into three groups. Group A ejidos normally pay their debts and distribute profits to their members; they represented 59 per cent of all ejidos financed by the bank in 1948. Group B contains societies which for special reasons were in arrears but which have removed the causes of their delinquency and are now making current payments, plus installments on back debts. Group C consists of poor ejidos which do not pay their debts but which the bank is trying to put on their feet by securing more or better land elsewhere or by aiding the society to reorganize and improve its work. Groups B and C represented 29 and 12 per cent of the total respectively. This grouping must be seen as involving a fluctuating number of ejidos as completely insolvent groups are denied credit, as has been pointed out on page 98, and as weather conditions occasionally favor even the poorer villages.

The average daily income from cotton and wheat was officially estimated at 2.25 pesos ($.45) in 1938; 3.04 pesos ($.61) in 1939; and 4.25 pesos ($.88) in 1945. The best societies averaged around twice that amount. Additional income is often found in the sale of truck from individual garden plots or of chickens or goats,[41] and increasingly from other crops such as alfalfa and grapes.

These amounts might be compared with the incomes of the migratory seasonal workers who have been as much a part of the Laguna economy as of the California fruit regions. Cotton picking time has brought around 13,000 to 16,000 migratory workers to the region ever since it became a great cotton-raising center. Whole families travel on foot or burro from nearby parts of Coahuila, Durango, and Zacatecas. They live in reed huts or lean-tos which they erect wherever they are allowed to camp. The money they earn generally is the only cash income the family has for the entire year.[42]

Migrants are paid by the weight of the cotton they pick. Rates vary with supply of the *braceros* (literally, those with arms) and the amount of cotton to be gathered. Women and children usually join the men. Estimates of the amount which can be earned by a family of three vary from 17.50 pesos ($3.50) to 52.50 ($10.50) weekly on the basis of seven days' work. If the family secured work every day throughout the three-month picking period, it would earn, according to these estimates, from 210 pesos ($42) to 630 ($126) on which to exist for the entire year.

DISEASE AND PEST CONTROL

The damage done to crops in the region by disease and pests has always been great. Before the expropriations there was little cooperation between the various owners. Although there had been an agency of the Department of Agriculture in the region for some years, it had been inadequately staffed and financed. From 1936 to 1939 it attempted to get the ejidos and the private proprietors to undertake disease and pest control, each on their own land. These measures did not bring the proper results because of the ease with which diseases and pests moved from one field to another. The Comité de Plagas was created in June 1939 and a quota of two pesos per *hectárea* of cotton was established. The life of this committee was short and its end ignominious.

The presidential decree which abolished the committee turned the supervision of this work back to the Department of Agriculture, with power to levy fines against either ejidos or private owners who did not follow a set of directions for the clearing of the fields and the combating of diseases and insects.

The department broadened the base of its work in 1947 by creating a new organization: Comité Regional de Defensa Agrícola. It consists of representatives of the Department of Agriculture, the state governments of Coahuila and Durango, Banco Ejidal, Banco Agrícola, Veterans of the Revolution (a group of colonists), the small property owners association, Centro Bancario, a Torreón private banking group, the Unión de Sociedades Ejidales, and the Liga de Comunidades Agrarias.

There has been a downward trend in losses of this character since the expropriations. The amounts lost from 1937 to 1941 were as follows: 17,232,209; 12,916,072; 12,382,625; 11,048,949; and 7,840,900 pesos. The loss in 1945-1946 was 17,500,198 pesos ($3,608,288). The ejidos accounted for 7,795,086 pesos and the private properties for 9,705,111. It should be noted that cotton and cottonseed prices were about double those of 1937 so that the deflated figure of around 8,500,000 pesos should be the one to compare with the 17,000,000 eight years before.

Climatic conditions often interfere with disease control. A rain causes an almost total loss of the insecticide sprayed on the plants. Ejidos of the Torreón zone began using two airplanes to dust their cotton in August, 1947. Other ejidos have since adopted the same practice.[43]

On every hand, the peasants find that life has become more complex, that they are involved in both political and technical decisions, and that the answers to their problems often have roots running far back into the history of the region and of Mexico, as well as out into the world far from their area.

There are few aspects of the economic life of the region in which the *ejidatarios* are not now deeply enmeshed, as citizens of its economic government. They have found that, difficult though the creation of the formal structure of democracy was, achieving a functioning democracy is immeasurably more difficult.

Chapter 6

PROBLEMS AND PROGRESS IN BUILDING
AN AGRARIAN DEMOCRACY

*O*NLY THOSE who free themselves are truly free. Destruction of rural feudalism can be accomplished; it was in La Laguna, and in Mexico generally. A framework for democracy can be created from above; that has been described largely in formal terms in the preceding chapter. These are necessary but not sufficient conditions for the existence of democracy. Democracy, in our terms, can be achieved only after intense and prolonged struggle by the people themselves. They must often rid themselves of old habits inherited from the past; habits growing out of historical conditions which vary greatly from place to place. How do people only just released from a state of virtual serfdom, with its attendant ignorance and provincialism, go about building democracy? What handicaps do they encounter? What help do they receive from those superior to them in knowledge, experience, and in political power?

PEASANT PARTICIPATION

The last factor in many respects is the most crucial. Federal officeholders generally tried valiantly for about four years following the expropriations to help the Laguna peasants to build in ways which appealed to them as sound. The attempt was continued during the remainder of the Cárdenas administration to secure the participation of the *ejidatarios* themselves in all aspects of the new

118

social structures in the region, but the essential impetus from the nation's capital failed after the change of presidents. The peasants of La Laguna received little support from the next two national administrations in their attempt to build a functioning democracy. There is some evidence of a more encouraging attitude in the past few years.

For years prior to the change in the region the owners had been organized into the Cámara Nacional Agrícola de la Laguna. It was formed in 1917 as part of a national organization of large rural property owners. The peasants were unorganized or temporarily organized into short-lived groups. It was not until the 1930's that their groups began to have any influence in the region.

After the reorganization of the region one of the most serious questions was that of the relations between the Banco Ejidal and the *ejidatarios*. The original theory was that the ejidos would be adequately represented within the bank by their ownership of Class C stock. It soon became apparent that this theory was not working satisfactorily. The bank officials in charge of the organization of collective credit societies faced a dilemma. The tactics of struggle which had been used against the *hacendados* were not applicable under the new conditions. At the same time it was realized that some form of self-organization for the *ejidatarios* was vitally necessary if the democracy which was sought in the region was to be achieved.

Several competitors appeared on the scene, striving for the right to represent the peasants. The heads of one of the national labor organizations, the Confederación de Trabajadores de México (CTM), who had helped the peasants bring their complaints before the president, expected to represent them before the Banco Ejidal. There were several other labor organizations, all composed predominantly of city workers, who challenged this contention. Politicians in both states, Coahuila and Durango, organized peasant groups through which they expected to be able to exert influence. There were also remnants of the "company unions" which had been recognized by the *hacendados*. Several competing organizations of peasants with strength in other parts of Mexico made appeals to the Laguna *ejidatarios*.

The bank's first attempt to cope with the situation was the creation of a complaints office, later named the Social Research

Bureau. This bureau attempted to create a general committee representative of the various organizations pretending to represent the peasants. Jealousies between the various groups wrecked this attempt.

The organization department of the bank, in consultation with the more responsible peasant leaders, then began to organize advisory committees of *ejidatarios*. They represented the *ejidatarios* of each of the fifteen zones into which the region had been divided by the bank originally. Their function was to meet with the zone-chief and help him with the settlement of complaints brought by members of the ejidos. During 1938 these advisory committees grew in importance. They settled many disputes within and between ejidos and between ejidos and the bank. They began to play a more important role in the entire range of peasant activities.

As the organization became more formalized, the advisory committees, which consisted of six members, were divided along functional lines. Conventions were held in each zone to elect members. Each member was assigned the responsibility of attending to a specified field of activity such as education, administration, health, credit, grievances, or agricultural matters.

A convention of the committees from the various zones was held and a central committee was set up with an office in Torreón and with full-time representatives of the membership.

The work of the zone delegate was to check on the functions of the community which came within his field, and to initiate activities on behalf of the regional organization. The regional delegates dealt with zone delegates to increase inter-ejido communication and competition. In cases of dispute, one member or the full central committee presented the peasants' case to the bank.

The duties of the delegates were as listed briefly below.

Education—to see that schools were built; watch school attendance; investigate motives for nonattendance; check schools and playgrounds for adequacy and hygiene; help form parents' associations; work up community support for school gardens and parcels of land tilled in common for the benefit of the school; help organize and supervise night schools and outside lectures for adults; and encourage sports, with games in and between ejidos.

Grievances—to investigate complaints against the personnel of the bank, authorities of the ejidos, or the federal authorities in contact with the ejido; and act as mediator in internal disputes over lack of discipline and similar conflicts.

Agriculture—to visit the fields continuously; to cooperate with the bank's agronomists; help educate the peasants to the need for scientific agriculture, pest control, use of fertilizer, crop rotation, use of machinery, planning land use; keep track of how the work-chief functions; check on market quotations for ejido crops, machinery, and food requirements; stimulate the formation of small community or individual supplementary farming activities, such as pig or chicken raising and vegetable gardens.

Health—to promote public health activities in the community, such as the establishment of dumps at a safe distance from the village, street cleaning, public laundering facilities, and public truck gardens to help vary the family diet; arrange lectures on health; help in sanitary campaigns carried on by the socialized medical service of the region; see that aid is given families of sick members, and that arrangements be worked out for the families of disabled or deceased members.

Administration—to check on the running of the ejido, keeping of books, accounting, holding of monthly assemblies, preparation of members for various jobs, and their competence after being elected.

Credit—to reconcile the budget of the society with its past and expected future performance; see that costs are not excessive; advise on proposed expenditures; deal with firms selling goods wanted; and deal with the bank on applications for credit.

The new organization was known as the Central Committee of Ejidatarios. It soon built itself thoroughly into the new economic and social structure of the region. It relieved the bank of part of the load of nursing ejidos along and trying to conciliate or arbitrate the disputes within and between them.

The committee became such an important contribution to Mexican agrarian developments that President Cárdenas recommended to Congress that *ejidatarios* in other collectivized zones of the country should be organized along the same lines. The agrarian code was amended in December, 1939, giving legal personality and increased powers and responsibilities to such organizations under the name of Central Union of Collective Credit Societies.

Side by side with the development of the advisory committees another type of organization was created. Several of the ejidos banded together to purchase and manage an electric power plant. Others took over cotton gins, several shared ownership of heavy farm machinery. These organizations had a legal personality under the agrarian code and were called Sociedades de Interés Colectivo Agrícola and were known by their initials, SICA.

The most important SICA became that which took over a large portion of the heavy farm machinery and built several "machinery centers" in what was one of the few direct borrowings from Russia in the entire Mexican agrarian program. The purpose was to concentrate machinery at several convenient spots and rent it to the societies as needed. Repairs were made at the central shops or by mechanics working out from them.

The Central Union of Collective Credit Societies, when the law was changed to give it legal status, took over the functions and assets of the SICA. The machinery center was run by it from June, 1940, to December 31, 1941. At the end of that time it owed the Banco Ejidal approximately 2 million pesos. The bank took over the center on January 1, 1942, and is still managing it in 1958. It also took over seventeen cotton gins, four electric light and power plants, 579 water pumps, and four vías de Decauville which had been owned and operated by ejidos or groups of ejidos. All these properties are now managed by the trust department of the bank.

The action of the bank gave rise to a tremendous outburst on the part of the organized ejidatarios. The bank had found itself faced with an extremely difficult situation. Its position was that the peasants had not demonstrated their ability to manage the various properties without tremendous losses. It charged that on the machinery center alone the SICA had lost 450,000 pesos and the Central Union 300,000 pesos. It alleged that the Central Union heads had loaded onto the machinery center the overhead of their entire organization. In addition it claimed that books were not kept properly and that the institution was run on the basis of "brotherly love" instead of on a strictly commercial basis.

The peasants answered that they had been given machinery in such bad condition that it was unserviceable. The bank's answer was that during the first year of its operation a profit of 57,167 pesos had been made.

The institution had available for rent by local societies in April,

1947, the following farm machinery: 45 wheat combines, 16 threshers, 338 arsenic sprayers, 52 alfalfa balers, 5 seed selectors, and 2 caterpillar tractors. This machinery is used by the ejidos which are too small to make feasible the purchase of their own equipment. A building for the main offices and shops for the machinery center were opened in January, 1944. They are valued at 110,000 pesos. In addition to the central shops in Torreón there are five located in convenient places throughout the region.

The Central Union has been petitioning for a return to its management of the various properties, especially the gins which it claims the bank runs at too high a cost. The bank recently installed two modern gins and has built a five-battery wheat elevator near Torreón. The percentage of *ejidal* cotton ginned by the bank's plants rose from 35 in 1936-1937 to 99 in the past few years.

Although the Central Union was developed out of the advisory committees, the amendment to the Ley de Crédito Agrícola which made it into a semigovernmental organization gave it far-reaching powers. It is authorized to borrow and lend money and carry on other banking operations. It may create commercial or industrial organizations for the handling, classification, packing, sale, or processing of farm products, on behalf of its member societies. It may buy for and distribute to its members, seeds, breeding or work animals, tools, fertilizer, and machinery and may construct or purchase and administer warehouses, elevators, dams, canals, or wells. It has the power to sell its own bonds to obtain the money needed for the activities it may carry out. It also represents its associations in situations involving municipal, state, or federal governments and may mediate in conflicts between or within its member societies. In a word, it represents the peasants in the same manner in which the central advisory committee did, but it has broad powers to carry out additional functions.

The Central Union in the Laguna region was formed on May 24, 1940, at a convention of delegates from local unions which had already been formed in each of the zones. The meeting elected a management commission and a vigilance board. The management commission consists of a general manager and five assistant managers. The latter were to handle the following subjects: finance, insurance and commercial matters, machinery, agriculture, and social services. The position of assistant manager in charge of machinery was abolished when the bank took over his functions. The board of directors of the union is made up of the management commission, the vigilance board of two members, and fifteen counselors. The latter are the general managers of the local unions. The general manager acts as the representative of the organization in all legal, administrative, and economic affairs. He may carry out transactions involving up to 10,000 pesos without the approval of the board of directors, but his checks and orders to pay must all be countersigned by the head of the vigilance board. In general, the functions of the other assistant managers are approximately the same as those outlined for the delegates of the central committee. Health and education have been consolidated under the title of social services.

PEASANT OWNERSHIP OF MACHINERY AND ANIMALS

Peasants throughout Mexico greatly increased their working equipment, both animal and mechanical, between 1936 and 1950, as has been seen.[1]* The *ejidatarios* of La Laguna made great strides in this respect also, with one interesting difference. Generally, Mexican peasants increased the number of mules by 339 per cent, but mules in the Laguna ejidos no longer were looked upon as signs of, or necessary to, progress. The number of mules in the Laguna ejidos dropped from 21,731 in 1940 to 9,195 in 1952. The number of tractors, owned directly and not held in trust through the machinery centers mentioned above, grew to 610 in 1952 from none in 1936. There were, in addition, 141 combines, 506 pumps, 286 trucks, 155 automobiles, 452 tractor-drawn harrows and 461 animal-drawn, 540 tractor-drawn and 6,073 animal-drawn plows, 4,869 cultivators, 2,078 seeders, 6 electric light and power plants, 4 gins, and 2,624 horses.

A number of observers, in addition to the author, have noted the care taken with the machinery in the "average" ejido. Sometimes the machinery shed is the most modern and best equipped building in the ejido village, aside from the school.[2]

RIVALRY AMONG PEASANT GROUPS

The first flush of enthusiasm among the peasants gave a tremendous advantage to the Central Union. It seemed obvious to

*Notes to this chapter begin on page 229.

everyone that "one for all and all for one" was a slogan that would bring results. Gradually the high morale of the early days declined. Personality difficulties, political interference, differences in judgment on such matters as the best method for marketing crops, defalcations by several minor officials, and antagonism on the part of some Banco Ejidal officials all played a part in the decline. Even international politics became a factor in the decline of morale.

A small but vociferous Communist group, mostly urban intellectuals, had been on the fringes of the peasant movement for some time. When it had attempted in 1936 to join the Torreón parade celebrating the expropriations, it had been elbowed out by the remainder of the paraders from peasant unions and urban labor groups. During the first four years of the experiment, the Communists carried no weight and remained a semiconspiratorial group which had strength in the region mostly as a reflection of its influence with highly placed persons in the national administration and in the "official" labor movement, the CTM.

The change of federal administrations in 1940 brought a substantial shift in emphasis in the agrarian field. Several important programs of the Banco Ejidal were crippled or eliminated by the "economy-mindedness" of the new administration. Increasingly, emphasis was placed on its commercial aspects; the organizational aspects diminished in importance. The reaction of many of the peasants strengthened the hands of the Communist groups. The following year, as a result of the invasion of Russia by the Nazis, the "party line" changed, and it became "patriotic" to aid Russia. The Communist group was able to achieve some public prestige which aided it in electing key members of the Central Union.

The Union in November, 1941, requested each of the credit societies to donate two bales of cotton or one ton of wheat to be sent to Britain and to Russia as a concrete expression of the belief of the Laguna peasants in the fight against the Axis. When Mexico entered the war, the peasant organizations promoted the formation of rural militia for which uniforms were provided from community social funds. They were drilled by regular army officers. At a meeting called by the Central Union in July, 1942, to discuss the war it was voted to contribute 150,000 pesos ($30,000) toward the purchase of a bomber to be donated by the Mexican peasants to their government.[3]

Shortly the lines began to be drawn in a struggle which weakened the Central Union and strengthened the hands of the employees of the Banco Ejidal. The initial public move was supplied by the Communists when they ran a prominent Central Union official for Congress in 1943.

At the height of the cotton-picking season, when every day counted, the group organized a caravan of approximately four hundred peasants for a trip of almost two weeks to the national capital. While ostensibly the trip was to protest against certain economic actions of the bank, it was interpreted both in the region and in Mexico City as a move on behalf of the Communist candidate.

The reaction on the part of the majority of the leaders of both peasant and urban labor organizations was vigorous. A call was issued by the seven leading worker and peasant groups of the region for a congress which would set up an organization to coordinate the activities of all the "constructively revolutionary" forces. It was understood from the first that the Communist group was to be excluded. Seven hundred fifty delegates from 517 organizations participated in an all-day session, attended by the writer, at which there was fervent discussion of many of the region's problems. Resolutions denouncing the Communists as saboteurs of national unity were unanimously adopted.

The leadership of the *ejidatarios* then hung in the balance for about seven years, with two major groups striving for dominance. The Communist and allied group leading the Central Union gradually began to lose out to a group with more powerful national connections. The sectarian judgment and decisions of the Union leaders themselves have contributed greatly to their defeat. The defeat was accomplished only at the price of splitting the *ejidatarios* into two competing central unions. Reduction of Communist influence was hampered by attacks on the Laguna experiment as "Communistic" and on any militant union or peasant leader as a Communist.[4]

Indicative of both tactics and the decline of the "original" Union are the developments during the 1952 presidential campaign. The Communists and their allies put up their own ticket, headed by Vicente Lombardo Toledano. The faithful were told, however, to vote for General Henríquez Guzmán, the major opposition candidate. Henríquez was declared defeated but he issued a challenge to the winning party which sounded like a call to rebellion. Nation-wide demonstrations were called for August 15 to "protest." According to evident plans of at least some of the organizers, an outpouring of peasants would have been a signal for next steps toward rebellion. Armed outbreaks were confidently predicted by the Henríquez forces interviewed by the writer in Torreón in early August. The old Central Union leaders organized the Laguna demonstration. It was a dismal failure: between one hundred and one hundred fifty peasants gathered, listened to the reading of the Mexican equivalent of the "riot act," and peacefully dispersed.[5]

The organization chosen by officials of the Banco Ejidal to replace the original region-wide peasant leadership was the League of Agrarian Communities. During the days of the Central Advisory Committee it was one of the organizations competing for the representation of the *ejidatarios*. In 1938 the National Peasant Confederation was organized and the leagues became their state affiliates. At the present time the national confederation has some 2 million members. Its influence in public affairs in 1943 was indicated by its forty-nine congressmen, seventeen senators, fourteen governors, and three cabinet members. It has since lost some of the influence thus indicated but it is still an important factor in national politics.

At the time of the organization of the Central Union there was a tacit division of labor between the two organizations. The leagues were supposed to do the agitational and political work. The unions were supposed to concentrate on the legal functions as part of the economic structure of collectivized agriculture. In practice this line has been a difficult one to maintain. When the Secretary of Agriculture came to the Laguna region in 1941, he was presented with a list of questions and demands formulated by each organization, which overlapped considerably.

The past twenty years have shown the development of the league into a full-blown rival of the union. The union originally carried on far more educational activity and political agitation than the league. The league, however, through its superior political influence, was able successfully to block the application of the agrarian credit code to the union. A showdown came early in 1948. The union applied to the federal government for a loan of 5 million pesos to be used to plant grapevines in a number of ejidos deemed suitable for grape production and to furnish processing plants and equipment for *ejidal* vineyards already in production. The league successfully opposed the application, although it had no positive program to substitute.

Technical experts for the union had prepared a six-year plan for the planting of 20,000 *hectáreas* to grapes, grouped in three main zones where soil conditions are propitious, with three supplementary refrigeration and wine-making plants.

Both groups presented requests for a 3-million-peso loan for a program of leveling *ejidal* lands to prepare for the new type of irrigation which they foresaw must follow the damming of the Nazas.[6]

The use of credit, political pressure, public disapproval, plus lack of realism on the part of the old group, gradually weaned the peasants away from them. The 1950 split and creation of two central unions dramatized a situation which had been gestating for over a decade. The old leadership has now been removed from almost all the important peasant posts in the region.[7]

CONSUMER COOPERATIVES

Organization of the *ejidatarios* as consumers was one of the main tasks of the Banco Ejidal in its early years. Each credit society was asked to elect a man to take charge of a local cooperative store. Enthusiasts organized stores without a study of the economic situation. Often stores were opened with so little capital and such small stock that they were doomed to failure. The bank began to insist on capital of 100 pesos ($20 at that time) per capita before a store was set up. There were other equally serious handicaps. The village storekeeper usually carried his customers on the books during the idle weeks. The cooperatives sold for cash. When they sold on credit, their lower prices left them no margin for losses.

Competition for the centavos of the peasant family is fierce. Most villages are oversupplied with "stores," usually small, rickety shacks with stock worth only a few dollars. During difficult times, many unemployed persons invest a few pesos they may have saved in goods and become shopkeepers. Peddlers regularly visit the villages and can undersell the local retailers. The big Torreón stores send truckloads of goods to the ejidos whenever profits are being distributed.

Poor management of the cooperative stores was another factor, and several stores were robbed. By 1941, in spite of all handicaps, 105 stores were reported in existence.[8] The war added to the troubles of the cooperatives, raising prices, cutting supplies, and forcing the cooperators either to deal with black market racketeers or go under. Some of them became branches of the official government retail system set up to combat high prices. The office for the promotion of consumer cooperatives in the Torreón agency was abolished in the 1940-1941 economy move. Without constant encouragement and advice of the bank employees the few *ejidatarios* with any real idea of cooperation sank under the weight of the adverse environment. No trace of cooperative stores was found in the summer of 1947, but there were 43 stores being run under the auspices of the Central Union. All of these had disappeared by the summer of 1950.

From time to time ambitious plans have been announced for exchange of products between ejidos in various parts of the country. Wheat, beans, sugar, and other commodities would be shipped from surplus areas to market areas and distributed through a cooperative wholesale society. Thus far nothing has come of the idea.[9]

The outstanding cooperative successes in the region have been registered by 61 women's groups running corn-grinding machines. The use of the machine saves several hours a day over use of the Indian grinding stone, the *metate*. In several ejidos the women's league runs the community store in the building which houses the corn mill. Since the women have a more immediate interest in saving on purchases than do the men, they have sometimes taken over the cooperative store. Technically it ceases to be a cooperative. Practically, it serves the village to the same economic end.

Women's Share in Reconstruction

Women were early assigned an important function in the reorganization of life in the Laguna region. The former German Kaiser might well have been describing the role of Mexican women when he made his famous statement that women should be concerned only with *Küche, Kinder, und Kirche*. Cárdenas, in his presidential campaign, had called upon Mexican women to participate in civic affairs. The first widespread attempt to apply this concept took place in the region.   *

The wife of the president and the wife of the head of the Agrarian department travelled from village to village throughout La Laguna. They spoke to the women personally and in mass meetings. They pointed out the job which needed to be done in eliminating superstition, illiteracy, drunkenness, and vice. They formed women's civic leagues and helped clean up poor conditions through education of children and adults.

Each league which was formed had a general secretary, recording and financial secretaries, and secretaries whose job it was to pay special attention to hygiene, to education, to organization, and to propaganda. The activities of the league varied from one ejido to another. Several dozen operated corn-grinding mills, as mentioned above. In this manner the women have been emancipated from the backbreaking task of grinding corn on the Indian *metate*, over which probably the majority of rural Mexican women spend from four to eight hours daily. The profits from the corn mills and other services are used for improvement of the school, for the building of a headquarters for the league, or for some other community projects. Most of the leagues have one or more sewing machines which are used by all of the women of the village. A sewing machine is too expensive to be purchased for one family's use.

Some of the leagues have secured from their ejido a small plot of ground which they themselves cultivate. On one occasion, after a women's league had made a profit of several thousand pesos from the sale of products from its lot, the men who controlled the ejido voted to take away the plot and put it into regular *ejidal* production. The women promptly called upon their sisters in nearby leagues for support and their protests forced the men to retreat from their position.

The women help promote supervised play for school children and baseball and basketball teams for older boys and men. They have proved to be a valuable adjunct to the rural medical service, particularly in combating superstitions which interfere with utilization of modern medical techniques. One of the women, speaking to a 1940 Torreón conference of persons from the United States interested in rural life, said very frankly, "The task which the rural woman has taken upon herself is hard because she must fight absurd prejudices and hostile attitudes." She mentioned specifically the struggle going on in some villages to get the peasants to agree to vaccination against smallpox and the heated discussions which were taking place in other parts of the region about the morality of birth control.

In the first fervor of the change women broke with their traditions and joined the leagues in large numbers. Local leagues were organized into *municipio* federations and they in turn were organized into the Confederation of Women's Leagues of the Laguna region. Disputes over leadership and conflicts between personalities occurred. The confederation was finally eliminated as a contender for feminine leadership, partly because it followed the "party line" of the old central union and affiliated with the World Federation of Democratic Women, a Communist-front organization. The various local leagues now function within a section of the new central union. "About a dozen" remained affiliated with the confederation, in the words of a vice-president of the old central union interviewed in 1952 by the writer.

The decline of the confederation has not meant the wiping out of activity in the ejidos themselves, however. Although the women have not succeeded in building a region-wide organization, they participate in large numbers in ejido assemblies; in school affairs, in the promotion of sports, in health and sanitation campaigns, and in the management of corn-grinding mills and sewing machine cooperatives.

INCREASED ACCEPTANCE OF RESPONSIBILITY

That the Laguna peasants are learning to accept increased responsibilities is demonstrated in several ways. When the bank agency was opened, the books of all the ejidos were kept in the Torreón office. Some members had to travel for as much as fifty or sixty miles to see their accounts. The bank announced that this was a purely temporary arrangement which would be changed when the *ejidatarios* themselves could supply competent bookkeepers. The bank created short courses in the fundamentals of accountancy, and a course in the subject was offered at the regional agricultural school established shortly after the expropriations. The books were moved to the zone offices in 1940 and *ejidatarios* are the bookkeepers. By 1947 two-thirds of the ejidos were keeping their own accounts; by 1952, all were.

A similar course of action was followed with regard to cotton and cottonseed classifiers and water gagers. A group of the most intelligent and best prepared *ejidatarios*, together with a small number of Banco Ejidal employees from various cotton regions, attended courses in cotton and cottonseed classification at Texas State Agricultural and Mechanical College each year for a decade following the expropriations. Water gagers are trained locally.

The central union early established a staff of expert accountants, classifiers, and gagers who themselves educated other *ejidatarios* in these techniques. The members not only participated in discussions of generalities but had their own trained representatives on the committees which decide upon the amount of water to be distributed in the principal and secondary canals. They also are involved, along with representatives of the private property owners and the government, in classification of cotton and cottonseed.

The experience of the Tlahualilo Union of Credit Societies provides evidence of the willingness of the bank to allow rather wide latitude for action by local organizations when they have demonstrated their capacity for assuming responsibility. The original twelve societies, later increased to seventeen, have maintained an outstanding record of hard work and productivity, in spite of several serious problems which arose out of the manner in which they were given land. The unity of the large-scale agriculture which had been built up by the Tlahualilo Company was broken. Small sections were sold to 142 *fraccionistas*, most of whom do not live in the zone. Their homes are in Torreón, Lerdo, Gómez Palacio, and even Monterrey. Locally they are ironically called "remote control farmers." An additional disadvantage was the donation to 1,305 peasants of an area of land on which the company had used an average of only 523 peons all year. Working against these handicaps the Tlahualilo *ejidatarios* achieved higher yields of wheat and cotton than those secured by the company and until recently usually made higher profits than most of the other ejidos.

As peons, men had received an average of 356.35 pesos ($71.27) per year. As *ejidatarios*, twice as many received 1,080.31 pesos ($216.06) in the 1937-1938 season, which has been studied carefully. In addition, they invested 23,832 pesos ($4,766) in medical services for the members and their families, 64,674 pesos ($12,935) were placed in the social funds for community improvements, and 12,512 pesos ($2,502) were used for the purchase of stock in the Banco Ejidal.

Unfortunately, the Tlahualilo experience also provides an object lesson in the dangers of expansion on the basis of unsound, and perhaps prejudiced, technical advice and in the difficulties of operating a business as a direct democracy.

After some five years of negotiations with the company the ejidos came to an agreement by which they purchased the cottonseed oil pressing plant, the gin, light plant, water system, warehouses, shops, and *vías de Decauville* which had been owned by the company. They made a down payment of several thousand pesos from a Banco Ejidal loan to complete the transaction.

Difficulties were overcome somehow in the first two years of operations, although the machinery which the *ejidatarios* took over was antiquated and it was almost impossible to secure repair parts during World War II. The oil plant was forced to shut down during the third year because of competition from more modern mills which were more conveniently located.[10] The easing of the world vegetable oil situation lowered prices and added to the troubles of the group. Dissension began to break out within the membership over the election of managers and others to paid posts, and attacks on administrators for their decisions became more frequent. Political parties began to help increase the confusion for their own ends. Seven of the ejidos split into conflicting camps; for or against the industrial managerial group. The writer sat in a convention of all the Tlahualilo *ejidatarios* in July, 1947, and listened to a marathon discussion of the situation which started at 10 a.m. and adjourned at 6:30 p.m.—with no time out for lunch!

The peasants, many unmistakably of Indian descent, took the debate most seriously. They had within three or four years shifted from a solvent organization to one with a debt of 1,133,400 pesos ($233,690). The previous fall the majority had turned the industrial properties over to the Banco Ejidal in trust to be administered for them. They listened to the bank's report and recommendations and accepted them by an overwhelming vote. Engineers and accountants had mapped out a plan of retrenchment which they hoped would put them on their feet.

It was brought out many times during the meeting that there were several factors responsible for the failures. First, many enthusiasts were anxious to repeat what they conceived to be the financial triumphs of the company without knowing the true economic situation. Second, it was frequently charged that two former bank officials had privately urged the purchase of the industrial equipment so that they could make a deal with a soap company in which they had an interest. Third, a former occupant of a high post made a full public confession of how he had misspent ejido funds on behalf of the Communist party in which he had been a key official. The party had contributed greatly not only to confuse the situation but also to cause financial losses.

Eight of the seventeen farming societies made profits in 1946 in spite of the chaos. They had 499 out of the 980 members. Eight more, with 479 members, ran from 1 to 5 per cent behind in their payments. Only one society, with twenty-two members, dropped below 95 per cent recuperation—it went down to 72. The debt of the farming societies then totalled only 151,700 pesos compared with the 981,700 pesos owed on the industrial properties. The latter were currently valued at 1,050,000 pesos on the books of the bank. With proper economies and administrative reorganization the bank's officials were hopeful that the group might yet pull back to its former secure financial position.

CROP INSURANCE[11]

Talk of insurance against hail, frost, fire, disease, and insects—the principal risks to regional crops—became general soon after the expropriations, but it took more than five years to get a hail and frost system working successfully in wheat and six years in cotton. It was on the initiative of the peasants that an organization called Mutualidad Comarcana de Seguros Agrícolas de la Laguna was formed by cooperation between the Banco Ejidal, Banco Agrícola, and the collective credit societies, on March 4, 1942.

The president was the manager of the Central Union of Credit Societies; the secretary the head of the Torreón agency of the bank. Three peasant representatives were the other members of the board which directed the organization.

This mutual system has worked so well that *ejidatarios* in 26 other areas of the country have copied the structure and functions of the Laguna organization. It now has its own office building in Torreón, and repair shops for trucks, station wagons, well-drilling equipment, pumps, and other equipment. It has built a "house of the peasant" in each of the Laguna *municipios* for meetings and other functions helpful to peasant groups.

The *ejidatarios* alone now manage the organization through a council of representatives of each zone in the region and a board of directors it elects. A general manager is appointed by the board. He was, in 1957, a young *ejidatario* who has also risen to become a deputy in the Mexican Congress.

The total value of wheat and cotton crops insured against loss from hail or frost by the Mutualidad from its inception to the middle of 1946 was 84,222,220 pesos ($17,365,406). The amount paid out to ejidos suffering damages was 1,453,390 pesos ($299,668). The total paid out in the 5 years ending the middle of 1957 was 27,398,509 pesos.

The value of crops insured had risen by 1954 to 118,829,024 pesos ($24,500,829); payments to 2,759,023 pesos ($568,871). Ejido buildings and automobiles are now covered against fire losses and, since 1948, life insurance has been written. Profits have been used to expand the operations of the company in a number of ways. It now drills wells for ejidos and claims to have forced a 30 per cent reduction in previous private drilling prices. It owned seven drills, eight trucks, and a pipe manufacturing shop in 1952.

It listed such "social services" as the following in a recent report:[12]

Free drilling of 20 wells for poor ejidos.
Donation of three ambulances to the *ejidal* medical services.
Gifts of paper, pencils, and chalk to 323 schools.
Assistance in repairing a number of rural schools.
Donation of 300 medicine kits to women's civic leagues.
Help in feeding "wet-backs" deported from the United States when their trains stopped in Torreón on the way south.
Gift of DDT to numerous ejidos participating in a campaign against flies.
Aid to flood victims in several recent years.
Free repairs for a number of trucks of ejidos hit by drought conditions.
Seven water tanks donated to ejidos needing more dependable supplies.
Baseball uniforms and equipment donated to ejido sports clubs.

The activities of the Mutualidad fluctuate with the economic fortunes of the *ejidatarios;* they also help greatly in building agrarian democracy.

THE DEMOCRATIZATION OF PELF

Graft under Díaz was a monopoly of the members of the ruling oligarchy and their obedient servants. Since the government belonged to the oligarchy, it did not have to be "corrupted." The situation changed after the revolution. Corruption in La Laguna, until the revolution reached the region, was monopolized by the *hacendados.*

One of the outstanding men in the region stated to the writer a few years ago that "the Laguna proprietors have the grave responsibility of having been among the greatest corrupters of the public administration." This has manifested itself in such moves as the one originally used by her enemies against the widow of Zuloaga, in their attempt to have her properties confiscated, alleging that she was pro-Maximilian during the French invasion. Rumors of large payments for favors from the commission regulating the Nazas river flow were in constant circulation during the period of its existence. The peasants charge that at the present time there are attempts made to bribe irrigation authorities for tips on the relocation of the canals.

Before the expropriations, some of the *hacendados* of the Laguna region followed the practice of their fellows in other parts of the country and destroyed peasant villages so that their peons would not be legally competent to petition for the application of the Agrarian Law. The 1928 survey listed Santa Teresa, California, Lucero, San Lorenzo, and Concordia among others as haciendas on which this practice had been carried out. The practice was illegal but was condoned "for a consideration."

A campaign contribution offered by the landowners to Cárdenas in 1934 has been mentioned. It deserves mention not because it was made but because it was refused!

The monopoly was broken by the creation of the new agrarian institutions. At the time of the expropriations Torreón was flooded with salesmen from United States seed and machinery concerns offering bribes to Banco Ejidal employees to assure favors for their products.[13]

The experience of many motorists in the United States includes solicitations of bribes by traffic officers. Those who have passed too rapidly through certain small towns may have had their attention drawn to a complete system of graft involving policemen, jailkeeper, and judge. Russian collective farms are not free from theft on the part of members, according to a recent study which reports on "the great problem of pilferage."[14] The same sort of thing is present in the Laguna region.

In 1939 the Government created a Comité Regional de Defensa Agrícola de la Comarca Lagunera, known locally as the "Comité de Plagas," to administer disease and pest control. Each grower was assigned a quota of two pesos per *hectárea* planted to cotton. Private property owners, *ejidatarios*, and Government officials were all represented. It was abolished within less than two years when it was found that out of the thousands of pesos collected, slightly over seven pesos had been spent for insecticides, slightly over one hundred pesos had been spent for the collection of infected cotton bolls, and the rest had been spent in regular and overtime salaries, traveling expenses, and other administrative charges. The local saying was: "The 'Committee on Plagues' has itself become a new plague in the region!"[15]

The organized peasants of the region staged great demonstrations in 1937 demanding that the Banco Ejidal be "cleaned up," that the salaries of some of the officials be reduced, and that surplus employees be fired. Charges were made that some of the bank's employees had bought secondhand machinery from the *hacendados* and sold it to the peasants. These and a number of other charges were investigated by a congressional committee headed by a large landowner. It was found that all but one of the specific charges which came to the attention of the committee arose from misunderstandings and unfounded expectations rather than dishonesty.

The bank did not come off so well in succeeding years, however. Peasant demonstrations continued to be held in protest against what was considered evidence of graft and other unfair practices. In 1942 it was charged, first, that the Banco Ejidal was forcing the peasants to buy an expensive foreign lubricating oil; and second, that a number of zone-chiefs had been persuading peasants to cultivate plots of land for the zone-chief's personal use. The executive secretary of the Department of Agriculture made an investigation of these charges during the summer of 1943. Eleven employees of the bank were discharged. The number included seven of the fourteen zone-chiefs in the region. The head of the agency was ordered transferred to a less important post because he had not discovered and stopped the practice. He was not charged with participation in it.[16]

The selection of an honest and competent man as regional head of the bank usually meant a reduction of official graft almost to the vanishing point. The opposite type of agent found it impossible to resist the multiple temptations of his position.

A new agent appointed early in 1953 found that he could not clean up the mess he had inherited because he could not get backing from Mexico City. Ing. Gonzálo Blanco Macías, an outstanding agronomic engineer, had only recently returned to his country from twelve years in the service of the Pan American Union when he was appointed to the post. He soon learned that fraud against the bank and the peasants had been widespread. He published the names of businessmen and bank employees who had been involved in shady transactions involving millions of pesos. Political pressure in the capital brought about his discharge, in spite of widespread newspaper publicity about the "cleanup" campaign of the new government. The two daily newspapers in Torreón supported him; one referred to his "offense" as the "enormity of being honest." Some peasant groups backed him; others joined the national administration of the bank in calling him a "troublemaker."[17]

Cotton theft and illegal sale has become probably the most widespread regional form of illicit enrichment. *Algodón de luna* (moonshine cotton!) is an expressive phrase in common use in the region. According to local newspaper reports, large fortunes have been made in commerce with stolen cotton. The names of six persons engaged in the business were published in a Torreón paper of August 1, 1943. Local and state officials have been involved and in 1942 a member of the federal Congress set himself up in business as a buyer of *algodón de luna*.

Owners of small plots who participate in the illegal traffic send out gangs or individuals to steal cotton piled up in sacks awaiting collection by burros or trucks to be transported to gins. The cotton is then placed on the owner's lot and sent to a gin as his own production. This has given rise to local jokes about "miraculous yields." An owner of a ten-*hectárea* plot (24.7 a.) in 1942 sold an amount of cotton which could not have been raised on less than four hundred *hectáreas* (988 a.). The *ejidatarios* maintain "home guards" armed with rifles to police their lands. On occasions when a high price for cotton has given rise to greater activity by the robbers, the federal army garrison has been utilized to patrol the region. Several Banco Ejidal employees were caught buying unginned cotton by peasant patrols in 1945. They were promptly discharged.

The Banco Ejidal has found itself in competition with some of the more prosperous illegal buyers who have offered to supply credit for ejidos at extremely low rates of interest in order that they might have a base of operations without purchasing land of their own. Ejidos have been duped into withdrawing from their connections with the Banco Ejidal by such moves.

A drastic federal decree which attempted to cut down on this traffic was issued in 1943. It forbade free commerce in unginned cotton and set up elaborate regulations providing that only licensed gins may purchase such cotton. Through a system of identification by the gin and checking back on private and *ejidal* production, it was hoped to get to the root of the problem. It turned out, however, that since the thieves could bribe soldiers, police, and government officials successfully, they continued to operate under the new law, even though it was more difficult.[18]

There have been scattered cases of defalcation among officers of the ejidos themselves, as would be expected. One local treasurer fled from the region with 300 pesos. A work-chief was found pocketing 371 pesos which represented the payroll for his group for two weeks. Such incidents seem to be relatively few.[19]

Experience in other parts of Mexico indicates that the presence of a strong independent peasant organization which can organize demonstrations, make charges against bank officials, and petition the president of Mexico for redress if they can not find it locally, has contributed greatly to making graft on the part of Banco Ejidal officials a relatively minor matter in the region. This is not enough, however. We have seen that the bureaucratic interests of the Banco Ejidal employees led to the splitting of the peasant movement and the encouragement of an organization which could be manipulated by them. Unless there is a strong and independent peasant movement nationally which can support local or regional peasant organizations, the local group will be defeated.

Graft has been democratized, as it is in the United States. Twenty years ago, Tannenbaum pointed out that

Mexican politics revolve about the treasury [and that this will be] inevitable for a long time to come. Outside the government there are no sources of income in Mexico that are secure, definite, self-perpetuating and available. All wealth is precarious, limited, constantly subject to danger from public attack or theft through robbery or rebellion, and this has been so for 120 years.[20]

This explanation of the widespread corruption in Mexico stresses two factors: economic and, by implication, sociological. The situation, Tannenbaum says, will improve when people can make money some other way than by either working for or cheating the government. The history of dishonest means of amassing fortunes in both England and the United States indicates that there is weight to this explanation.[21]

Almost every newspaper in the United States supplies qualifications daily, however, and the millions of dollars of which the public is cheated by business frauds force us to maintain Better Business bureaus, Pure Food and Drug Act machinery, the Federal Trade Commission, Senate investigating committees, and other expensive policing of business habits. Obviously, something more than an economic explanation is needed.

The sociological explanation seems to lie in the strength of a Mexican heritage, not in the absence of norms, as seems to be indicated by Tannenbaum. The country has a long tradition of accepting graft as an essential ingredient of its governmental and private business: that *is* the norm.

Gruening points out that municipal offices in Spain were openly for sale in the sixteenth century and that "high office was a perquisite . . . which sanctioned pillage from the top."[22]

The scarcity of opportunities to become wealthy, plus the intense individualism also inherited from Spain, helped make "short cuts to success" accepted. Since most of the natural resources and public utilities of the country were monopolies of foreigners, the Mexican with better than average schooling who could not get a government post had to "sell out" to the foreigner. It became patriotic for those who could not or would not do so to make money at the expense of the foreigner.

There are two interlocking groups with which the Mexican usually will share his wealth—family and friends. The extended family system—the *compadrazgo*— which has its roots in both Spanish and Indian traditions, is responsible for much of the public and private nepotism which helps exploit the Mexican people.[23]

The outstanding Mexican sociologist Lic. Lucio Mendieta y Nuñez describes the results in damaged morale when "aviators" are put on the payroll of a government office with nothing to do in the office but draw their pay. He also notes that supplies for public clinics and even food for hospitals are often inadequate because of minor officials lining their pockets.[24]

Exposés of graft and fraud during the Alemán administration started exploding immediately after it went out of office in the fall of 1952. The amounts pocketed by the government clique must be astronomical for a poverty-stricken country such as Mexico, even if they do not reach the frequently quoted figure of $800 million.[25]

President Adolfo Ruiz Cortines took occasion in his inaugural address to lash out at the grafters and to promise a "cleanup." He chose a device tried thirteen years before by President Cárdenas: "the law of responsibilities of public employees."[26]

The Cárdenas and Ruiz Cortines laws provide that public officials and employees shall declare their wealth and income under oath upon assuming and again upon leaving office or job. Undue enrichment is punishable. The newer law also states that an investigation of an official's wealth may be undertaken at any time, with the onus on him "to prove that his property and possessions do not exceed his 'economic possibilities.' "[27]

Other strong voices have been raised in recent years against graft and corruption. The daily and weekly press consistently attacks and exposes one or another aspect of dishonesty in public life. Outstanding public figures such as university professors, labor leaders, and publicists have taken heart from the increase in public criticism.[28]

This will indicate why President Ruiz Cortines received such an enthusiastic outburst of approval for his "moralization campaign."[29] The leadership of the president is of enormous importance in Mexico. If it supplies insistent and consistent pressure during the six-year term, and if it is seconded by important organizations and individuals through the social structure and·in all parts of the country, real strides forward may be made.

It should be remembered that the cultural heritage of the United States also included a tradition of governmental graft and corruption which marked our public and private life for most of our history and has by no means been eliminated.[30] It has receded partly because of an aroused and organized public opinion. The democratization of corruption can be the forerunner of improvement only if private attitudes are changed from "He's getting his now; wait till I get my chance" to "Let's change the rules so that nobody can get rich without working honestly for his income."

The building of democracy in La Laguna started with a new legal frame of reference within which the peasants were to work. The old order of society provided no place for their initiative, participation, or exercise of responsibility. The new order required these in large measure. To a high degree the demand brought forth the supply—among the peasants. They were playing a new role in society—one which many of them had thought about, dreamed about, discussed and planned for during the years between the civil war and the belated arrival of revolutionary rewards.

The Banco Ejidal and other government employees were also expected to do something new for which they had developed no patterns—to help bring the peasants into real participation. Some of them had the "living convictions" which Sorokin lists as essential to wholehearted support of social norms.[31] Others did not. They readily fell into playing the exploitive, or at least manipulative, role which superior social status had always meant in Mexico. It was relatively easy for them to betray the democratic program since they, and even many of the more idealistic, wanted to "do something *for* the peasants." It is difficult to realize and even more difficult to carry out a program based on the democratic process, which means to "do something *with* the peasants."[32]

Insistent and persistent national leadership by the president, the head of the Departamento Agrario, the Banco Ejidal, or the Mexican Society of Agronomists might have gone a long way toward strengthening those in the bureaucracy who believed in agrarian democracy. Such leadership left the scene, at least temporarily, at the end of the Cárdenas administration.

The Laguna experience would indicate that democracy does

not grow spontaneously after land reform but must be deliberately promoted. Furthermore, the social norms of various groups involved in the reform must be recognized as playing at least as vital a role as new legal and economic arrangements.

REGIONAL LEVELS OF LIVING

Substantial improvements in levels of living have been indicated, but a more adequate picture of how the people of the region live is needed than can here be presented. Only two studies have been made which provide insight into rural levels of living generally in the Laguna region and both are now out-of-date, having been made in 1939 and 1943. A sketchy survey in one ejido in 1953 is helpful in supplementing the earlier data, as are minimum wage reports. The 1939 survey of 400 peasant families was made in twenty-three villages. It lasted three months and produced adequate data on 328 families. The results of the survey and comparisons with a similar survey made among families of industrial workers in Mexico City in 1938 supplied important though fragmentary data on rural life in the region in that year.[33]

Families in the Laguna region are larger than those in Mexico City, with an average of 4.54 consumption units per family, compared with 3.98 units per family, a mode of four members as compared with three, and 21.04 per cent of the families with over seven members contrasted with 4.65 per cent.

Comparison of expenditures on food shows people in the Laguna region spending more than five times as much on cereals, more than twice as much on sugar and on condiments; less than one-half as much on meat and milk, slightly more on fats and oils and fruits and vegetables, and only a minor fraction of the Mexico City expenditure on beverages. Although data on calory values of the various foods are not available, obviously more protective foods are badly needed by Laguna families.

When all expenditures are broken down, it is seen that Laguna families spend approximately the same percentage of their total on food and on domestic services as those in Mexico City. They spend almost twice as much on clothing, but only 1.83 per cent on shelter as compared with 9.40 per cent spent by Mexico City families.

Prices have risen very considerably in the Laguna region since this survey was made. Data made available by the Secretaría del

Trabajo y Provisión Social in the spring of 1943 indicated that in the Laguna region as a whole minimum family budgets accounted for 103 per cent of average family incomes.

A seven-month study of levels of living in El Cuije in 1953 throws light on the damage done by over four years of drought in what had been a fairly well-off ejido.[34] All but four of the sixteen families studied (about one-fourth of all the families in the ejido ran into debt in the year studied. Much of the debt was carried by the communal store run by the ejido itself. The daily expenditures per adult ranged from an incredible low of 4.67 pesos ($0.51) to a high of 21 pesos ($2.31). Corn, rice, potatoes, or other starches made up the principal items of food. Fortunately, as Miss Kelly points out, almost all of these were served with tomato sauce, chilis, onions, or other ingredients which supply vitamins. The starch consumption was about the same as that in several Mexican Indian towns studied. Sugar intake was high, about 30 per cent above that of the average for the United States. Meat had all but disappeared from the diet, and only half the families ate eggs with any regularity. Beans, as in most of Mexico, were the chief source of protein.

Miss Kelly felt that one of the reasons the peasants in El Cuije were not doing more for themselves lay in malnutrition. Unfortunately, no data are available for comparisons with the family diets when the ejido was prosperous and some of the members were receiving as much as 10,000 to 14,000 pesos ($1,100 to $1,540) per year in profit.

Some idea of incomes may be secured from sketchy data available for both urban and rural wage rates fifteen years ago.[35] At the top of the wage and salary pyramid stood the skilled metallurgical workers. Wages in 1942 ranged from 68.07 pesos ($13.97) per 45-hour week for foremen to 15.54 pesos ($3.19) for 40 hours worked by the apprentices and 15.30 pesos ($3.15) per 34 hours worked by janitors and similar unskilled workers. Common mill labor received 27.27 pesos ($5.62) for 39 hours. The average for mine and metallurgical labor in 1941 was 37 pesos ($7.63) for 45 hours.

A higher average wage was received in 1941 by the small number of light and power workers, who drew 48 pesos ($9.89) for a 42-hour week, and the printing trades workers who earned 48 pesos ($9.89) for a 43-hour week. The workers in the two small foundries in Torreón averaged 46.68 pesos ($9.63) for a 45-hour week. Following in order were workers in breweries, with a weekly average in April, 1941, of 35.92 pesos ($7.41); railroad workers (Gómez Palacio has a roundhouse and Torreón is a division point on two railroads) with 35.11 pesos ($7.24); woolen textile operatives with 34.73 pesos ($7.16) (1945 average); soap factory labor with 38.07 pesos ($7.82); garage mechanics with 27.90 pesos ($5.75); workers in Torreón commercial establishments with 27.30 pesos ($5.63); and bakery workers with 25.90 pesos ($5.34). Workers in the numerous small mills which grind corn for tortillas averaged 25.08 pesos ($5.17). The municipal services average was 21.69 pesos ($4.47) and building labor got 17.28 pesos ($3.56).

The 186 school teachers of Torreón received an average of 23.08 pesos ($4.76) per week in 1943. The nine highest-paid received 200 pesos ($41.24) a month, the six lowest-paid, 30 pesos ($6.19).[36] Their salaries were raised an average of 54 per cent in the next two years.

The wages of the skilled and semiskilled workers mentioned above have been recorded in special studies. The wages of other workers are not available, but an idea of unskilled wages is furnished by the legal minimum wage rates set every two years since 1934 by joint government-employer labor boards.[37]

The averages of the legal minimum wages in the region for city and rural workers are given in Table 9. Since the decision of the

TABLE 9
LEGAL MINIMUM WAGE INDEX
LAGUNA REGION
1942-1955
(*pesos per day*)

Municipio	Urban			Rural		
	1942-1943	1952-1953	1954-1955	1942-1943	1952-1953	1954-1955
Coahuila						
Matamoros	2.75	7.45	8.60	1.90	4.75	5.70
San Pedro	2.75	6.90	7.90	1.90	4.75	5.70
Torreón	2.75	7.60	9.10	1.90	4.75	5.70
Viesca	1.75	6.30	7.23	1.50	4.35	5.25
Durango						
Gómez Palacio	2.75	8.00	9.55	1.90	4.75	5.70
Lerdo	2.00	8.00	9.55	1.75	4.75	5.70
Mapimí	2.00	5.00	7.20	1.75	4.50	5.70

Source: Dirección General de Estadística.

boards is based on the cost of living in each *municipio*, the average minimum wages set for five periods of the past eighteen years are given for Coahuila, Durango, and Mexico as a whole in Table 10. The rates for the Laguna region parallel the state rates closely. Nationally, urban rates rose 89 per cent from 1936-1937 to 1946-1947, rural rates 69 per cent. Coahuila's urban and rural rates rose 120 and 74 per cent respectively, while Durango's went up 73 and 55 per cent. Again in the interval from 1946-1947 to 1954-1955, Coahuila and Durango rates rose somewhat more than national rates. This did not hold for the following year, however.

Legal minimum wages are generally actual wages in unorganized

TABLE 10

LEGAL MINIMUM WAGE AVERAGES

1936-1955

(pesos per day)

	1936-1937	1940-1941	1946-1947	1952-1953	1954-1955
Coahuila					
Urban	1.43	1.99	3.14	5.28	6.91
Rural	1.17	1.42	2.04	3.97	5.38
Durango					
Urban	1.09	1.52	1.89	4.43	5.99
Rural	1.06	1.34	1.64	3.20	4.08
National Average					
Urban	1.31	1.52	2.48	5.35	6.66
Rural	1.21	1.30	2.05	4.55	5.68

Source: *Anuario Estadístico, 1940; El Salario Mínimo, 1946-47,* Secretaría de la Economía Nacional, p. 4; *Compendio Estadístico,* 1951, p. 294; Dirección General de Estadística.

occupations, so that the rates given may safely be assumed to be close to the prevailing wages by the day. Unfortunately, no surveys have been made of the number of days worked by the unskilled urban worker. Therefore, the average annual income is unknown for this group. Rural laborers usually work 200 to 250 days a year, except in drought years.

Inflation has held back rises in the real value of money wages in La Laguna, as in Mexico as a whole. Real wages of the nation's industrial workers fell 27 per cent from 1939 to 1947, recovered about 5 per cent in 1948 and 1949 and then lost some ground in the following two years. It is probable that even the agricultural workers in La Laguna (and other commercialized farming areas) have experienced the same tendency since they must "import" from other regions most of what they consume, just as do urban workers. It is often pointed out that one of the results of the land reform has been that the producers of food crops eat better now, but often at the expense of production going into market channels.[38]

Beds have been one of the household items most prized by the *ejidatarios* since they have had more money to spend. The 1939 housing census showed all but three Laguna *municipios* with higher than the Mexican average for beds per one hundred persons. The straw *petate* stretched on the floor was still in the majority, however (Table 11).

Next to beds come sewing machines. All regional *municipios* showed a greater number per one hundred persons than the national

TABLE 11

BEDS, SEWING MACHINES, AND RADIOS PER 100 PERSONS
MEXICO, COAHUILA, DURANGO, AND LA LAGUNA
1939

	Beds per 100 persons	Sewing machines per 100 persons	Radios per 100 persons
Mexico	25.5	4.8	1.6
Coahuila	32.3	7.9	2.1
Durango	28.6	7.7	.9
La Laguna			
Gómez Palacio	31.7	8.3	2.1
Lerdo	31.5	8.4	1.7
F. I. Madero	21.1	6.7	.4
Mapimí	28.2	7.6	.4
Matamoros	23.7	7.5	.5
San Pedro	26.9	7.8	.8
Tlahualilo	29.2	9.3	.4
Torreón	40.3	9.1	4.2
Viesca	22.0	7.2	.1

Source: Censo de Edificios, 1939 (México: Dirección General de Estadística, 1939).

rate. Radios, being more expensive, needing electricity and having less utility, lag behind the national rate, except in the cities. Most of the ejidos own community radios.

Hacendados generally supplied housing for their peons rent free before the expropriations. Most were one-room adobe huts usually measuring approximately ten or twelve feet square. Cooking, heating, and sleeping were all done in the one room. "Living" was done outside! In addition there were many reed and mud huts' and even some caves in hillsides or along river banks which were used by migratory workers. Adobe houses, which had represented slightly more than three-fourths of all the houses in the region in 1939 (Table 32, Appendix), had risen to almost nine-tenths in 1950. Reed and daubed reed huts had begun to disappear from the region by the time of the 1950 census. Only 864 were found in that year compared with 3,364 just eleven years before.[39]

One of the first efforts of many of the peasants after they began to receive a larger income was to improve their housing. In several dozen cases the approach was a fundamental one. The village was moved away from its former site and laid out anew near a road or highway. A school was built first in nearly every case, and the homes were then grouped around the school, which served as the community center. Attempts were made, in those ejidos which could not move, to build at least one model house. Plans for these homes were drafted by the engineering section of the Banco Ejidal and the *ejidatarios* were aided in planning the houses. The bank's plans provided for a bedroom 13 x 13 feet, a kitchen 9 x 13, and a living room 13 x 13. The kitchen contains an open fire place for heating the house and for cooking. The cost of materials for building such a house in 1937 was 450 pesos ($90.00).

The social fund of an ejido was used in some cases to build several model houses. The members then drew lots to see which families would occupy the new houses. It was hoped in this way to provide an incentive for other *ejidatarios* to build their own new homes from their own funds.

Nueva California, an ejido of twenty-six families, handled the matter another way. It borrowed money from the Banco Ejidal after several successful seasons during which it established a top credit rating. An architect was hired to design a home to the liking of the group, and all twenty-six houses were built on the same model. The housing loans ran for twenty years.[40]

A larger-scale attack on the problem of rehousing the Laguna peasants was started by Marte R. Gómez, Secretary of Agriculture, in 1942. At his suggestion the bank drew up plans for a "model of urbanization." The ejido of Ana was moved almost a mile and relocated along the Torreón-San Pedro highway. The new location was planned so that houses are supplied with safe drinking water and drainage. Streets are wide and there is a market place and a playground. Sixty houses were included in the project, which was to cost 150,000 pesos ($30,000). The cornerstone of the first house was laid on June 2, 1942. Most of the houses had been built when the village was revisited in June, 1943. The new homes are outstandingly different from most peasant dwellings in their provision for drinking water and adequate drainage.

Even so, Table 33, Appendix, shows that the more rural of the *municipios* still had considerable distances to cover before they matched the improvement shown by Torreón.

ADVANCES IN HEALTH AND SANITATION

Poverty, illiteracy, and superstition, plus almost complete absence of medical facilities, presented President Cárdenas with another difficult complex of problems to be faced in changing the social system of the Laguna region. Smallpox, endemic for about two hundred years, was usually treated by *curanderas*, or witch doctors. Although the peasants of the Laguna region were more advanced in their thinking than those of most other regions of Mexico, there was still great dependence on "folk medicine." Among many, the practice was to "scare away evil spirits which cause smallpox." Neighbors would gather around the victim in an attempt to drive away the spirits. Smallpox has been wiped out in the ejidos, in spite of this discouraging background. The story revolves around hard-won cooperation between the *ejidatarios* and medical personnel.

Only near the cities were there doctors available before the expropriations, even in cases serious enough to result in death. While the region was ahead of Mexico as a whole in this respect in 1930, the situation was far from satisfactory. Sixty-three per cent of all deaths were unattended in Mexico as compared with the following experience of the Laguna municipios:

Gómez Palacio	29.3
Lerdo	51.9
Mapimí	48.1
Matamoros	58.9
San Pedro	56.2
Torreón	2.8
Viesca	68.5

The difference between city and rural experience is very evident.

This vast problem was attacked first in a number of small-scale preliminary attempts. The first *ejidal* medical unit was 'established in November, 1936. By February of the following year twelve units had been established. Each succeeding month brought increased expenditure, but the peasants were disappointed. They found that the doctors were city born and trained and did not know how to cope with the problems which faced them. A convention was held by the *ejidatarios* to discuss the medical services in August, 1937. Over two hundred speeches were made by peasant delegates in three days. Most of them contained sharp criticism of the organization and its personnel. The *ejidatarios* had added 300,000 pesos to the 200,000 the government had budgeted for the first year's work. They felt that they were not getting their money's worth.[41]

As a result of the criticism there was a house cleaning. New personnel was brought in and the organization was improved administratively with peasant participation as an outstanding innovation. Its name, Servicios Coordinados de Higiene Rural y Medicina Social en la Comarca Lagunera, indicates the scope of its work.[42] Activities have increased steadily and the financial support coming from the *ejidatarios* increased 212 per cent from 1938 to 1952, being 1,327,573 pesos in the latter year. The federal government added 1,088,582 pesos. Crisis conditions in many ejidos in 1946 and 1947, and again in 1951 and 1952, caused a slight drop in contributions in those years. The Central Union in 1947 agreed to share with the federal government the cost of building a 250-bed hospital, which was opened three years later.

From the first the organization stressed preventive medicine and set as its ideal 70 per cent of its resources for prevention, 30 per cent for cure.[43] The region was divided into nineteen zones and in each one a medical unit was housed. It consisted of a doctor, a nurse, a midwife, and a pharmacist. Each unit was equipped with a stock of the more common drugs and equipment sufficient to take care of all but serious cases of illness or accident. Each unit had two ambulances for emergency service as far as roads would take them. Eight first-aid stations and five clinics were established in isolated spots which could not be reached from the units. A central hospital for more serious cases and more lengthy treatment was created in Torreón. Another hospital for contagious diseases was built later. There were 45 full-time doctors in 1952, assisted by two dentists, 18 midwives, 118 nurses, 21 pharmacists, and 184 other employees. Patients hospitalized averaged 2,550 per year from 1940 to 1950, and 2,097 operations were performed annually.

Peasant participation is open to ejidos only, but the "free" ejidos may join it. Services are available only through membership by the ejidos and the whole machinery of the organized *ejidatarios* is used to build and maintain confidence in and utilization of the medical facilities supplied. The section of the services which attends to hygiene and sanitation in the villages has built a close working relationship with the women's groups, the rural school teachers, and the *ejidal* unions. A travelling sanitary brigade systematically visits every ejido in the region, checking up on the regular work of the service and pointing out conditions which should be remedied either by the services themselves, by the villagers, or by cooperation between the two.

The factors involved in assessing the success of the services are many. There is no doubt that there has been an increased acceptance of the newest medical and sanitary techniques. During the first several years a great deal of time had to be spent breaking down mistrust and "selling" the *ejidatarios* and their families on the advantages of the service. The medical personnel was aided greatly in this by the peasant leaders, both male and female, who had lived and worked in the United States. The next phase was reached with an acceptance of the doctors, but they were called on only when sickness occurred. For the past fifteen years the services feel that they have entered a third phase. The peasants no longer wait until they are ill, but take an active interest in preventive measures. For example, in the summer of 1943 twelve cases of smallpox appeared in the town of San Pedro, which is not within the jurisdiction of the *ejidal* services. Nevertheless the *ejidatarios* came to the doctors with the plea that the people of San Pedro be vaccinated against smallpox. They pointed out the danger to the peasants of contagion when they went to San Pedro to market or to attend meetings. They also secured the approval of the local authorities. Then the *ejidal* services concentrated all available doctors and nurses in San Pedro and vaccinated the entire population of over 16,000 in a few days.

Vaccinations against smallpox have won increased acceptance year by year, gaining more than ten-fold from 1937 to 1942 (4,082 to 42,427). Vaccinations for the 1940-1950 decade totalled 141,728.

The campaign has been carried on so assiduously that the services could boast that within their own sphere of activities, which includes approximately 100,000 persons, smallpox had been brought down to one case in 1941 and no cases in the following years.

Child births provide another indication of the increased acceptance of the medical services. Women usually refused to come to them when the hospitals were first set up. Even after this attitude had been broken down, largely through the wholehearted support of the women's civic leagues, many who came felt so uncomfortable in beds that the nurses found them sleeping on the straw mats on the floor. With this background in mind the advance indicated by the percentage of births attended at *ejidal* medical centers as compared with homes is more meaningful. From 1938 to 1942 the percentage rose as follows: 3, 9, 11, 16, 24. The proportion had risen to 52 per cent by 1950.

This is most unusual in Mexico. Doctors are "rarely called in to deliver a child, even in the upper-class segment of the population" in a Jalisco town studied by Norman D. Humphrey,[44] and "virtually all births occur in the home."

The work load of patients attended in 1950 averaged 372 per cent higher than in 1938, and totalled 160,399. Some 369,500 therapeutic injections were administered.

Venereal disease had been a serious problem in the area before the expropriations, as it is in most of the underdeveloped areas of the world. The incidence of syphilis seems to have increased as transportation to the large "red-light" district of Torreón became easier and the peasants had more money to spend. Reduction of morbidity rates from 793 per 100,000 in 1938 to 572 in 1950 has been achieved in spite of male resistance to the use of modern prophylactic precautions. Norman Humphrey found the same reaction in Tecolotlán, Jalisco: "Prophylactics are sold in the town but evidently are employed only by some upper-class men, and here largely in extramarital areas and with reluctance."[45]

Tuberculosis has shown an impressive decline in cases reported: from 1515 in 1938 to 200 in 1950. Pneumonia cases dropped from 240 in 1938 to 112 in 1950.

Typhoid showed a drop from about 400 cases in 1938 to 200 five years later. Safe drinking water was available in 1943 in only 46 ejidos out of 310, or 14.8 per cent. Typhoid incidence had by 1952 been reduced to around twelve per 100,000 through more general provision of safe drinking water.

Dysenteries and undulant fever are serious diseases against which real headway has been slow in spite of intensive efforts. The region for years has had a widespread reputation as a center of undulant fever (also known as brucellosis, Malta fever, or goat fever). A reduction of two-thirds was achieved between 1946 and 1952, although the summer peak still reaches 200 cases, compared with about 600 in the earlier year.

Mexico's infant death rate has been reduced from 286.8 per 1,000 in 1900 to 125.7 in 1940, and 95.8 in 1950. The reduction in the United States in the same period was from 138.2 to around 30, and it is far surpassed by New Zealand. Most Laguna *municipios* lagged behind the 1940 rate for the entire country, but by 1950 the situation had improved appreciably (Table 17, p. 171).

Diarrhea and enteritis rank first as killers of adults in each Laguna *municipio*. Infants have even less chance against them than adults. Therefore, until safe water supplies are provided for all the villages, and the peasants are thoroughly imbued with the need for extraordinary precautions, the infant death rate will continue high.

One important gap in the *ejidal* services is absence of any provision for education of women in the rudiments of the physiology of reproduction, to say nothing of contraception. The attitude, expressed by doctors interviewed on the subject over the years, has been a mixture of fear and futility. "We can't afford to broach the subject, since contraceptive devices are illegal," "the people are opposed to any discussion of the subject," "the men won't use condoms even with prostitutes so how could we get them to use them with wives?" Only the older doctors mention religious feelings; the younger ones are somewhat more apt to be influenced by the nationalistic demography dealt with later.

Two women active in the *ligas femeniles* expressed a desire for information in this field at the Laguna conferences organized by the writer in 1940 and 1941. They claimed that a considerable number of women had become aware of the possibilities of preventing unwanted conceptions, but that there was no place to turn for help. Inquiry revealed that both these women had lived and worked in the beet fields of Colorado and had learned of contraception there.

That Mexican women in regions far less "advanced" than La

Laguna are beginning to feel the need for some intelligence applied to childbearing is indicated by a recent study in Morelos.[46] The general attitude of the Tepoztecan women seems to be expressed in the statement:

There is no way out. I have a husband. If more children come, what can we do? We will endure it even though like pigs they come one after another.

But the attitude is changing. Lewis reports:

Many women actively express interest in birth control. There is no doubt that if such information were available, and if permitted by their husbands, a large number of women would practice birth control. Abortion, although very secretive, is not uncommon, and it is said that many women take medicine to make themselves sterile.

It has been shown that rural-urban fertility differentials were already present in Coahuila and Durango in 1939. The spread of the urban pattern will undoubtedly continue, and speed up, as it has in Western civilization generally. Class and sex barriers hamper such diffusion; the extension of democracy will facilitate it.[47]

The *ejidal* services in 1943 covered 310 ejidos with 125,100 persons, counting *ejidatarios* and their families. Crisis conditions had reduced the number to 95,000 by 1952, or 45 per cent of the rural people. This leaves over half of the rural population of the region dependent on almost nonexistent private facilities. This gap is regrettable not only from the humanitarian standpoint, but because it endangers the advances made by the *ejidal* services. It is an old medical aphorism that "germs are no respecters of boundaries."

The urban population is only slightly better situated, except in Torreón where medical and dental facilities are more adequate than in Mexico as a whole. Mexico had one doctor for 9,100 persons in 1938. The United States had one for each 750. Torreón, in 1939, had one for each 1,500 and it had 41 more doctors in 1947 than in 1939.

EDUCATION IN THE NEW ORDER

The crucial role of education was appreciated by President Cárdenas and his co-workers at the inception of the Laguna experiment. This was in the tradition of The Revolution.

Public education in rural Mexico was all but unknown before 1910. It existed to a very small degree even in the cities. Literacy in the nation increased only 5.8 per cent between 1900 and 1910 (Table 12). In spite of the fact that Mexico was in a state of civil war most of the next eleven years, there was an increase of 4.8 per cent. A federal department of public education was formed in 1921 and since that time large increases have been shown most years in the budgets for education, both urban and rural. Literacy figures show no progress between 1921 and 1930, probably because of continually disturbed conditions. The 1940 census showed Mexico 41.7 per cent literate, which would mean an increase of 8.3 per cent between 1930 and 1940, and 12.9 per cent between 1910 and 1940.

TABLE 12
LITERACY: MEXICO, COAHUILA, AND DURANGO
1900, 1910, 1921, 1930, 1940, 1950

	1900*	1910	1921	1930	1940†	1950
Mexico	23.0	28.8	33.6	33.4	41.7	55.9
Coahuila	36.4	43.7	60.5	47.5	62.0	72.8
Durango	22.7	27.5	52.3	38.0	49.9	67.7

Source: Censo General, 1900; Anuario Estadístico, 1938, 1940; Dirección General de Estadística, 1952.
*The 1900 census included those who could read only, while later counts included only those who could both read and write. Thus the 1900 figures are relatively higher than later figures.
†The 1940 census lowered the age of inquiry to six. The age of ten or over was used in previous censuses. Thus the data are not strictly comparable.

Data for 1950 indicate some increase in the rate of progress, with a gain of 14.2 per cent since the previous census.[48]

Rural education has been stressed heavily ever since the federal department was created. The Cárdenas government, with its orientation toward rural reorganization, placed special emphasis upon the education of the peasants. The schoolteacher was expected to be the "dynamo" of community life and the school was to be considered "a center for the study and solution of all community problems in their economic, social, recreational, and cultural aspects."

From 1921 to 1936 rural education in the Laguna region was found in an anomalous position. The schoolteachers were supposed to explain the Mexican constitution to the pupils, but this did not fit into the plan of the hacendados. There were a number of incidents arising from this contradiction.

The tempo of rural education in the region changed with the October 6 decrees. The singing of the agrarian hymn opened school sessions. The teacher found herself serving as an aide in the reorganization of rural life. In addition to regular classroom work, which included explanations of the Mexican revolution, especially in its agrarian phases, the teacher had many outside jobs. *Ejidatarios* crowded the schoolrooms at night to learn about the agrarian code and the new ejido system in all of its aspects. Meetings were held in the afternoons to give a boost to the women's leagues. Plots of land set aside for cultivation by the school children had to be managed. The teacher was also involved in the extracurricular teaching of personal and community hygiene, in the promotion of consumer cooperatives, theatrical clubs for children, musical groups for adults, and sports groups for the youth.

Some 280 rural schoolteachers were employed in 1936. By 1947 there were 441, with many petitions for teachers still unfilled. One of the earliest jobs of the teacher under the new regime was to help in the building of a schoolhouse. Schools had been held in makeshift buildings, in unused corners of warehouses, in one of the larger village huts, or even under trees. Around 250 new school buildings were erected in the region between the fall of 1936 and the end of 1947. Now each ejido has a school, but some of the other villages still lack them. Enrollment for the 1946-1947 school year was 26,829. Data for the number of schools by *municipios* are not available, but Table 13, showing the number of primary schools in Mexico as a whole and in the states of Coahuila and Durango for 1927, 1937, 1940, 1950, and 1952, shows the tendency.

TABLE 13

PRIMARY SCHOOLS: MEXICO, COAHUILA, AND DURANGO
1927, 1937, 1940, 1950, 1952

	1927	1937	1940	1950	1952	Increase 1927-1952
Mexico	14,188	20,423	23,434	24,075	25,613	80%
Coahuila	568	628	708	749	795	40%
Durango	175	555	797	856	965	451%

Sources: Anuario Estadístico, 1938, 1940; *Compendio Estadístico*, 1953; Dirección General de Estadística.

Data are not available for 1910 or 1921 on literacy in the Laguna *municipios*, but Table 14 shows the situation in 1900, 1930, 1940, and 1950. The lowest literacy rates are found in San Pedro, Viesca, Matamoros, and Mapimí, as would be expected, since they include the poorest parts of the area. The three *municipios* with the largest cities show the highest rates of literacy, of course.

TABLE 14

LITERACY: LA LAGUNA

1900, 1930, 1940, 1950

Municipio	1900	1930	1940	1950
Gómez Palacio	*	42.8	60.9	75.8
Lerdo	24.1	45.3	59.3	71.1
Mapimí	27.3	41.3	51.4	60.2
Matamoros	23.7	47.6	51.9	65.0
San Pedro	31.6	37.5	56.4	64.4
Torreón	41.1	54.5	77.6	79.5
Viesca	45.0	35.0	50.4	65.2

Source: *Censo General*, 1900, 1950; *Anuario Estadístico*, 1938, 1940, 1952.
*Formed part of Mapimí district in 1900.

The region as a whole was only a few points above the national average in 1900, except for Torreón and Viesca. The latter lost ground between 1900 and 1930, in contrast to all the other Laguna *municipios*, and was still lagging in 1950. The rest of the regional units all came at least close to doubling their literacy rate in the first half of the century; Lerdo almost tripled its rate.

Informal education now plays a far greater role than previously. Each day now contains new experiences of an educational nature for many of the *ejidatarios*. Discussions carried on in ejido meetings impress one with the wide range of decisions which are now being made by men who a few years ago were either illiterate or had had only two or three years of elementary schooling. The meetings deal with such subjects as the acreage of the various crops to be planted during the next season, the way in which irrigation water is measured and the irrigation district managed, the supply of credit and the advantages and disadvantages of working with the Banco Ejidal. Representatives of the *ejidatarios* sit on committees which make decisions affecting the welfare of the entire region and almost invariably are obviously greatly impressed with the responsibility which has been placed upon them. They make trips to the center of the *municipio*, to Torreón, to the state capital, and to Mexico City representing their fellows before government bodies. They go to other parts of Mexico to explain happenings in the Laguna region to *ejidatarios* of other zones. To aid them in their new responsibilities the public school system holds classes during the late afternoon and at night, in which some 5,000 persons were enrolled each term during the early years of the reform.

The peasants of La Laguna are more fortunate than those of many other regions in having had greater possibilities of contact with the outside world via the printed page.

Both Torreón and San Pedro have been noted publishing centers for north-central Mexico. The latter has been eclipsed by Torreón for three decades, but from the days of Madero to the early 1920's it saw more than a dozen influential newspapers and reviews published. Torreón now has two dailies—one founded in 1917, the other in 1922—several weeklies, and several organs of special groups. Periodicals published during the 1900-1926 period numbered thirty-eight and included organs of the Chamber of Commerce, Rotary Club, the Spanish colony, as well as labor and socialist papers. From 1902 to 1913 there was an English paper, *The Torreón Enterprise*. Important dailies from the nation's capital now sell several hundred copies each in Torreón.

There have been contacts with the outside world and new ideas practically from the founding of the city. There has been nothing like the isolation of most of rural Mexico, except for distant villages on the periphery of the region. The potentialities for broadening the horizons of the people which these contacts afforded have become actualities since the expropriations. Although the writer could not quantify the trend, observation over sixteen years indicates a tremendous increase in the circulation of printed material in the villages. Even Torreón had no bookstore in 1937, for example; by 1953 there was one which would do justice to a town in the United States perhaps twice the size of Torreón, plus several smaller stores.

Technical agricultural education was, of course, completely unknown to the Laguna peasants, except for the few who had been taught by hacienda foremen to run tractors or tend water pumps. The government created a school of regional agriculture on the old Hacienda de Santa Teresa. This school has expanded its curriculum and the length of its courses each year. It now offers the material shown in Table 15 during three terms of ten months each. Two students are selected by each zone from among the *ejidatarios* who have shown the most initiative, intelligence, and leadership ability. The selections are made by agreement between the ejidos and the Banco Ejidal zone-chiefs. They are usually in their middle or late twenties, although there has been a tendency toward lowering the age in the past several years.

The Santa Teresa school is run as an ejido. The students, with the advice of the faculty members, cultivate the land assigned to the school, sell the surplus products, and distribute the profits in the same manner as the regular ejidos. There is a small experiment station at the school where the students and teachers together try

TABLE 15

CURRICULUM, SCHOOL OF PRACTICAL AGRICULTURE
SANTA TERESA, COAHUILA

Subject	Terms Taught		
Drawing	I	II	III
Geography	I	II	
History	I	II	
Arithmetic and Geometry	I	II	
Nature Study	I		
Physical and Premilitary Training	I	\II	III
Elementary Agriculture		II	III
Rural Industries		II	III
Practice with Farm Tools	I	II	III
Domestic Husbandry		II	III
Civics		II	III
Practice with Farm Machinery			III
Cooperative and Ejidal Bookkeeping			III
Economics			III
Elementary Chemistry			III
Elementary Physics			III
Farm Machinery Management			III

Source: Personal visit, August 6, 1947.

out crops which are new to the region and which might be recommended to the *ejidatarios*.

The Coahuila government founded an agricultural school in San Pedro in 1940. It is also a boarding school, but the students are much younger and are offered a four-year course which includes both secondary subjects and agricultural training. It has a capacity for 100 students. At Saltillo the state government also has maintained for some years a school of agriculture on a late secondary and junior college level. Students attending it number 150.

In addition to these schools the Banco Ejidal and the Central Union of Collective Credit Societies early carried on educational programs. *Ejidatarios* have been training as water gagers, cotton and cotton seed classifiers, and bookkeepers. For several years the Banco Ejidal sponsored educational radio broadcasts from Torreón stations. Since 87 per cent of the ejidos had radio sets for community use in 1941 this was thought to be a valuable technique of reaching the members of the local credit societies. The *ejidatarios* themselves took part in both the musical and educational aspects of the programs.

The bank published a regular printed bulletin which went to all members of the credit societies for four years following the reorganization. It contained material on the region itself and on agrarian and agricultural experiences of peasants in other parts of Mexico. During the economy moves within the bank in 1940 both the radio programs and the bulletins were discontinued. This left no way in which the membership could be reached regularly except through the cumbersome process of regional delegates' reporting to zone meetings from which local delegates took the message to their own ejido meetings.

The same economy wave, plus jurisdictional jealousies, wrecked the regional federal education office in 1941. For the first four years under the new system the region had been treated as a unit. The schools helped build up a feeling in both children and adults that they were part of an increasingly important integrated community which was the object of attention throughout the rest of Mexico and even in many foreign countries. Attached to the federal office was a staff of physical education specialists who built up regional basketball, baseball, and softball leagues.[49] All of this work suffered severely when the educational administration of the region was split up between the two states. During a field trip in 1943 it was found that to discuss educational problems in the region one would have to visit one administrator in the city of Durango and another in Saltillo.

The peasants consistently demanded the re-establishment of the regional education office. Their active participation in the national campaign against illiteracy showed that they were in earnest about their desire for education. The campaign was probably the most thorough attempt to involve the entire population in a common cause ever undertaken in Mexico. It was a frontal attack, not only on illiteracy but on the general habit of concentrating on personal affairs to the exclusion of any interest in the community. A law was passed August 21, 1944, fixing on each literate person the responsibility for teaching an illiterate to read and write. An outstanding poet, Jaime Torres Bodet, outlined, organized, and conducted a brilliant campaign to involve all possible groups in the success of the drive to bring at least the rudiments of education to every Mexican. He later left Mexico to head UNESCO, in Paris. His departure coincided with a lessening of interest in the need for elementary education. Lately stress has been placed on technical and other higher education. The result was the slowing of the rate of advance in the struggle against illiteracy, already noted.

The Central Union participated in the literacy campaign by voting a fund to give teachers extra pay for afternoon and evening classes and a bonus of two pesos for each adult taught to read and write. Such persons numbered 2,635 during the 1946-1947 school year, out of 3,442 who attended literacy classes in 182 centers.

The federal office of education for the region was revived during 1944. The new director has been striving to overcome a number of handicaps in addition to the usual inadequate budget.

Difficulties in the provision and management of school parcels in the ejidos illustrate the problems arising from the Mexican cultural heritage which places serious obstacles in the path of peasant advance. The idea of the parcel is sound, and each agrarian community is charged by law with the creation of such a plot.[50] Children are initiated into farm and garden practices, including canning of products, and links between the parents, the teachers, and the children are built by work at this civic task. It often works.

The administrative committee consists of three members: the school principal, the president of the parents' association, and the chairman of the ejido. Profits from the sale of products from the parcel go 50 per cent to the purchase of school equipment, 25 per cent for equipment, seed or other material for working the plot, and 25 per cent as a bonus to the teachers who direct the work.

The value of the crops sold from Laguna *ejidal* school parcels was close to half a million pesos during the 1946-1947 academic year. "It could have been much more if the parcels had been worked properly" was the plaint of the federal director in his annual report.[51]

Examples of the faults he described give a measure of the cultural factors with which he must cope. Peasants seldom cooperate in the cultivation of the parcels; they demand wages for their work, then they cheat and charge "immoderate sums." The "egotism of many officials of the ejidos" expresses itself in demands for a free hand in managing the parcel and disposing of the product, sometimes pocketing the money obtained. The parcel is looked upon by some ejidos as an integral part of their lands to be managed as they please. Some of the teachers have had the same experience as that of the women's league mentioned previously. Occasionally the teacher herself will refuse to render an accounting. Lack of technically competent teachers is another handicap. Geographic factors add to these troubles. Water for irrigation of the plots is often lacking at the time it is needed. The writer has seen dozens of parcels which seem to have been planted and tended with care but which, in the absence of water, contained only plants shriveled by the desert sun.

The office is attempting to form a regional council on school gardens through which experiences can be pooled and lagging ejidos urged to fall into line. A regional museum and a text on the region for all schools are also being planned. There are about twenty school cooperatives in which the children may learn to work in many ways which are still strange to many of their fathers.[52]

RELIGION IN THE NEW ORDER

Religion enters onto the Laguna agrarian scene only in a negative manner, as might be expected from the history of the dominant church in the nation. The antiagrarian moves of the church left the peasants either hostile or indifferent. Religion in Mexico, as in Latin America generally, is a "matter for women."

However, there has been no antireligious agitation in connection with the social changes in the region since 1936. Most peasant leaders seem to take the position that the majority of their fellows are not greatly interested in the church and that a frontal attack on it would probably redound to its benefit. They point out that while people in the cities continue to go to church on Sunday with fair regularity, the vast majority of the country people attend services only on four occasions, in descending order of importance: death, birth, confirmation, and marriage.

Census figures on religious beliefs show slight decreases in the proportion of Roman Catholics from 1900 to 1950 for each Laguna *municipio.* There were small increases in the number of Protestants in all *municipios,* but even in Torreón they number only 2,933, or 2 per cent of those reporting their religious beliefs.

Religious influence on Torreón marriage customs might be judged from the following figures on civil status. There were 3,820 united in religious bonds only; 4,838 persons married by civil ceremony only; and 5,867 living in "free union" in 1930. Presumably the second and third groups, which total 10,705 persons, do not take their church membership too seriously. Add to these 270 divorced persons.

The 1950 census data show an increase in each of the categories: 8,861 married by civil ceremony only; 8,675 *uniones libres* and 579 divorced persons. There were 2,467 persons married by religious services only. What might be indicated as convinced Catholic marriages were, therefore, reduced by 36 per cent while those frowned upon by the church increased by 67 per cent.

Indicative also are data on buildings used for church purposes. There were reductions in Roman Catholic churches of 9.8 per cent and 10.2 per cent in Coahuila and Durango, respectively, from 1929 to 1939. In Mexico as a whole the number increased 5.6 per cent. Protestant churches showed decreases in Mexico and the two states (Table 34, Appendix). No data are available by *municipios.* However, some former churches are now used as meeting halls for ejidos, women's league headquarters, warehouses for ejido goods, or storehouses for wheat. Some have simply been boarded up by the former *hacendados* on whose remaining lands they stand. Sometimes the church is within the walls surrounding the *casa grande* and the *ejidatarios* are not welcomed inside. In any case, Sundays are for ball games, trips to the city, or extra work in the fields for most of the *ejidatarios.*

Judging from sermons heard occasionally in the Catholic and in four Protestant churches in Torreón during sixteen years, neither offers leadership toward democracy in public affairs. The only civic comments ever heard of were those from the Catholic clergy on behalf of the 1940 presidential candidate who was also approved by Generalissimo Franco.

There are a few centers of *sinarquista* agitation in the region. Four leaders of the National Union of Sinarchists were arrested in Gómez Palacio in January, 1944, for distributing leaflets urging drafted men to refuse to report for induction. The Allies were fighting to "bolshevize the world" was the reason given.[53] While the archbishop of Mexico announced that the group had no official connection with the church, the sinarchist movement used religious shibboleths and paraphernalia, maintained relations with clerico-fascist groups in Latin America and Europe, and was directed by an outstanding Mexican Jesuit priest.[54]

In the summer of 1943 peasant leaders reported some sinarchist agitation in the villages against conscription and against the collective system. A huge mass meeting of workers and peasants was held in Torreón in January, 1944, to warn against this agitation as an attempt to disrupt the unity of the Mexican nation behind the war effort.

Acción Nacional, the political expression of the extreme "right" in Mexico, has paid a good deal of attention to La Laguna since the sinarquistas were forced underground by the national government in 1944.[55] The writer collected its literature and talked with its leaders on field trips in 1947 and 1952. Torreón headquarters resemble the forlorn meeting halls of radical political sects in the United States, but the personalities are different. No "proletarians" are apparent, either rural or urban. Instead a seedy lawyer in an old but expensive black suit with white piping on the vest explains how the peasants are being oppressed under a "Communist regime." The major plank in his group's program, he explains, is to give each *ejidatario* possession of his "plot of land" in fee simple.[56] It developed that no one in the "regional committee" had figured out what this would mean in peasants displaced or what it would do to the successful ejidos. It "probably" would mean an extensive transference of population out of the region to the "vast undeveloped areas in the deserts, and the tropics," according to the spokesman interviewed.

Mexico's agricultural problem, according to the official literature distributed by Acción Nacional, arises from actions in 1856 and 1857 which divested the church of its vast landholdings.[57] Actually, both the church and its supporters and many of the revolutionaries still think of the fundamental struggle in Mexico as the maintenance or abolition of the Constitution of 1857, if not of 1821! The theme ran through all public statements, articles, speeches, banners carried in parades, and other aspects of the celebration of the two-hundredth anniversary of the birth of Miguel Hidalgo, excommunicated by the church and executed with its approval for his role in securing the independence of Mexico. Even more open conflict arises each year when the birth and death of Júarez are commemorated.[58]

The contrast between the wholehearted acceptance by the peasants, on one hand, of such forward-looking measures as modern health and sanitation techniques, their hunger for education for themselves and their children, and their responsible participation in civic and economic affairs, and, on the other hand, the yearning for the "good old days" under Porfirio Díaz (if not under Spain) of Acción Nacional, is startling. Evidently, many middle-class Mexicans are still not certain whether they want their society to be democratic or authoritarian.

Chapter 7

POPULATION PRESSURE AND
AGRARIAN PROBLEMS

*T*HE LAGUNA REGION PRESENTS, in a microcosm, the
same acute problems arising from overpopulation
which are now hampering economic development and social reorganization in many areas of the world.[1]*

THE "SURPLUS" POPULATION

Excess population has plagued the Laguna experiment from the
start. Three factors contribute to the presence of more people than
the economy of the region can support at adequate levels of living:
speculative overdevelopment; the inclusion of migrant workers in
the 1936 agrarian census; and a high rate of natural increase.

Speculative Overdevelopment.—This has been mentioned above.[2]
Throughout the central plateau and the northern states the "bonanza"
which might be found by those of few resources brought the foot-
loose and the adventurous seeking quick improvement in their
fortunes. This was encouraged both by those who had land to sell
and by the *hacendado* who wanted a plentiful supply of "hands."

Agents covered the desert and mountain villages shortly before
harvest time spreading the word that *bonanceros* were wanted.
Migrants were as much a part of the Laguna economy prior to the
expropriations as they are now of the California fruit regions.

*Notes to this chapter begin on page 232.

Cotton-picking time had brought migratory workers to the region ever since it became a great cotton-raising center. Whole families travelled on foot or burro from nearby parts of Coahuila, Durango, and Zacatecas.

Inclusion of Migrant Workers in the Census.—The presence of some 16,000 *bonanceros* at the time of the expropriations presented the agrarian authorities with a mixed legal and humanitarian problem. It is quite doubtful, legally, that they were entitled to be included in the land distribution. Two major requirements are found in the agrarian code: (1) residence within seven kilometers of the land to be expropriated, and (2) six months work preceding the application of the law. A strict application of the law would have meant denying the migrants an opportunity to become full-time instead of part-time participants in the agricultural life of the region. The *bonanceros* formed committees to press their case. They reminded the settled workers that many of them had taken an active part in the general strike. The representatives of the resident workers responded in the revolutionary spirit of the occasion and asked that the migrants be included in the agrarian census. Two crucial results followed: (1) overpopulation, and (2) the inclusion of many persons not as familiar with the year-round agricultural cycle as were the resident landworkers. It is easier to demonstrate the influence of the first factor than of the second, although Banco Ejidal employees have often expressed to the writer the opinion that the failure of certain ejidos is at least partly due either (a) to conflict between older residents and migrants grouped together in the same ejido, or (b) to the inexperience of those *ejidatarios* who formerly were migrants.[3]

The disequilibrium in the man-land ratio may be stated as follows, if we leave out of account for the moment the minority of workers left on the haciendas:

Seventy per cent of the land now supports 172 per cent of the population which 100 per cent of the land formerly supported. In other words, there is 30 per cent less land to support 72 per cent more workers. These averages somewhat oversimplify the problem, but data have already been given in the treatment of land tenure and irrigation to show how serious the situation is.

Another approach to quantification of the "surplus" population lies in following up the irrigation data set forth on pages 108 to 110.

Completion of the Lázaro Cárdenas dam was followed by an unbroken series of seven "dry" years. Thus even the most "pessimistic" forecasts of the benefits from the dam have proved too optimistic. Assuming that no drastic changes have taken place in the long-range habits of the cyclonic storms off the Pacific Ocean, however, it seems that land formerly considered "irrigable" has actually turned out to be some 47,832 *hectáreas* (118,145 a.) less than supposed. It must now be admitted that there exists a serious imbalance between land available and persons attempting to make a living from working the land.

If it be assumed that it is good land, and that each six *hectáreas* of it could support an *ejidatario* and his family, the livelihood of 7,972 ejido families would be jeopardized if all the difference were taken from the *ejidal* sector of the economy. If small owners were dispossessed to correct the unbalance, 2,391 of them would have to move if the limit were the twenty *hectáreas* they are now allowed for irrigation purposes.

Another approach would be further to subdivide those lands in excess of twenty *hectáreas* and allow sales only to present inhabitants of the region. The official average area per private farm was 91.7 *hectáreas* in 1943 and 25.7 in 1950, but this is a considerable understatement in both cases. Landowners have boasted to the writer that they "sold" their holdings to their brothers, uncles, aunts, and cousins. Like the relatives of the captain of the Pinafore, they are "numbered by the dozens." Figure 5 (p. 92) gives an example of the method.

Application of our own laws and practices in regard to irrigated land to determine the "ideal" size of farms in the Laguna region would wipe out ownership for the majority of present proprietors—both private and *ejidal*. For example, if the average-size irrigated farm in the United States in 1944 were the criterion (42 a.), there would be 10,584 farms instead of 33,920. Or, if the legal limit of 160 acres contained in the Reclamation Act of 1902 were to prevail in the area, there would be only 2,778 owners. One of the major factors in the evolution of our own irrigation policy was the lack of population pressure on land resources.[4]

The ejidos have attempted to cope with the problem by closing their books and refusing to admit new members. Subdivisions of other properties have gone to outsiders, however, as has been seen.[5]

Thus not only have more people been brought in, but one of the possible solutions has been weakened.

There were 20,000 sons of *ejidatarios,* according to the Central Union, who had come of age to be admitted to membership, but for whom there was no land in 1947. In some other parts of Mexico it is felt that the collectivized ejido has solved the problem of the emigration of farm children. This is true, however, only because there has been additional land to be brought under cultivation by the enlarged group.

High Rate of Natural Increase.—The third factor contributing to overpopulation in the region has been a high rate of natural increase. Birth rates are high, as in the other "underdeveloped" areas of the world. Crude rates per 1,000 inhabitants for each of the *municipios* in the region (Table 16) show a range of from 47.9 in Gómez Palacio to an improbable high of 61.2 in Mapimí for the year 1950.[6]

TABLE 16

CRUDE BIRTH AND DEATH RATES AND
NATURAL INCREASE OF POPULATION
MEXICO, COAHUILA, DURANGO, AND LA LAGUNA
1940 AND 1950

| | Per 1000 Inhabitants | | | | Annual Rate of | |
| | Birth Rate | | Death Rate | | Natural Increase | |
	1940	1950	1940	1950	1940	1950
México	44.3	45.6	23.2	16.1	2.1	2.9
Coahuila	63.1	49.5	23.5	13.9	3.9	3.6
Durango	51.0	47.8	19.6	11.7	3.1	3.6
La Laguna:						
Gómez Palacio	59.4	47.9	29.1	12.2	3.0	3.6
Lerdo	53.6	54.5	22.0	12.2	3.1	4.2
Mapimí	52.5	61.2	17.8	15.7	3.5	4.5
Matamoros	56.2	51.5	29.7	17.0	2.6	3.4
San Pedro	67.5	57.4	29.1	17.6	3.8	3.9
Torreón	57.5	51.9	30.3	14.7	2.7	3.7
Viesca	67.2	57.0	27.8	15.0	3.9	4.2

Source: Dirección General de Estadística.

Rates in the 40's and 50's are generally found today only in the poorer areas of Africa, Asia, and Latin America.[7] The Laguna region is beginning to show a slight but spotty decline, even on the basis of the admittedly deficient statistics. Rural-urban differentials were noticeable for the entire states of Coahuila and Durango in 1939, when the following crude rates were recorded:[8]

	Rural	Urban
Coahuila	66.2	54.7
Durango	55.2	44.3

Improvements in levels (and standards) of living are usually reflected slowly in a decline in the birth rate, but fairly rapidly in falling death rates. La Laguna in the recent past is no exception (Table 16). Death rates in the five most populous *municipios*, with 94 per cent of the regional population, fell in percentage points as follows between 1940 and 1950:

Torreón	15.6
Gómez Palacio	16.9
Matamoros	12.7
San Pedro	11.5
Lerdo	9.8

The smaller, outlying areas of Viesca and Mapimí showed decreases of 12.8 and 2.1 points, respectively. The latter was the only regional unit with a fall less than that for Mexico as a whole, which was 7.1 per cent between the census years.

La Laguna, as did Mexico as a whole, shifted in one decade from death rates characteristic of Asian and African countries to the intermediate position of Latin America generally. Further drops to around Oceanic and European standards of twelve to thirteen may be expected in the coming years—if economic development is not too greatly hampered by the growing gap between birth and death rates.

Even more sensitive as an index of improved levels of living is the rate of children dying before reaching their first birthday.[9] La Laguna shows much more noticeable improvement in this field than in crude death rates (Table 17). Only Mapimí failed to record more of a decline than for Mexico as a whole between 1940 and 1950. Mexico and the region as a whole now resemble the more advanced Latin American areas, although they still lag behind most of the Caribbean islands. Mapimí, however, about equals India in the past few years.[10]

La Laguna, as well as Mexico in its entirety, can thus be located in the demographic "stage" of "high growth potential" in which population is increasing rapidly and at an accelerating rate. Probably the majority of the world's people are now found in this stage.[11]

TABLE 17
INFANT MORTALITY
MEXICO, COAHUILA, DURANGO, AND LA LAGUNA
1930, 1940, AND 1950
(per 1000 live births)

	1930 Rate	1940 Rate	1950 Rate
Mexico	131.6	125.7	95.8
Coahuila	166.1	114.8	89.6
Durango	106.2	106.2	67.6
La Laguna:			
Gómez Palacio	154.5	141.0	77.3
Lerdo	138.8	112.4	70.1
Mapimí	154.2	77.8	79.4
Matamoros	188.3	156.6	122.1
San Pedro	205.2	146.3	100.3
Torreón	266.3	160.5	86.1
Viesca	120.2	137.0	99.2

Source: Dirección General de Estadística.

Mexico's inhabitants increased 2.9 per cent annually from 1940 to 1950; the lowest yearly rate for natural increase for a Laguna *municipio* was 3.4 per cent; the highest, 4.5 per cent (Table 16). Mexico's net increase in the decade was 6,052,906; La Laguna grew by 124,900 people, or 4.77 per cent annually.

It is obvious that there was some net in-migration into the region, although the unreliability of the data does not permit any clear estimate of the extent of the movement. An approach to an estimate might be made along the following lines. If one assumes that birth and death rates are likely to be more reliable in the comparatively highly consolidated *municipios* of Torreón, Lerdo, and Gómez Palacio, and further, that differences which might bias birth and death rates would about cancel out between these three *municipios* and the other four in the region, a weighted rate of natural increase would be 3.75 per cent. The actual annual rate of increase was almost exactly 1 per cent higher. If this were taken as the rate of in-migration, then some 12,500 more persons moved into the region than moved out between the census years. The number would rise as the recorded rate of natural increase is inflated by reported birth rates which magnify actual phenomena.

Torreón's annual rate of increase was 6.4 per cent during the decade, of which 3.7 per cent was reportedly accounted for by natural increase. Assuming the accuracy of birth and death rates, as well as census figures, the gross population growth of the metropolis of the region (57,530 persons) would owe 12,254 to natural increase and 42,276 to in-migration. What portion of the latter came from regional smaller towns and rural areas, and what from outside the region is highly uncertain. However, Mexico is one of the world's countries urbanizing most rapidly. The Laguna region is no exception; Torreón grew about 2 per cent a year faster than the region as a whole.

POPULATION PRESSURE AND ECONOMIC DEVELOPMENT

Mexico lived in a comparatively "boom" period from 1939 to 1950. Partly this was a result of the war, and partly of the tremendous efforts made to overcome its former semicolonial position through industrialization and improvement of agriculture. The experience of that period has recently been exhaustively analyzed by a capable and conscientious team of economists for the International Bank for Reconstruction and Development. Few recent studies so well show the discount chargeable to population growth which hampers raising of levels of living. Consumers' goods utilized by Mexicans rose 105 per cent between 1939 and 1950. Per capita consumption increased only 55 per cent; the "discount" for population increase was therefore 50 per cent of the total gain in the period. Per capita daily food consumption fell from 2,449 calories in 1953 to 2,257 in 1955, according to a calculation by an eminent United States agricultural economist. A similar trend is shown when the percentage rise in the real national income between 1950 and 1955 (25.6 per cent) is compared with the percentage rise in per capita income (8 per cent). There was thus a "discount" for population growth of 68 per cent.[12]

Possibly the first official notice ever taken of the pressure of population on resources in Mexico occurs in the 1953 annual report to congress by President Adolfo Ruiz Cortines, in which the facts of rapid population growth are brought forcefully to public attention and linked with the mass movement of Mexican farm workers from central Mexico to the United States, either legally or as "wet-backs."[13]

NATIONALISTIC DEMOGRAPHY

The inclination in the past has been not only to ignore population growth as a factor in Mexico's development plans but even to insist on the need for a greater population. The official position, established in a weighty tome in 1935, was "vigorously revolutionary and opposed to the neo-Malthusianism of the militarist and imperialist countries." It demands an increase in the population "by every means possible" and denounces as "imbeciles or cowards" those who "seek to raise levels of living in underpopulated countries without creating a vigorous increase in population."[14] Nationalistic emotions and dreams of the "historic destiny of the Hispanic-American peoples" seems to have been at least as large an ingredient as scholarship in this book, a product of Italian training in the Mussolini era. It reminds one of the "manifest destiny" slogans of John Fiske, who foresaw in 1885 a population of 700 millions for the United States.[15]

A contest to choose the "heroine of the year" is run by *Excelsior*, one of Mexico's largest dailies; the national heroine is the mother with the greatest number of living children. A diploma, a gold medal, and one thousand pesos ($120) are the first prize. The newspaper explains that it is moved to this patriotic effort by "the country's need of manpower."[16] Nationalistic delusions seem to be supplemented in this case by religious inspiration, perhaps not uncoupled with circulation promotion.

More somber thoughts, and perhaps different training, are reflected in a recent judgment that "the agrarian reform was inspired by static ideas . . . to cite only one example, future population growth was not considered."[17] It has been shown above that even in the supposedly more flexible cooperative ejidos of the Laguna region the problem of accommodating the children into the economy is a difficult one. That is virtually a world-wide problem which thus far no farming system seems to have solved satisfactorily, unless large amounts of new land are available.[18]

It has been pointed out that attempts to correct the disastrously low amount of land per *ejidatario* are blocked by the presence of too large a population dependent on working the land.[19]

MECHANIZATION AS A SOLUTION

The advocates of a larger population for Mexico were ready with an answer in the early years of the Laguna experiment:

"Mechanize the ejido! Mechanization will bring greater production, production will be more evenly divided, all will benefit." This was the theme repeated to the writer countless times in the early years of the new era.

Many ejidos in which this has happened can be found. Perhaps one-third of all *ejidal* farming in the region, given sufficient water, can be counted as successful in raising levels of living. They are the more highly mechanized. The monetary advantages of heavy mechanization are shown in Table 18, and are obvious whether calculated on the basis of total profit or return per man-day. An additional investment of only 89 pesos ($17.80) per year by the more heavily mechanized ejidos brought average higher profits of 3,181 pesos ($636.20). The crucial column of the table is that showing man-days utilized in the three types of operations. Lightly mechanized ejidos use 87 per cent more man-days than do the heavily mechanized. The ways they use manpower are shown in Table 35, Appendix.[20]

TABLE 18

INVESTMENTS AND RETURNS OF LAGUNA EJIDOS
ACCORDING TO DEGREE OF MECHANIZATION
1939

(per 100 hectáreas, in pesos)

Type	Investment per Crop Year	Value of Production	Profit	Man-days	Return per Man-day
Light	16,831	36,730	19,899	6,633	3.00
Medium	16,185	36,730	20,545	5,955	3.45
Heavy	16,920	40,000	23,080	3,542	6.51

Source: Carlos Torres Cordera, *op. cit.*

Why are not more ejidos heavily mechanized? One part of the answer seems to lie in what has been referred to as "one of the most definitely established agricultural facts—the tendency toward diminishing returns."[21]

How does this "principle" or "tendency" or "law" work out in actual practice in La Laguna? One group of *ejidatarios* works just as hard as another, let us assume for the moment. Therefore, their labor should, from a "social justice" standpoint, be equally rewarded. The landlord, who is the reason for the poverty of landworkers in Marxist and modern physiocratic (and even some of the classical)

economic theories, has been abolished.[22] In spite of this, one group averages 3 pesos return per day and the other averages 6.51 pesos— more than twice as much. If the difference lies in the comparative degrees of mechanization, why don't all groups mechanize?

Obviously, since land in possession of various ejidos differs in quality as well as in quantity, greater returns will flow from the application of more machine power to the better land. But there is another factor. It can be seen in a comparison of the extent of mechanization of the two major sectors of the Laguna economy. Private properties were rated as 75 per cent "heavily mechanized" in 1939 as compared with 23 per cent of the ejidos.[23]

Credit was available, in general, to all producing units (private or cooperative) for mechanization. In fact, immediately after the expropriations, there was such tremendous enthusiasm among the *ejidatarios* for buying farm machinery that the Banco Ejidal suffered many attacks while trying to establish rational economic bases for lending money for such purchases. Some ejidos sought private machinery loans after they had been adjudged poor risks because of lack of suitable or sufficient land, and overloaded themselves with obsolete machinery in the first flush of enthusiasm for their new status. This machinery, acquired almost exclusively from the former landlords, was generally secondhand. The *hacendado* kept the best for himself and sold the remainder on a sellers' market. Within a couple of seasons most of it was junk. Since farm machinery was difficult to purchase during the war, the ejidos which had bought secondhand machines were left holding the bag when they failed. Many of those ejidos which did secure better machinery lost it through mortgaging it to private money lenders. The poor land and location of many of the ejidos has made it impossible for them to acquire machinery in view of the probability that they would never be able to pay for it.

The writer has sat in on dozens of *ejidal* assembly or committee meetings at which there was serious discussion of "machines vs. men." The theme was always "we have x men available for doing our work; if we use machines, the work gets done more quickly and fewer of our men get their daily pay."

Pressure of population and the realities of the economic structure in the region specifically and Mexico at large make exceedingly diffi- cult the solution offered both by classical and Marxist theory—

"use the machines to produce more and share the increased production equitably."

An attempt was made to accommodate mechanization to population realities by pooling at least the heavier machinery. This allowed those ejidos which could benefit from greater degrees of mechanization to do so more economically. It did not solve the dilemma of the overcrowded ejidos.

One additional mention of mechanization needs to be made, in view of the participation of Laguna cotton in world trade. Neither of the newest developments in the mechanization of cotton fields—flame-throwing cultivators or mechanical pickers—has yet been seriously considered for use in the region, nor have new chemical weed-killers. Cotton production in the United States is taking giant strides toward modern technology. Less than 1 per cent of the cotton crop was picked mechanically in 1946; this had jumped to 18 per cent in 1952. The newer cotton areas of the West are racing ahead of the older states; in 1952, 59 per cent of California's cotton and 46 per cent of Arizona's were harvested by machine.

The combination of a flame-throwing cultivator and a mechanical picker is reducing labor force and costs to incredibly low levels. One Alabama farmer, using the two machines jointly, cut his workers from two hundred to four for each two thousand acres, and his labor cost per bale from $94 to $4.70.

The addition of the flame-thrower solves a problem that made mechanical picking difficult in the past by forcing the bloom up the stem where the machine can collect it without also gathering dirt which harms both the mechanism and the cotton. California experience has shown substantial savings even when the picker alone is used. Harvest labor time in 1945 was cut from seventy hours per acre to one and one-half hours.[24]

A "cotton mechanization conference" in October, 1953, was told by one Arizona planter, "When we can pick 85 per cent of our cotton crop by machine we will feel that our business is approaching the peak in efficiency. We will then be able to sell cotton on the world market in competition with any foreign crop or any synthetic and show a reasonable profit."[25]

The Laguna region, neither in its private nor its cooperative sector, can look forward with like confidence. One of the major reasons is the surplus of labor which makes such highly capitalized farming neither economical nor, in the short run, socially desirable. In the long run, of course, the only alternative is government subsidies, either outright or via the indirect method of tariffs.

POPULATION TRANSFER AS A SOLUTION

The first years of the experiment were marked by occasional talk of "transferring the excess population." Delegations of *ejidatarios* were sent to newly opened irrigated zones in other parts of Mexico. Plans were made, meetings were held; few moved. "We are the ones who belong here; let those move who own more than a just share, and give us more land" was the answer of the *ejidatarios*. Others placed their faith in the opening of the Lázaro Cárdenas Dam.

Seven drought years in succession made an impression on some of the optimists, although only after a "rainmaker" had been hired, and had failed, to fill the dam.[26]

The cumulative effect of increasingly dry years began to make itself felt by late 1951. Large-scale public works programs were put into effect by the federal and state governments. Sizable groups of those "displaced" by the continued drought have been aided in moving to such widely scattered spots as Cuatro Ciénagas, Coahuila; Huimanguillo, Tabasco; the Popaloapan valley and Acayucán, Veracruz.[27]

Indicative of the approach to the problem is the constant iteration of the phrase *pala de mano*, the equivalent of the "pick and shovel" ideology of WPA days in the midst of the 1929-1939 depression in the United States.[28] The situation was much more serious in the Laguna region than in depression United States; estimates of the proportion of the rural labor force without means of support ran as high as 50 per cent.[29]

President Ruiz Cortines announced a new program in May, 1953. It contained three major points:[30]

1. Reallocation and consolidation of *ejidal* and private properties to prevent evaporation of water in irrigation canals, and other wastage;
2. Limitation of population to the number the region can support (with no details given on mechanisms for reaching this objective);

3. Continued attempts to transfer the surplus population to other areas.

The most thorough student of Mexican internal migration, after lengthy review of past colonization efforts, recommends further movement of peasants from the overcrowded central plateau to the tropics. He sums up the entire man-land question in Mexico as follows, however:

We must not forget that we do not have enough land to satisfy the needs of our farm population . . . even if we do not take the natural increase of the coming years into account.[31]

URBAN MOVEMENT AS A SOLUTION

Companion to the slogan "industrialization" in the under-developed areas, is "urbanization." Underemployment in the country is to be solved by movement from the farm to the city. Often this simply transfers underemployment from a rural to an urban environment, where, incidentally, it may be more difficult to handle.

Mexico as a whole is no exception to the world-wide urbanization trend, as we have seen. Torreón grew faster than did the region, between 1940 and 1950 as in previous years. Regional growth was 47.7 per cent; the metropolis grew 66.4 per cent. However, the increase in the economically-active population of Torreón was almost exactly the same as the population increase. This would seem to indicate that relatively there was little improvement in this sector of the economy. There was however a small increase in the proportion engaged in industry.

The gainfully employed population in 1950 was 121,688 persons, or 31.5 per cent of the total. This was slightly lower than the proportion for Mexico, which itself was one of the world's lowest, 32.4 per cent.[32] Women accounted for 14,266 of the economically active persons; men for 107,422. There were only minor differences between the *municipios* in the percentage of the total population gainfully employed, but there was a difference of almost 400 per cent between Viesca and Torreón in percentage of women employed (Table 19, and Table 36, Appendix). This fact is probably linked with the low ratio of urban-industrial workers in Viesca as compared with the larger percentage in Torreón. Possibly the most significant shift between 1940 and 1950 was the considerable increase in proportions

TABLE 19

PER CENT OF POPULATION GAINFULLY EMPLOYED
LAGUNA REGION
1940 AND 1950

Municipio and State	Per Cent of Population Gainfully Employed		Per Cent of Males Gainfully Employed		Per Cent of Females Gainfully Employed	
	1940	1950	1940	1950	1940	1950
Coahuila	27.0	31.5	51.6	56.2	3.5	7.9
Matamoros	19.4	31.0	36.0	57.6	1.1	3.0
San Pedro	29.9	32.0	56.6	58.6	1.3	4.4
Torreón	28.0	31.4	52.1	53.7	5.7	10.9
Viesca	26.9	32.1	50.7	59.5	.9	3.1
Durango	28.9	31.5	55.5	56.6	2.0	6.0
Gómez Palacio	28.6	31.1	55.0	55.6	2.2	6.6
Lerdo	29.4	31.8	56.7	57.6	2.0	5.9
Mapimí	29.4	33.3	55.5	61.1	1.4	2.8
Entire Region	27.6	31.5	52.8	56.3	3.0	7.3

Source: Data supplied by the Dirección General de Estadística.

of women employed. The percentage of men employed rose only from 52.8 per cent to 56.3 per cent, but the proportion of women more than doubled, rising from 3.0 per cent to 7.3 per cent.

Just over half (50.6 per cent) of the economically active population of the region was engaged in agriculture, or 61,604 of the 121,688 persons so classified.[33] Next came industry with 21,281, followed by commerce with 13,791.

The city of Torreón of course shows a different pattern of occupational distribution from that of the region as a whole, and an interesting shift in occupational distribution between 1940 and 1950. Industry replaced commerce as the largest grouping, with 12,944 workers in place of the 4,605 of a decade earlier, an increase of 181 per cent. Commerce fell slightly, from 9,952 in 1940 to 8,238 in 1950.

The shifts just noted are particularly significant in view of the fact that between 1930 and 1940 industry had increased by only 753 workers, whereas commercial employees had risen by 2,648.

One important limitation on the ability of industry to provide employment for large numbers of in-migrants is found in the urban equivalent of the mechanization dilemma. It has already been reported that Mexican textile factories, which are important in Torreón, are technologically retarded and that increased efficiency would reduce rather than increase its labor force. The United Nations Economic Commission for Latin America has the following to say about underemployment in Mexican industry:

It has been noted that there is a surplus of labor in the textile industry in relation to existing equipment. Similar conclusions have been drawn in the cement industry, and are certainly applicable in a number of other cases, not excepting the railways.[34]

There is still a heavy concentration of Torreón's industry in areas which are heavily dependent on exports. This, plus the national lack of sufficient funds for the capital investment needed to raise low levels of income and keep up with the country's rapidly growing population, indicates that urbanization will provide neither a facile nor a substantial contribution to the relief of overcrowding on the ejidos.

Urban movement may help, indirectly, in that urban dwellers, as they acquire broader vision, higher aspirations, more education, and more knowledge of the "facts of life" do begin to plan their families both as to frequency and number of births. It is probable that some of the knowledge is then transmitted to "country cousins." There is some indication that the same process is taking place in the more successful ejidos.[35]

POPULATION PRESSURE AND SOCIAL STRATIFICATION

The ejidos were forced to close their books to new members, as reported already. We have seen that neither transfer of population nor urban movement has been adequate to cope with both the "built-in" overpopulation/with which many ejidos were born, nor with natural increase. What, then, happens inside the ejido village? The equalitarian social system of the cooperative ejido, originated to solve the problems of insufficient land for the peasants, has been split into two subsystems. The *ejidatarios* make up one system, with its rights, norms, and "network of expectations." What have come to be called the *libres* (the free ones!) often make up half or more of the population of the *ejidal* village. They are the sons and relations of the original member of the ejido and occasionally a recent in-migrant who has been allowed to settle in the village because of *compadrazgo* connections or because he came from the same Durango or Zacatecas mountain village as the original *ejidatarios*.

The "agricultural ladder" in the United States worked, at least for some years, because if the father could not divide his farm equally among his sons, at least he could help those who did not inherit part of his farm to purchase land if they wished to continue farming. This outlet for the surplus farm population, now largely closed in the United States, never existed in La Laguna, at least in recent times.

The *libres* have no rights to participate in ejido work, in the assemblies, in the medical services, or other forms of economic or political democracy. Neither daily advances for regular work nor participation in the annual sharing of "profits" is theirs. They sometimes are allowed to work by the day in the peak of the season. Generally, they attempt to "hire out" to the remaining private properties, to find occasional work in neighboring ejidos, or to get jobs in one of the urban areas and commute. They are, of course, the ones most likely to move to the city, to participate in population transfer schemes, or to enroll as *braceros* for seasonal agricultural work in the United States.

Kelly reports that in El Cuije "the attitude of the *ejidatarios* toward the '*libres*' is one of complacency and condescension." She feels that their presence has helped reinforce the old prejudice against doing any manual labor for which one is not directly paid.[36]

To build or remodel one's own home instead of hiring someone to do it would be to "act like a '*libre*.'" Whether this feeling, obviously arising from a desperate need for maintaining status, is widespread or not cannot now be judged. It does not coincide with usual attitudes encountered by the author in the early days of the experiment when peasants gladly participated in the joint construction of school buildings and other community facilities with the students of the American Friends Service Committee work camps.

Chapter 8

DEMOCRACY COMES TO A COTTON KINGDOM

*T*HE PRIME TASK of modern times is to make democracy a living, growing factor in the daily lives of men, women, and children of all creeds and colors, everywhere on earth. The American people, in spite of their rich heritage from fighters for freedom and of the great wealth which has lighted the path and lightened the load, still have far to go in achieving democracy. This is especially true in relationships built up around earning one's daily bread. Pendergast, Hague, Crump, Curley, and their peers show also that the people still do not live up to their responsibilities in the political field. The frictions in multiethnic communities indicate that we have not yet abandoned the utterly unscientific and antidemocratic belief that our group is inherently superior to the "lesser breeds."

Democracy, in other words, cannot be usefully defined in a two-value system of thought; it ranges toward or away from the central eight "goal values of democracy."[1]*

THE MEXICAN HERITAGE AND DEMOCRACY

"The world revolution of our times" gives relevance to an examination of Mexico's most ambitious attempt to overthrow feudalism and install a thoroughgoing democracy in its place. The present world-wide interest in land reform has provided an occasion for trying to assay the successes and, since human beings and not

*Notes to this chapter begin on page 235.

angels are involved, the failures, of the Laguna experiment. This has been attempted by one who from the first has hoped for the success of the experiment, but who is firmly committed to the collection and impartial analysis of facts to the best of his ability. A better world will never be constructed on the suppression of truth nor on the acceptance of half-truths.

Basic to our understanding of La Laguna, Mexico as a whole, and in fact much of the rest of the world, is the realization of how fortunate the United States is never to have known widespread, well-established feudalism. The weak feudal institutions which were brought to this country, such as primogeniture and entail, were destroyed by or soon after the Revolution.[2]

The Biblical singer of Psalms chanted, "The earth He hath given to the children of men." But much of human history has been concerned with man's attempts to secure a portion of earth on which to live or access to it on terms which would enable him to live above the level of animals. Only yesterday Mexico saw the *hacendado* as the absolute lord and master, ruling huge estates with his own armed forces or having those of the government completely at his command. Villages, stores, and churches on the hacienda were the property of the owner. The peon was expected to remove his hat and bow his head in the presence of the master even if the latter were demanding the medieval *droit du seigneur*. Schools and civil rights were nonexistent.

The Mexican Revolution was an attempt to solve problems left unsolved by the War for Independence a century earlier. Ernest Gruening has summarized the essential features of the colonial regime, which lasted from 1521 to 1821, in terms which could scarcely be improved:

It was a period of comparative peace—the peace of suppression, stagnation and decay. Its outstanding characteristics were: Politically—absentee absolutism resting on military and religious domination, with complete denial of local self-expression and self-training, and disregard by officials of laws that it was to their interest to disregard; economically—extraction of raw materials based on slave labor, with office-holding the universal desideratum; socially—splendor and privilege contrasted with misery and degradation; spiritually—corruption, ignorance, fanaticism, intercaste hatred.

Three hundred years rooted these traits deep into the Mexican social fabric—one century has not sufficed to eradicate them. No worse preparation for self-government and the evolution of a modern state could have been bequeathed to a people.[3]

The "reconquest of Mexico" by the Mexican people actually began seriously with the revolution and in many respects the revolution actually started with Lázaro Cárdenas.[4] More vigorous, widespread, and fundamental attacks were made on the colonial and feudal heritage under Cárdenas than under any other revolutionary president. That many parts of that heritage are still extant should surprise no one who is aware of the persistence of outmoded cultural traits even in more dynamic societies. Their persistence among relatively static peasant groups is readily understandable.

The Mexican Revolution is essentially an indigenous product, although it contains elements of all the vast sweep of social change represented by the Roman Gracchi of twenty-one centuries ago, the Peasant Revolts, the Renaissance, the Reformation, the French Revolution, the bourgeois national revolutions of Germany and Italy, the Industrial Revolution, the War between the States, modern antiimperialist movements for colonial independence, the "New Deal," and occasionally, a slight dash of the Russian Revolution. There has been no copying of essentials from the Russians, however. The basic ideas and institutions of revolutionary Mexico have grown out of her own culture. It must be remembered that the Mexican Revolution began seven years before the Russian and that the 1917 Constitution was adopted eight months before the October "ten days that shook the world."

One of the greatest causes for misunderstanding of modern Mexico by her northern neighbor has been her different attitude toward land tenure. The tradition of land being held in fee simple, dominant in the United States, is contained in neither the Indian nor the Spanish parts of the Mexican heritage.[5]

The Indian and Spanish heritage holds as queer and antisocial the doctrine that land can be bought and sold as can a sack of flour. Land is the property of the community, for the use of members of the community so long as they follow the socially-fixed rules for its use. This is a concept to which many cultures give their sanction.[6] Even Great Britain, the home of Adam Smith and the classical seat of laissez-faire, swung around to a similar position in the prelabor government Uthwatt reports and in the Agricultural Act of 1947.[7] The greater part of Australia's land area is publicly owned and the majority of her farmers hold leases rather than titles.[8]

There are those in our own culture who wonder whether the complete power to "use and abuse" land does not contribute to antisocial behavior and result in losses rather than gains to the economy. Restrictions on this right have been adopted piecemeal for many years. They have yet to be given an adequate, well-rounded public expression in policy. Scholars and publicists sound an alarm, however. An outstanding student of land problems states:

Private enterprise in the ownership, use and exploitation of most natural resources has not been justified by its results. One of the tasks facing our government during the next century will be to repair the ravages resulting from three centuries of waste and spoilage under private enterprise.[9]

The impact of capitalist ideas from the north, particularly during the Díaz regime, threatened the ancient Indian and Spanish heritage, but did not destroy it. The revolution had rubble to clear away in the field of land law, but no fundamental reconstruction. It had no such good fortune in the field of civic attitudes, however. The Laguna experiment would have been difficult enough in Switzerland, Denmark, Sweden, or any other land where democracy has historic roots and where there is a tradition of widespread participation in political life, solidly based on years of popular education and almost universal literacy. Mexico, instead, is still struggling to overcome the colonial heritage mentioned above.

The Laguna region had known, during the past century of its development, a somewhat different social system from that of most of the rest of Mexico. It was not so isolated, however, that it was not finally reached and profoundly affected by the revolution.

ASSESSMENT OF GOAL VALUES

An outline has been given of the major happenings since October 6, 1936, and the principal factors influencing them. We have seen that the old institutions were destroyed insofar as their legal bases were involved. Since institutions are, in the last analysis, only viable when they are buttressed by the values which are meaningful to the people, let us now turn to an assessment of the Laguna experiment in terms of the goal values of democracy adopted from Lasswell's study.[10]

Power.—The monopoly of power once held by the small *hacen-*

dado class in the Laguna region has been broken. Legally, the *ejidatario* now has a voice and a vote not only in political matters but also in complex economic decisions. He participates in decisions as to the crops he is to raise, the price and time of sale of his products, the use or nonuse of machinery, the distribution of water, and even the election of the "field-boss" who is to supervise his daily labor. He owns, jointly with the others of his ejido, the land on which he works and often sizable quantities of farm machinery. His and other ejidos jointly own electric power plants, cotton gins, and other capital equipment.

He belongs to the peasants' organization and in its meetings debates its policies. He and his wife and children now have schooling available; they travel as freely as their economic circumstances permit.

Violence, once the monopoly of their enemies, is now the function of an army which is sworn to maintain "revolutionary institutions," which include his right to land, to vote, to freedom from the wrath of any "lord and master." A dramatic illustration of the relations between the army and the *ejidatarios* was the appearance of a colonel to explain the army attitude to the first Laguna conference organized by the author in 1939. He pointed out that antagonism between soldiers and peasants was great before the expropriations and led to frequent clashes at village fiestas. Soldiers now are given "orientation" courses in the meaning of the land reform and are taught to see themselves as defenders of the peasant, rather than of the *hacendado*.

The *ejidatario* no longer must make his purchases at the hacienda store; he can shop in the community store or he can join his friends and drive the *ejidal* truck to the most convenient urban market, or to a cooperative store. His participation in social life, his status in society, the role he plays, all have changed in the direction of the sharing of power and a voice in the making of decisions.

The ejido itself has become the basic element in what is legally among the most fundamentally democratic political and social structures in the world. Its constitution provides for "checks and balances," for minority representation and protection. The personnel in charge of the crucial economic function of the direction of production is subject to the democratic process. Turnover of elected officials depends on the will of the majority in the ejido.

The "field-boss" no longer is appointed by an outsider, one who might even be considered an enemy of the land worker. The writer has attended many elections of ejido officials. He was accompanied at two by the president of the Farmers' Union of a midwestern state. "If I had one-tenth of my membership able to conduct meetings in such a responsible manner and participate with such wisdom," said the official after the second meeting, "I would have the most important farmers' organization in the United States." The writer has been similarly impressed at the overwhelming majority of the meetings he attended.

Not all ejido meetings are conducted in such a responsible manner, however. Cliques have developed around personalities, or ejidos have divided politically along family lines. Some elected work-chiefs have used demagogic slogans to gain re-election; some rivals have used similar tactics to displace a successful man who applied discipline against a popular member. Such hazards of any democratic political system are particularly important in an ejido since the economic welfare of the entire group is involved.

The writer has several times selected samples of the most prosperous and the least prosperous ejidos and then had four persons in the old Central Union and four in the Banco Ejidal characterize them as to their conduct of meetings, election of responsible officials, and similar qualities. Overwhelmingly the more prosperous ejidos were reported as being responsibly and democratically conducted, although there were significant exceptions. The ejidos listed as having less fertile land, inadequate water, an excess of population in relation to good land, and other economic disadvantages were generally listed as having the less-smoothly functioning democratic machinery.

But here also there were significant exceptions. Several prosperous ejidos had fallen into debt because of internal squabbles; one outstanding example of a poor ejido which held together for four years to the writer's personal knowledge was often cited. "When the *ejidatarios* see that they are getting someplace economically, they are not nearly so likely to quarrel among themselves," was what most of the persons consulted replied. Pursuit of this lead would bring us to the second goal value, but first we must look at La Laguna in the broader framework of Mexican political and economic institutions.

The highly centralized character of the Mexican social system has been noted before, as well as the crucial role played by outstanding personalities.[11] The ejidos which depend on the Banco Ejidal for credit find that such centralization hampers their economic development, since often their work plans for the coming crop season must be submitted to the national office of the bank before funds are forthcoming. This usually means interminable delays which take their toll in reducing the efficiency of the ejidos.

Laguna ejidos are affected by decisions made in Mexico City, but the organized *ejidatarios* in 1941 began to become aware that they were increasingly unable to influence such decisions. While Lázaro Cárdenas was president, the Central Union was able to reach him with complaints and suggestions. The climate changed when Cárdenas left office. A struggle then began between the bureaucracy of the Banco Ejidal and other government dependencies on one hand and the organized peasants on the other.

Gradually, every mistake made by the peasants began to be used by the government officials to discredit and eliminate those among the *ejidatarios* who had maintained an independent attitude. The governors of Coahuila and Durango were encouraged to promote their own peasant groups. The sectarian maneuvers of the Communists helped split the *ejidatarios* and aided the "bureaucrats" in their endeavors.

The original efforts of the bank's staff to secure the participation of the peasants in the reconstruction of the regional economy became a concerted drive to manipulate them in the interests of "normal, smooth functioning of the credit machinery," as it was expressed to the writer by a bank employee.

An indication of the lengths to which the subversion of the *ejidatarios* had gone is indicated by the reaction of the "captive" peasant group to the discharge of Ing. Gonzalo Blanco Macías. It joined the angry chorus of those who had been demonstrated to be robbing the ejidos in denouncing Blanco as a "disturbing influence."[12] Obviously, he was. The fact that he was disturbing their exploiters makes the affair an outstanding illustration of the need for "living convictions" (to use Sorokin's phrase) to give a content of social power to the legally created democratic institutions.

Wealth.—Both increased production and more equitable distribution of economic goods and services are subsumed under this goal value heading. "Land reform which does not increase production merely equalizes poverty," Chiang Mon-lin, chairman of the Joint Commission on Rural Reconstruction in Formosa, points out.[13] Production of cotton and wheat has increased in the Laguna region since the expropriations. The increase, ironically enough, has come mostly from the private properties. Their owners have been forced to intensify cultivation, using wells and machinery to a higher degree than before.

Productivity, the basic factor in real income, has risen for the private sector of the Laguna economy but, on average, has fallen for the *ejidal* sector. The total production of both cotton and wheat increased after the expropriations by 14 and 52 per cent, respectively, as we have seen. Yields fell, however, from an average of 396 kilograms of cotton per *hectárea* in the six years just before the change to 339 in the following ten years and from 1.19 metric tons of wheat to 1.14. Tables 20 and 21 show that the drop was greater in *ejidal* than in private production and that the latter exceeds the former in almost every year in both crops.

Our examination of the reasons for these phenomena must begin with a qualification of the accuracy of the figures. Reporting of

TABLE 20

COTTON: AREA CULTIVATED, PRODUCTION, AND YIELD
PRIVATE PROPERTIES AND EJIDOS
LAGUNA REGION
1936-1937 TO 1945-1946
(crop years)

Crop Year	Area Hectáreas		Production Bales of 507 lbs.		Yield Kgs. per *Hectárea*	
	Ejidos	Private	Ejidos	Private	Ejidos	Private
1936-1937	90,944	29,056	84,649	55,351	214	439
1937-1938	66,472	26,198	94,000	53,000	326	466
1938-1939	56,329	28,971	65,000	68,000	266	541
1939-1940	50,589	23,319	55,016	50,000	251	494
1940-1941	37,753	55,984	50,000	70,846	305	292
1941-1942	50,016	70,000	64,921	139,010	299	457
1942-1943	56,699	71,881	95,445	166,843	388	535
1943-1944	61,538	78,777	55,000	132,500	206	387
1944-1945	41,606	60,805	84,737	99,757	469	378
1945-1946	23,312	28,257	33,816	56,514	334	461

Source: Compiled from reports issued by: Secretaría de Agricultura; Banco Nacional de Crédito Ejidal; Departamento Agrario; Banco de México, Torreón office; Pequeña Propiedad Agrícola de la Comarca Lagunera, A. C.

TABLE 21

WHEAT: AREA CULTIVATED, PRODUCTION, AND YIELD
PRIVATE PROPERTIES AND EJIDOS
LAGUNA REGION
1936-1937 TO 1945-1946
(crop years)

Crop Year	Area Hectáreas		Production Metric Tons		Yield Metric Tons per Hect.	
	Ejidos	Private	Ejidos	Private	Ejidos	Private
1936-1937	7,093	19,407	7,835	21,616	1.10	1.11
1937-1938	33,329	19,024	37,452	29,487	1.12	1.55
1938-1939	51,136	18,364	53,000	32,000	1.04	1.74
1939-1940	39,401	19,620	54,683	35,317	1.39	1.80
1940-1941	43,278	14,500	47,957	16,000	1.11	1.10
1941-1942	55,420	15,000	41,479	15,000	.75	1.00
1942-1943	30,485	10,000	34,126	12,000	1.12	1.20
1943-1944	21,664	12,000	20,094	15,000	.93	1.25
1944-1945	33,991	23,051	32,999	46,955	.97	2.04
1945-1946	20,453	11,463	13,205	12,800	.65	1.12

Source: Compiled from reports issued by Secretaría de Agricultura; Banco Nacional de Crédito Ejidal; Departamento Agrario; Banco de México, Torreón office; Pequeña Propiedad Agrícola de la Comarca Lagunera, A. C.

agricultural data in the region, as elsewhere in Mexico, leaves much to be desired. Essentially, the figures are those provided by the interested parties; the *ejidal* by the Banco Ejidal and the private by the owners. The totals of some years exceed the crop figures of the federal agricultural department and in other years drop below it. The *ejidal* figures are published and subject to challenge, however, while the others are not. In all cases of discrepancy between what seem to be equally reliable sources, the more conservative figure was accepted.

Analysis of the causes for the difference in yields must of course take into account all the factors which influence production: the quality of the soil, water supply and timing, that is, river flows, rain, and wells; weather, application of labor to the land, that is, management efficiency; mechanization, and credit. Unfortunately, in the region, another factor must be included—cotton theft. Obviously cotton stolen from *ejidal* lands and sold as if raised on the private properties not only reduces the yield record of the ejidos but increases it on the private properties and thus counts double in any comparative figures. Theft of wheat is far less prevalent than that of cotton and therefore would be a minor factor in comparing yields. Cotton fields dropped noticeably more than wheat yields.

We may rule out rain, frosts, and hail as "falling on both the just and unjust." They are factors in the uneven chart of regional production, but not in differential yields between the two economic and social systems.

River water, in amount and timing, may also be ruled out, with one qualification. The irrigation laws provide for simultaneous distribution of river water in proportions roughly equivalent to the amount of land held by the two groups. The *ejidatarios* charge that the undemocratic organization of the canal-users committees gives the private sector an advantage. There are persistent charges of favoritism and bribery of water gate tenders.

Wells are an important factor in water supply. We have seen (p. 107) that both cotton and wheat yields are raised substantially by irrigation with well water, which can be timed exactly to suit the crop needs. The private owners now have 65 per cent of the wells in the region for 30 per cent of the land.

The fertility of the soil obviously plays an extremely important role in production. There are no soil maps nor analyses of private as compared with *ejidal* lands, but it will be recalled that the *hacendado* was free to choose at least 150 *hectáreas* (370 a.) of his holdings. Obviously he generally would choose the most fertile soil. It may reasonably be assumed, therefore, that the private lands contain the choice soils of at least the zones in which they are located.

It has been pointed out that the amount remaining under one management is often considerably more than 370 acres. The private farmer has the advantage of unified direction of a larger area. He does not cut his land into plots to be worked by families. The private owner has a completely "collectivized" farm, but of course run under a more or less modified dictatorship, not a democratic collective. It may or may not be more efficient than a farm run by a committee. One finds a wide range of overlapping between the efficiency curves of private farms and ejidos, with some ejidos ranking above some private farms and vice versa.

The relative position varies widely by zone and by crop, as indicated in Table 22, which takes the average private property yields in cotton and wheat for the year 1945-1946 as a basis for comparison between the two systems.

A crucial factor in modern farming is mechanization. Other

TABLE 22

YIELDS, WHEAT AND COTTON
COMPARISON OF EJIDAL WITH PRIVATE PROPERTY
LA LAGUNA
1945-1946
(per cent of all ejidos in relation to average private
property yield)

Zone	Wheat			Cotton		
	Above Average	Same as Average	Below Average	Above Average	Same as Average	Below Average
1	27.8	33.3	38.9	—	—	100.0
2	18.2	13.6	68.2	—	9.1	90.9
3	50.0	16.7	33.3	4.2	8.3	87.5
4	34.8	17.4	47.8	4.3	—	95.7
5	13.3	3.3	83.4	3.3	3.3	93.4
6	8.9	11.1	80.0	—	—	100.0
7	37.1	14.3	48.6	2.9	—	97.1
8	65.0	—	35.0	20.0	5.0	75.0
9	55.2	6.9	37.9	3.4	—	96.6
10	—	—	100.0	—	—	100.0
11	48.7	9.8	41.5	12.5	10.0	77.5
12	33.3	13.3	53.4	20.0	6.7	73.3
13.	16.7	4.2	79.1	8.3	—	91.7
14	9.1	9.1	81.8	—	10.0	90.0

Source: Compiled from reports issued by Secretaría de Agricultura; Banco Nacional de Crédito Ejidal; Departamento Agrario; Banco de México, Torreón office; Pequeña Propiedad Agrícola de la Comarca Lagunera, A. C.

factors being equal, a well-mechanized farm will far outstrip a non-mechanized or poorly mechanized farm. It has been seen above that the returns are appreciably higher on the heavily mechanized ejidos. It has also been seen that whereas 75 per cent of the private properties were heavily mechanized in 1939, only 23 per cent of the ejidos were. The influence this fact has on yields has been reported.

Inadequate credit completes the picture. The private owner generally may be able to get credit fairly quickly and simply since he can mortgage his property, although even he is hampered by the general lack of farm credit facilities in the country as a whole. Government credit suffers from a complicated bureaucratic system of so many checks that as much as six months may pass from the application date before money is available to an ejido.[14]

"Lack of discipline among the membership" and many other factors are often stressed as causing the difference in productivity between the private properties and the ejidos.[15] This would lead to the conclusion that the *ejidal* form of organization is the reason for the difference in yield, even though we have pointed out other factors which reasonably can be linked with the observed differentials.

There is a statistical technique available for analyzing this problem somewhat further, the analysis of variance.[16] Application of this technique to data for the 1945-1946 crop year adds weight to the indications from the previous examination of factors affecting productivity in warning against any generalization that the cooperative ejido is inherently less productive than the private farm.[17]

There is a less involved manner of demonstrating that the decisive factor is not a constant (the *ejidal* form of agricultural organization) but variables (including amount and timing of water flows, and other geographical factors as explained in Chapters 4 and 5). Table 36, Appendix, shows that the profits from cotton of the *ejidatarios* working with the Banco Ejidal over a period of 18 years from 1937 to 1954 varied from a low of 692,012 pesos in 1940 to a high of 45,578,423 pesos in 1954. The high is 65 times the low. The difference between the second highest year (1950, with 24,276,498 pesos) and the 1940 low is 35 times. The extreme fluctuations of the annual returns, added to the null hypothesis tests, should indicate that at least a major part of the answer to *ejidal* failures lies in the variables and not in the constant.

There will be no widespread recognition of this fact until all the geographic and economic factors contributing to the lack of financial success of most of the ejidos have been eliminated. Obviously, this is not likely to happen in the foreseeable future.

Indications of greater economic welfare have been given in Chapter 7: including better housing and clothing, more beds, radios, group possession of capital equipment, garden plots, domestic fowl and animals and horses. La Laguna cannot be separated economically from the rest of Mexico, however. Relatively more prosperous than the country as a whole, it still suffers from the raging inflation of recent years, from the general overpopulation of the country in addition to its own specific population problem, from the dislocations of unplanned and uncoordinated economic development, and the interference of self-serving politicians in regional economic matters.

One significant area in which the increased economic welfare of the region as a whole may well help toward building democracy in Mexico is increased support for local and state governments. There was a weak tradition of local autonomy in the Spanish heritage of Mexico, but it has never firmly taken root. There has been increased agitation for greater "home rule" in recent years, but the overwhelming majority of local governments do not have an economic basis for autonomy. The local government unit, the *municipio* (comparable with counties in the United States rather than municipalities), usually contains a large percentage of rural people. Within the *municipio* there are cities, towns, and villages, with definitions and powers which vary from state to state. All are closely supervised by the state governments. The Torreón budget, for instance, has to be approved by the state government. Relationships between the smaller entities and the *municipios* are not too clearly defined.[18]

Far less local police power is characteristic of Mexico than of the United States. Federal garrisons stationed throughout the country quite often act as local peace officers in the absence of anything resembling a local police force. In the Laguna region, as has already been noted, the chief of the federal garrison usually had been one of the region's important *hacendados* up to the time of the expropriations.

A Mexican student of fiscal affairs has said that "of all the tax systems in the world the most backward, unjust and irrational are those of the Latin American countries."[19] Sales taxes, stamp taxes, and taxes upon the movement of goods from one place to another (known as *alcabalas*) play an important role in Mexican public finance. *Alcabalas* were blamed as early as 1788 for greatly increasing the cost of living and interfering with development of the country. In addition it was reported that they lent themselves easily to graft.[20]

Alcabalas were forbidden by the constitutional convention of 1857. They were again "abolished" by a reform of the Constitution in 1896 and again in the Constitution of 1917. In spite of all these decisions a committee of the federal senate found that there were more than thirty such taxes existing in 1943. In July of that year the Continental Rubber Company applied for an injunction to restrain the state of Durango from enforcing an *alcabala* of 5 per cent of the value of guayule, lechuguilla, candelilla, and similar products. *Alcabalas* were again "abolished" by a bill sponsored by President Ruíz Cortines in November, 1953![21]

Federal, state, and local governments all levy taxes. The federal government has always collected more taxes and a larger share of taxes than have local and state governments. A large proportion of the total governmental revenues comes from export and import duties, although in recent years there has been decreasing dependence upon these sources and increasing dependence upon taxes on industry and commerce. The income tax until a few years ago yielded only a small percentage of governmental income.[22]

The Laguna *municipios* increased their income from 1,540,716 pesos in 1940 to 22,937,000 pesos in 1950, a gain of 1,388 per cent. The states of Coahuila and Durango raised their incomes 673 per cent and 611 per cent, respectively, in the same period. All state government revenues together went up only 367 per cent; the national government raised its income by 589 per cent. Thus, the Laguna local governments and the two states containing the region showed considerably higher gains in income than did the federal and all state treasuries.[23]

Well-Being.—It is toward this goal value that the Laguna experiment has made the most progress. Much of the advance is now past quantifying. One thinks, for example, of numerous reports of eye-witnesses and participants in whippings of field workers only a few months before the expropriations; of houses destroyed and peons driven off haciendas only a few years before 1936. One remembers hundreds of meetings in which men and women vibrated with a new dignity and determination to work hard and make a success of the "land which is now ours." One recalls the mixed meetings of *ejidatarios*, private owners, urban businessmen, and government officials into which the former day-workers came armed with facts and figures, presenting well-reasoned arguments for their position with calmness and determination. One rereads the annual reports of the old Central Union in which a recommendation was made that a mutual crop insurance fund be created, and follows this through the years to the present thriving organization which could well serve as a model for farmers in other nations.

It is possible roughly to quantify one crucial index to the feeling of security which has been won by the *ejidatarios* of La Laguna.

On the writer's first visit to the region, March, 1937, a count of all peasants visiting the Torreón office of the Banco Ejidal showed nine out of ten wearing at least one revolver, supported by a well-loaded cartridge belt; there were many "two-gun" men! Each succeeding visit found a decreasing number of guns. All had disappeared by 1939. A gun-carrying official of the bank was encountered in 1943; a surprised query brought this response from a peasant leader: "He has just been transferred here from Jalisco and he hasn't got used to our ways yet!"

The reply indicated a glaring difference between the region and many other sections of Mexico where frequent *despistolización* campaigns have been conducted intermittently ever since the writer's first trip to the country in December, 1936. The Mexican is still "quick on the draw," although an improvement may be noted between 1940 and 1954. There were 13,175 homicides registered in the former year, to 10,954 in the latter, in spite of a substantial increase in the population in that period. The rate dropped from 66 per 100,000 to 38. That was still the highest rate reported by the United Nations for 1954.[24]

Gun carrying is still common enough even among students at the University of Mexico so that its rector announced the "extirpation of the *pistoleros*" as one of his aims in the 1953-1954 academic year.[25] The federal police launched a "disarmament campaign" in the nation's capital in October, 1956, and estimated that "at least" 10,000 persons carried fire arms in the city, according to the United Press.

This is all evidence of regional progress in the field of what might be called psychic well-being. The record of the *ejidal* medical services, mentioned in Chapter 7, speaks for itself in the field of somatic health. They have by all means the most brilliant record of overcoming handicaps, adapting to realities and solid accomplishment of any institutional aspect of the new regime.

Skill.—It is in this area of values that one of the most interesting changes has occurred among the *ejidatarios*. Almost all the skilled personnel in the region before the expropriations worked for the *hacendados*. The more highly skilled ate at the table of the land-owner, swam and played golf at the country club, and gambled at the casino. They were naturally lumped with the *hacendados* as "enemies of the peasant." The peasant had no skills, no reason for having skills, and no opportunity to acquire them if he wished. The sons and daughters of the peasants were in the same situation. The expropriation gave rise to a tremendous demand for skilled and semiskilled persons. A new attitude was needed, as well as new facilities for acquiring skills. The latter were furnished quite promptly, as indicated before. Changing attitudes was somewhat more difficult. There was a fairly widespread disposition to repeat the same naive democratic shibboleths so often encountered in the United States in past times: "Any good man is capable of filling any good job—and I am the man." The presence of a corps of agrarian technicians in the entourage of Lázaro Cárdenas helped overcome that attitude as land was being distributed.

The world suddenly became a much more complex phenomenon than it had been. Bookkeepers, water gagers, cotton classifiers, mechanics, electricians, well-tenders, drivers, and even economists and lawyers were needed to help the new landowners find their way along strange and untrod paths.

Now, as has been seen, the *ejidatarios* either do these jobs for themselves or hire those who know how to do them. Their experience has taught them the value of skills and through the public educational system both regional and national, they are able to acquire those they need.

One of the great handicaps to Mexican progress until the past two decades has been the paucity of adequate facilities for training competent technicians, especially in the agrarian and agricultural fields. The National University has, until recently, often been a breeding place for enemies of democracy, both Communist and fascist. The National School of Agriculture, until the Cárdenas regime, often turned out "swivel chair" agronomists accustomed to giving orders and with the "Spanish gentleman's" horror of performing useful work with his own hands. The son of a peasant who occasionally found himself attending the school was often weaned away from his attachment to the soil. That some outstanding leaders of the agrarian movement did come from the school is a testimony to Merton's "stress and strain" concept.

Simpson pointed out in 1937 that:

. . . the Mexican student who actually goes out in the field and looks for facts about his own country is so rare as to be a curiosity. I could name on the fingers of one hand the research monographs dealing with modern Mexican social problems published by Mexican students in the last decade which by any stretch of the imagination could be called scientific.[26]

Considerable strides have been made toward remedying that situation, as is shown by the well-grounded scholarly current output of scientific monographs and of articles in such journals as *Cuadernos Americanos, Investigación Económica, Problemas Agrícolas e Industriales de México, Revista de Economía, Revista Mexicana de Sociología,* and *El Trimestre Económico* and in the progress since 1943 of the Comisión de Fomento de Investigaciones Científicas under the direction of the world-famous atomic physicist, Dr. Manuel Sandoval Vallarta.[27]

Shared Enlightenment.—Information and interpretation available to the most remote reaches of the region, the smallest and the largest ejido, to the poorest and the best endowed was part of the original frontal attack on the heritage of feudalism.

Much has been done. Schools now mark each ejido (one has two within fifty feet of each other because of the rivalry between the directors of the Coahuila state department of education and the federal organization!). However, the education of the *ejidatarios* themselves in a manner designed to involve them in "problem-solving" has been neglected in a most irresponsible manner. There are several reasons for this. First, the drive for education was supplied initially by the Cárdenas administration. When it went out of office the key post of secretary of education was occupied by a political appointee whose chief qualification seemed to be a hatred of democratic ideas. The regional education office was abolished and a wet blanket was thrown over the enthusiasm of both teachers and inspectors. Second, an economy wave hit the Banco Ejidal, resulting in the discontinuance of the *Boletín Ejidal* and the weekly educational broadcasts.[28] Third, a "commercial" orientation was adopted by the bank, as we have seen. Seemingly it was oblivious to the fact that its clients could not make a complete transition in a few years from virtual slaves to self-reliant members of a far-reaching democracy. Fourth, employees of the bank who either did not share the democratic ideals for which the institution was supposed to work or who wanted to capitalize on the ignorance of the *ejidatarios* often did not carry out even those plans which were authorized.

Mexico as a whole and the region in particular have partially made up for this situation, however. The almost universal aspiration for education and information has resulted in the proliferation of sources of news and discussion of public issues in the daily press, in magazines, and on the radio. The country in 1954 counted 127 dailies and 1,128 magazines, most of them weeklies, compared with 60 dailies and 159 magazines in 1935. The circulation of periodicals of all types doubled between 1930 and 1954.[29]

Furthermore, individuals of standing and ability have for some years felt free to criticize governmental policies and can depend on most organs of mass communication to give circulation to their statements. The revolution, as a matter of fact, is officially represented by only one inadequately-staffed daily newspaper in the capital and one radio station; the "opposition" has all the other hundreds of outlets for "news and views." Also, there is an old tradition of "wall newspapers" and handbills which comment on public affairs.

It must be noted that standards of truth and reason are not universally observed, either by the often anonymous authors of the posters and leaflets or editorial writers and newscasters. Political controversy, especially, reminds one of our own tradition of violent attack and counterattack, with "no holds barred."[30]

Caveat emptor should be recognized as one of the corollaries of democratization of the distribution of piffle and poison.

Shared Affection and Respect.—Lasswell defines the former expression as meaning the acceptance in the culture of "the desirability of congenial human relationships." Here we find in La Laguna, and other parts of Mexico, many expressions of such revolutionary slogans of human brotherhood as solidarity of the worker and peasant. The feelings extend even to "workers and peasants" throughout the world; delegates and "fraternal visitors" from other groups and other countries are welcomed cordially at labor union and peasant conventions. Many times real friendships grow out of contacts made in working for "the common cause." This would seem marginal to the major patterns, however. Actually, it is in this goal value that Lasswell's schema seems least applicable to the Mexican culture, unless one confines the word "congenial" to its root meaning of "kindred."

Mexico has been in a state of social disruption so often and so much of the time for the past four centuries that the family (biological and ritual) is almost the only place in which a man can "let down his guard." Expression of pleasant and sympathetic feelings toward persons outside the family do not seem to be as common as in the United States, except among the small but growing urban middle class.

Much has been made of the key role of the family in the Mexican culture by social scientists and journalists, both foreign and domestic. Unfortunately, the vast majority of Mexican ethnographic studies treat of relatively isolated rural or village "folk."[31] However, some of the aspects of family structure and function are fairly widespread. Most observers seem to agree with Redfield that "there is no open conflict within the family," that the father wields undisputed authority, that submission is the role of the other members, that the family plays a vital role in economic and political life, especially in small villages.[32]

Humphrey notes that, although there is "little spanking or ordering and forbidding in the training of children," they are fairly rigidly disciplined by threats of withdrawal of affection. He found a noticeable amount of "repression of elements of self" which he felt is "dynamically related to the exaggerated necessity of maintaining 'face' or 'honor' as adults and to violent expressions of revenge and sudden anger."[33]

Lewis reports on "the quality of inter-personal relations" in Tepoztlán as follows:

There is a readiness to view people as potentially dangerous, and the most characteristic initial reaction to others is suspicion and distrust. Lack of trust is not only present among non-relatives but also exists within families and affects the relations of husbands and wives, parents and children, and brothers and sisters. This is not a neurotic distrust, but one rooted in the hard realities of Tepoztecan social and economic life, in patterns of child training, and in a long history of conquest, colonial status, and internal and external political and economic exploitation. In Tepoztlán, the motives of everyone are suspected, from the highest public officials of the nation, to the local priest, and even to close relatives. It is assumed that anyone in a position of power will use it to his own advantage at the expense of others. Honest government or leadership is considered an impossibility; altruism is not understood. The frank, direct person, if he exists anywhere in Tepoztlán, is considered naive or the greatest rogue of all, so powerful or shameless as to have no need to conceal his deeds or thoughts. An individual who is obliging without cost to those who seek his aid is understood to have some as yet unrevealed plan for capitalizing on his position.[34]

The greater degree of social participation among the peasants of La Laguna seems to have eliminated some of the traits reported from other areas of Mexico, if it may be assumed that they were once present due to a common cultural tradition. For instance, cordiality and hospitality of the Laguna *ejidatarios* to the writer and his colleagues of the American Friends Service Committee and the college students from "north of the border" many times have been embarrassingly fulsome.

The original suggestion that college students would be willing to come from the United States to help build rural schools was greeted by a puzzled lack of belief that anyone, especially those with the superior status of college students, would "do something for nothing." After several days in which the students worked side by side with the peasants, mixing straw into mud with bare feet to make adobe bricks, word spread from ejido to ejido that the *Americanos* actually were working with their hands (and their feet). The appearance of the students at any rural event after that was always followed by effusive expressions of good will. Many students to this day maintain correspondence with their former fellow workers.

The same acceptance was never achieved with the Torreón middle class. Many business and professional people grudgingly expressed their interest to the writer, but usually ended by regretting that the students "couldn't see the *real* life of the Mexicans instead of living and working with those peasants." The consular representatives of the United States in Torreón in the early days of the work-camp program invariably were critical of it on the ground that it "impaired the dignity of the American" in the eyes of the only Mexicans their staff knew—the urban middle class.

These experiences might indicate that as changes of the kind experienced in recent years in La Laguna continue, the narrower family-centered culture begins to give way to class-oriented culture.

The demand for "respect," the insistence on authority, the double standard of sexual morality and monetary responsibility, all militate against expressions of affection in the family.[35] On the other hand, as Mexican social contacts become increasingly "secondary" instead of "face-to-face," the need for dependable friendships arises. Several of the informal groups which have ruled the country have been based on friendships forged during the civil war, during student strikes at the universities or normal schools, or during exile for political activities. Once formed, such friendships often take precedence over any idea of the public interest, as pointed out by several outstanding Mexican students.[36]

Shared respect is somewhat more nearly universal in Mexico. Lasswell defines it as "absence of discrimination on grounds other than merit." However, the opportunities to achieve prestige, power, and wealth are so limited in Mexico that competition may become fierce and bitter. The idea of civil service is officially accepted but of no importance in practice; "to the winner go the spoils" as in Jackson's day. Thus merit for the greatest single source of employment is usually meaningless.

Next, the widespread *compadrazgo* system and the tightly knit friendship cliques rule out nonmembers when opportunities open. Even broader is the still-present antagonism around the concept of "Spanish origin." One is white (no matter what the skin color) if one is "pure Spanish." The writer heard an extremely dark lawyer once start a speech, "*Nosotros de la raza blanca . . .*" ("We of the white race . . ."). Iturriaga[37] points out that "to indicate that someone is white, it is said that he has '*cara de gente decente*' (literally 'face of decent people') and, on the other hánd, one uses the brusque expression '*cara de pelado*' for an Indian or Indian-looking mestizo." (The closest English equivalent is probably "nobody.") This vestige of colonialism and feudalism is declining but still evident in many aspects of human relations. It is lent support by some of the sociologists who still follow the "primitive mentality" concept of Lèvy Bruhl, long discredited in the United States.[38]

Rectitude.—This goal-value includes not only the dichotomous concept good-bad, but the far more fundamental idea that "each person ought to feel, think and act responsibly for the purpose of perfecting the good society (defined as the maximum sharing of all values)."[39] This is a large and serious requirement, but obviously one crucial to a successful democracy.

It has been already reported that numerous actors in the Laguna experiment have fallen short of their goal: business men, government officials, labor representatives, *ejidatarios,* lawyers; the highly-placed and the lowly. One is tempted to compare those who complain about graft and corruption with those who wanted simply to replace old men with new (themselves) in the "Diazpotism." Nevertheless, old institutions were destroyed and new ones were created. Social change can start only with an awareness of the need for change. It can come about only when large numbers of persons share the awareness, desire a change, and reach some consensus about the direction of change. We have seen that it is only when this consensus is organized that it begins to bring results. In the field of private and governmental graft and corruption in the United States the relatively recent past has witnessed a multiplication of such organizations as the National Civil Service League (1881), many municipal governmental research bureaus, the National Tax Association (1907), the Governmental Research Association (1917), and the Association of Better Business Bureaus (1921). They make investigations, hold open meetings for discussion of their research results, issue public denunciations of improper behavior, and in other ways serve as "watchdogs" over our business and political morality. They are now joined by hundreds of groups formed for civic purposes; for the promotion of responsible citizenship, for example, the influential League of Women Voters and the "service clubs."[40]

The realization is growing in Mexico that the same thing can be said about widespread graft that Tawney said about capitalism:

The poor do not always realize that capitalism is maintained, not only by capitalists, but by those who, like many of themselves, would be capitalists if they could, and that the injustices survive, not so much because the rich exploit the poor, as because the poor, in their hearts, admire the rich.[41]

Mexico is just beginning to organize civic clubs, thus far mostly branches of "international" bodies, started in this country; for example, Rotary, Kiwanis, Lions, and others. The disposition to criticism is present; it seems as if organization for acting on the criticism may not lag for many more years. There is as yet only a rudimentary beginning of public forums, "round tables," discussion groups, "Let's Find Out" programs, and the thousands of other informal educational groups which abound in the United States.[42]

The fact that some such groups are being organized is hopeful for those seeking a greater sense of responsibility in civic life. Intense individualism has served Mexico well in helping break up some attempts to "turn the clock back"; pushing ahead will be more difficult.

"The first rule of the social code," states Anita Brenner, a veteran observer of and participant in the Mexican culture, "is 'you live your way; I'll live mine.' It's the unwritten supreme law; the one law everybody meticulously respects. The rules of polite behavior work all the time to allow people to live as they choose without paying the slightest attention to what you or anyone else is up to." She adds a most significant comment, "It's an incoherent spectacle, like a society of sleep-walkers."[43]

Spanish thinkers have minced no words in characterizing the Mexican cultural background in Spain in terms which aid in understanding the difficulties of cooperative action in Mexico. "Anarchy is the natural state of the Spaniard," wrote Salvador Madariaga. "In Spain, nobody agrees with anyone," says Rufino Blanco-Fombana. Santayana thinks that "The Spaniard . . . distrusts everything and everybody."[44] Obviously the building up of a consensus on social matters and the application of "sanctions" is difficult under such conditions.

One may now frequently read or hear such denunciations as the following by an outstanding economist, professor at the National University and former government official, Jesús Silva Hérzog:

Politics alters and corrupts everything. . . . There are big, medium and small politicians, giants and dwarfs, and they are found everywhere: in the offices and reception rooms of officials, in the schools, in the labor unions, in the co-operative societies, in the ejidos. The politician is not often considerate and honest, he is only interested in personal gain, and is a profiteer of the Revolution: in the ejido he exploits the *ejidatarios,* in the labor unions he exploits the workers and employees, and in the schools he deceives his companions. It is the easiest and most lucrative profession in Mexico. Culture is not necessary, it is a detriment; what is necessary is boldness, lack of scruples and being an authentic representative of Mexican *machismo* ("masculinity"). Everything has been corrupted. In the ejido it is common for the peasant, exploited by the political leader, to try in turn to exploit those who are economically weaker than he is; there are many peons working the lands of the new miniature landlord: the *ejidatario*. There has been a lack in the ejidos, as well as in the labor movement, of political education and of good teaching not only regarding rights but also regarding social duties. In the labor organizations the immorality of a good number of leaders is notorious.[45]

On another occasion, Silva Hérzog attacked the immorality and lack of any sense of responsibility of merchants, industrialists, and professional men.[46] Another economics teacher recently published a book denouncing graft and corruption.[47]

One aspect of the heritage of Spain, colonialism, feudalism, and the days when the revolutionary governments maintained themselves by naked force is the persistence of the citizens' feeling of alienation from the government.[48] The fact that governmental activities in Mexico so profoundly affect persons in all walks of life might have led before now to a "governmental reform" movement but for three factors:

1. So many of the revolutionaries thought that the only enemy was in the economic field; "abolish economic exploitation and governmental corruption will clear up."
2. The previously noted persistence of the hope that one might himself get into the "racket."
3. The feeling that the situation is "natural" and therefore nothing can be done about it.

A powerful challenge to the old habits was issued by the newly inaugurated president, Adolfo Ruiz Cortines, in the fall of 1952. He "cleaned house" in a number of government departments, held up the payment of bills left by his predecessor, refused to accept expensive gifts, began arriving for work at 8 a.m., obeyed traffic regulations, commended a traffic policeman for stopping his chauffeur for a forbidden U-turn, and in many other ways set a high standard of probity and responsibility for his appointees to meet. Collection of taxes was reorganized to put an end to tax evasion which, in the words of *The Financial Times of London*, "had risen to the level of an economic system."[49] The old idea of a "law of financial responsibility" was revived; government officials elected and appointed now must declare their personal wealth and income as they take office and as they leave, with records being open to the public.

An example from the occupant of a position of such prestige in the Mexican social system may be expected to encourage numerous persons down through the social structure to emulate the president. If they are backed up, the progress toward greater rectitude may well be considerable. La Laguna was unfortunate in being given an example of a man who took the president's example seriously and lost his position as a result.[50] Generally, reports from various other sections of Mexico report more favorable consequences, although the Mexico City daily, *La Prensa*, alleged in the spring of 1954 that 10,000,000 pesos ($1,250,000) annually was mulct from the merchants of the capital.[51]

AGRARIANISM—UTOPIAN OR SCIENTIFIC?

Land reform will continue—that is not the question. Peasants depending on land for a livelihood but denied access to the land will sooner or later demand a change in "the rules of the game." This will be particularly true where the lords of the land do not have enough self-discipline to keep from abusing the dignity and self-respect of the peasants and their families, and where the peasant has begun to be aware of the vast currents of social change in the world.

These are the areas in which the problem is that of the latifundia. There are other, and in some respects even more complex, questions to be resolved in the areas where the problem is of the minifundia. Our concern here has been with the former only, since that was considered Mexico's major obstacle to democracy in 1910 and the Laguna's in 1936.

Our attempt has been to examine Mexico's experience in regard to the three basic questions raised in the Preface in hopes that whatever lessons might be learned could be called to the attention of two groups:

1. The policy-makers and the publicists of the advanced nations (which largely have passed beyond their agrarian reforms). Understanding on their part may well help avoid both economic and political mistakes in dealing with agrarian phases of the "world revolution of our time." Land reform is taking place, and demands for more will arise in the "underdeveloped" regions of the world, especially those with colonial or semicolonial economies. A United Nations report issued in February, 1954, states that "many millions

of former tenant farmers throughout the world have become owners of their lands since 1950 and other millions have similar prospects.[52] Our relations with the leaders of agrarian movements in such regions may well determine the course of the future history of the world and the role of the "developed" countries in it. The United States officially has expressed little positive interest in land reform since the first chapter of this study was written, that is, since the 1953 change in administration.[53] Bolivia did receive a $9 million loan from this country to "provide farm credit for the host of new landholders established through its agrarian reform," however.[54]

2. The second group includes those in position of authority in international technical and financial institutions, both public and private, and both policymakers and technicians in those countries facing the prospect of land reform. They are in a position to antici-pate problems which may arise and to contribute to their solution in a less wasteful manner than "trial and error" experimentation usually involves. A person may become sensitized to the possi-bilities and probabilities of future needs and future programs in his own economy and culture by becoming aware of parallels and differences between his situation and those in other cultures. He must, of course, be constantly on guard against viewing the prob-lems of others with the distortions provided by the lenses of his own culture. Probably few persons have ever fully achieved this objective, but it must be attempted.

Since the end and justification for social science is "prediction and control," what kinds of generalizations can be hazarded on the basis of our study of La Laguna which might add to our abilities to follow the old motto: "Forewarned is forearmed"? It must be said that they are in all truth modest and elementary. The justifi-cation for presenting them is that: (1) so much is written in the "advanced" countries on land reform which ignores social realities, (2) one knows of so many action programs in which the most elementary precautions are not being taken against some of the mistakes made in La Laguna, and (3) a check list based on the experience of others may at least save time for persons usually harrassed by demands for plans "day before yesterday," and for *immediate* action.

1. It is often unlikely, even though highly desirable, that, to quote the World Land Tenure Conference and the International

Bank, "ownership rights . . . of dubious origin and legally and morally not well established" on which are based "oppressive systems of land tenure" will be given up peacefully.[55]

2. Commentators in the countries comfortably far beyond their own periods of violent action to break the bonds of the past would be well advised not to take an unctuously moralistic attitude toward sincere attempts to obtain for the people a voice in their own destiny.

3. Violence might be avoided if the owning classes were far-sighted enough to help the peasants work out a peaceful transition. The recent actions of the shah of Iran and the "land gift" movement in India might be used as positive examples, if the fate of the aristocrats in the French, Mexican, and Russian revolutions are not impelling enough as warnings.

4. Recent resolutions and studies of the United Nations and other international bodies may well serve to weaken the "living convictions" of latifundistas and their intellectual retainers about the sacredness of their right to control the lives and destinies of those who depend on their land for a livelihood. The "transfer of the allegiance of the intellectuals," has been called the "first master-symptom of revolution."[56]

5. A softening of intransigent attitudes on the part of latifundistas may help make the transition more peaceful. It will not contribute toward making peasant ownership more productive unless steps are taken well in advance of transfer of ownership to prepare the peasants technically to overcome their centuries of deprivation of human rights.

6. Agrarian reforms probably will take place at least as often as a result of explosions arising out of "strains and tensions in the social system" as they will as a result of long-range planning.[57]

7. In either case (5 or 6), there are a number of technical measures which could be prepared and introduced in advance and which can be justified as being necessary under either democratic or predemocratic land tenure patterns. Among them are: maps of soil, topography, land use, property boundaries, and irrigation and drainage canals; the building of proper facilities for increasing productivity, for example, irrigation canals; the creation of plague and pest control machinery; the introduction of better varieties of crops and breeds of animals, and the whole galaxy of technological

improvements which have raised productivity in agriculture so greatly in some cultures in the recent past.

8. These seem to be purely technical matters but Laguna experience indicates that they may become involved in the social struggle. The building of an irrigation dam was opposed by some of the big owners in La Laguna, it will be recalled. The peasants, on the other hand, may feel that the increased intensity of effort which might be required represents just that much more "exploitation." Participation in the new agrarian structures on a democratic basis will help motivate the peasant.

9. Adequacy of land for productive farming is also often looked upon as solely a technical matter. It is a technical matter, but it is also a political matter during land distribution. If the *latifundista* is allowed to choose the best land and leave only the marginal or submarginal land for the peasants, obviously the peasants will suffer.

10. Technically, land distributors would benefit by remembering the warning of Pearson and Harper that for full productivity there must be at least the following physical factors:

favorable temperature
sufficient but not too much rainfall
reliable, well-timed rainfall
slopes not too steep
fertile soil

"Few persons recognize the veto power of any one factor," they point out.[58]

11. Overloading even good land with a population too dense for it to support may sound like good humanitarianism when it is being done. It might more properly be compared with the action of a captain who allows a lifeboat to be loaded far beyond capacity. A miracle might save the passengers (or the peasants) but miracles happen as infrequently in land reform as in lifeboats.

12. Such a mistaken step is made easier by those who refuse to recognize that population is often the major independent variable contributing to the poverty of an economy. Probably the most glaring example of such thinking is the recent book which states its thesis as follows:

The crucial point of this essay is the argument that overpopulation does not cause starvation in various parts of the world, but that starvation is the cause of overpopulation.[59]

13. Motivation to work, and to work more productively, is a matter needing study and experimentation in many areas even before land reform takes place. It becomes more urgent if land ownership shifts to the formerly landless peasant who has never been given a chance to exercise the slightest degree of judgment or initiative, nor assume any responsibility. Here psychology and economics mix, since increased income (both monetary and psychic) must demonstrably flow from increased exertion.

14. An understanding of what social change is and what social institutions are would be helpful to agrarians. Too often physical analogies used by reformers and revolutionaries lead to highly simplistic thinking in the field. "Tear down the old structure," "smash the capitalist system," and similar slogans have been used for many years. The idea that society is like an outmoded building which can be razed and rebuilt with new materials following a new blueprint has marked both "scientific" and Utopian revolutionaries in their work-a-day moods, even though some of their greatest mentors have warned against such patterns of thought. Even Lenin spoke on several occasions about the need for convincing "the overwhelming majority of the population"[60] if a real socialist transformation was to take place.

15. Mexican experience indicates that the scientist most likely to be called upon after agronomists and related workers in the physical sphere is the economist. This is highly necessary, but not sufficient. For instance, Gordon summarizes what many, if not most, Mexican economists believe:

To increase production substantially in areas of inadequate water supply, it will be necessary to build great dams and to farm most of the land in large blocks, that is, to farm most of the ejidos as collectives.[61]

It has been seen that this is the Laguna plan. It has also been pointed out that the ideological basis for the plan was the supposed relevance of the Aztec heritage to the new agrarian structure. This type of *Indianismo* in the absence of Indians or any real identification with the Indian cultural heritage proved illusory.

This does not mean that the cooperative ejido cannot work and contribute to both economic and social betterment. The fact that at least a third of the Laguna ejidos usually do so, and far more are viable when favored by a sufficiency of water, belies the negative. It does mean that more attention must be paid to both structure and the motivation which makes the structure function acceptably.

This sociologist would like to see a further, intensive experiment carried out in the Laguna region and elsewhere as Mexican agrarianism proceeds. It seems quite probable that careful selection of members of an ejido plus a period of training and even probation might well give the new organization a better chance to succeed economically. Experimentation with a few selected ejidos on a carefully controlled basis might well give a clue to a program for helping revitalize those which are lagging. Suggestions for testing and selection of members as well as analysis of the experience of the kvutza of Israel are available as background and guides.[62]

16. The sociological analysis of a stable social system as "highly dependent upon the motivation of the participants" opens up a field of endeavor technically much more difficult than the admittedly serious problems of land fertility, farm layout, credit, and other areas in which agronomic engineers are becoming increasingly competent. Here the social scientist who works with the agronomist may find himself in a dilemma. He knows that he must secure the participation of the peasant if democracy is to be built on the basis of a more equitable distribution of land. He knows also that he must start with the "felt needs" of the peasants, with their aspirations. But while the "broadest possible participation" of the peasant, his wife, and his children in education, recreation, production, and civic and religious affairs is an easy prescription to write, it is exceedingly difficult to follow.

Analysis of agrarian history indicates that many times the program "land to the landless" is based on an idea (perhaps partly true but usually wholly or partly false) that his ancestors lived an idyllic life before the ancestors of the present lord of the land took the land away from them. This may lead, as it did in many instances in Mexico, to a completely static approach to production, based on a feeling of psychic satisfaction in merely owning the land and in being able to meet minimum subsistence needs.

Obviously new wants must be aroused before new techniques will be adopted. Vast social changes over centuries have been needed in the past to produce the dynamic societies of "Western civilization." They are based on attitudes and sentiments and concepts which may be quite strange to the new landowner.

17. Possibly the greatest single contribution the sociologist can make toward helping policy-makers formulate a workable program for building democracy is to analyze the major social institutions of the society involved as they affect the agrarian program. They must be democratic, actually or at least potentially, if the new agrarian structure is to be functionally democratic.[63]

We have seen that it has thus far taken Mexico some forty-five years since it started its efforts to democratize its political structure; and that such effort in turn required democratizing agrarian, industrial, educational, and other institutions. Such a vast change in the social system can benefit from the sociologist's training in the analysis of social institutions. The sociologist can make plain that, if a fundamentally sound democracy is the aim, the eight goal values outlined above must all be considered as part of the agrarian movement. He will need to suggest plans for arousing new wants along nonexploitive lines, since economic, political, and administrative exploitation must be avoided. Many times the power to correct such situations will lie far from the hands of the scientist, but knowledge of the ways in which ideas are transmitted and become accepted by the people can help both policy-makers and the people work toward the goal of functional democracy; toward the acceptance and implementation of the concept of the dignity of man.

Notes

1. Harold D. Lasswell, *The World Revolution of Our Time: A Framework for Basic Policy Research* (Stanford: Stanford University Press, 1951).

2. Paul Louis, "Agrarian Movements in Rome," *Encyclopedia of the Social Sciences*, I (1938), 494-95. See also M. Rostotzeff, *The Social and Economic History of the Roman Empire* (Oxford: Clarendon Press, 1926), pp. 23-25, 196, 245, 620-21; and the schematic diagram showing the frequent occurrence of agrarian revolts running back to 800 B.C. in C. P. Loomis and J. A. Beegle, *Rural Social Systems* (New York: Prentice-Hall, Inc., 1950), p. 621.

3. *New York Times*, December 28, 1955. See also the background story by Albion Ross, "Mau Mau Rising Called Outburst of Native Grievance Over Land," *New York Times*, October 26, 1954.

4. Dean Acheson, "World Land Tenure Problems," in *Land Reform—A World Challenge* (Washington: Department of State, 1952), pp. 27-51; Isador Lubin, "Hope of the Hungry Millions," *New York Times Magazine*, February 10, 1952, pp. 18, 49, 52, 54.

5. Lubin, *op. cit.*, p. 53; Arthur F. Raper, *et al.*, *The Japanese Village in Transition* (Tokyo: General Headquarters, Supreme Commander for the Allied Powers, 1950); Lawrence I. Hewes, Jr., *Japan—Land and Men, the Story of Land Reform in Japan* (Ames: Iowa State University Press, 1955).

6. C. Clyde Mitchell, *Land Reform in Asia* (Washington: National Planning Association, 1952).

7. *Fourth Annual Report, 1948-1949* (Washington: International Bank for Reconstruction and Development, 1949), pp. 8-9.

8. *Conclusiones de Manizales* (Des Moines: National Catholic Rural Life Conference, 1953); *New York Times*, April 17; April 23, 1955; April 6, 1957.

9. The author found, among the many works in this field, the following especially relevant to an understanding of these three phenomena: Devere Allen, *What Europe Thinks About America* (Hinsdale, Ill.: Henry Regnery Co., 1948); Norman S. Buchanan and F. A. Lutz, *Rebuilding the World Economy* (New York: Twentieth Century Fund, 1947); Louis Fischer, *Empire* (New York: Duell, Sloan & Pearce, 1943); W. E. Moore, *Industrialization and Labor* (Ithaca: Cornell University Press, 1951); National Planning Association, *America's New Opportunities in World Trade* (Washington: National Planning Association, 1944); Fritz Sternberg, *The Coming Crisis* (New York: The John Day Co., 1947), chap. iii, vii, viii; Barbara Ward, *The West at Bay* (New York: W. W. Norton & Co., 1948); Harvey Perloff, *Puerto Rico's Economic Future* (Chicago: University of Chicago Press, 1950), especially chapters xii and xiii; Karl Polanyi, *The Great Transformation* (New York: Rinehart & Co., 1944); Chester Bowles, *The New Dimensions of Peace* (New York: Harper & Bros., 1955); Chester Bowles, *American Politics in a*

213

214 NOTES (PAGES 5-11)

Revolutionary World (Cambridge: Harvard University Press, 1956); Richard P. Stebbins, *The United States in World Affairs* (New York: Harper & Bros., 1956); Evron M. Kirkpatrick, *Target: The World* (New York: Macmillan Co., 1956); C. L. Sulzberger, *The Big Thaw* (New York: Harper & Bros., 1956); William O. Douglas, *Strange Lands and Friendly People* (New York: Harper & Bros., 1951); Erich H. Jacoby, *Inter-relationship between Agrarian Reform and Agricultural Development* (Rome: Food and Agriculture Organization of the United Nations, 1953); Arthur T. Mosher, *Technical Cooperation in Latin-American Agriculture* (Chicago: University of Chicago Press, 1957); Food and Agriculture Organization of the United Nations, *Report on the Latin-American Seminar on Land Problems* (Rome: Food and Agriculture Organization of the United Nations, 1953); Food and Agriculture Organization of the United Nations, *Report on the Center on Land Problems in Asia and the Far East* (Rome: Food and Agriculture Organization of the United Nations, 1955).

10. Douglas, *op. cit.*, chap. xxvii.

11. "First World Land Tenure Problems Conference and Report of Its Steering Committee," *Land Economics*, XVIII, 1 (February, 1952), 77.

12. Loomis and Beegle, *op. cit.*, p. 622.

13. P. A. Sorokin and C. C. Zimmerman, *Principles of Rural-Urban Sociology* (New York: Henry Holt and Co., 1929), p. 458. One is tempted to question the adjectives "programless" and "objectiveless," in view of the consistent use of the slogan "land to the landless," or "land and liberty," or "bread, land and liberty." It seems likely that these two students are reflecting, unwittingly, their own comfortable positions in a society which is now aware of agrarian needs only intellectually.

14. Henry G. Bennett, "Land and Independence—America's Experience," in *Land Reform*, pp. 71-72.

15. Isador Lubin, "Land and the Free World," in *Land Reform*, pp. 15-16.

16. Robert K. Merton, *Social Theory and Social Structure* (Glencoe: Free Press, 1949), p. 116.

17. Among the sounder works are: Ernest Gruening, *Mexico and Its Heritage* (New York: Century Co., 1928); Frank Tannenbaum, *The Mexican Agrarian Revolution* (New York: The Macmillan Co., 1929); Eyler N. Simpson, *The Ejido—Mexico's Way Out* (Chapel Hill: University of North Carolina Press, 1937); Nathan L. Whetten, *Rural Mexico* (Chicago: University of Chicago Press, 1948); Frank Tannenbaum, *Mexico: The Struggle for Peace and Bread* (New York: Alfred A. Knopf, 1950); and Andrés Molina Enríquez, *La Revolución Agraria de México* (México: Talleres Gráficos del Museo Nacional de Arqueología, Historia y Etnografía [five volumes issued from 1933 to 1937]).

18. In *Land Reform*, p. 53.

19. A. Whitney Griswold, *Farming and Democracy* (New York: Harcourt, Brace and Co., 1948), p. 45.

20. *Ibid.*, pp. 147-55.

21. Food and Agriculture Organization of the United Nations, *Report of the Director General, 1950-51*, (Rome: Food and Agriculture Organization, 1951), p. 3.

22. W. S. Woytinsky, "India Facing Destiny," *The New Leader*, August 13, 1956.

23. John Dewey, *Freedom and Culture* (New York: G. P. Putnam's Sons, 1939), p. 76.

24. Charles E. Merriam, *The New Democracy and the New Despotism* (New York: McGraw-Hill Book Co., 1939), p. 109.

25. Lawrence K. Frank, *Society as the Patient* (New Brunswick: Rutgers University Press, 1948), p. 251.

26. Robert S. Lynd, "Foreword" to Robert Brady, *Business as a System of Power* (New York: Columbia University Press, 1943), p. viii.

27. Robert S. Lynd, *Knowledge for What?* (Princeton: Princeton University Press, 1946), p. 214.

28. Lasswell, *op. cit.*, pp. 5, 6, 14-26, 41-44.

29. It is not contended that the eight elements listed by Lasswell are accepted by any specific agrarian movement as defining democracy. It is a matter of personal value-orientation which, as Parsons points out, "provides the standards of what constitute satisfactory 'solutions' of . . . problems." Talcott Parsons, *The Social System* (Glencoe: Free Press, 1951). The "goal values" of Lasswell are here treated as a summary of the normative "ends, values, and sentiments in the minds of the people" which are viewed by the "voluntaristic" school of sociology as basic to the unity of society. See Talcott Parsons, *The Structure of Social Action* (Glencoe: Free Press, 1949), especially Part IV; and Kingsley Davis, *Human Society* (New York: Macmillan Co., 1949), pp. 121-22, 145, 633.

CHAPTER 2

1. Details and references are to be found in Wilfrid Hardy Callcott, *Liberalism in Mexico, 1857-1929* (Stanford: Stanford University Press, 1931), pp. 120-95, and Gruening, *op. cit.*, pp. 55-65.

2. The Indian worker's daily wage purchased about 33 litres of corn in the decade of 1900, against 8 litres in 1910, says Gruening, *op. cit.*, quoting Francisco Bulnes, *El Verdadero Díaz y la Revolución Mexicana* (México: E. Gómez de la Puente, 1920), p. 218. Another estimate, along the same lines, has it that agricultural wages remained constant from 1810 to 1910, but that the cost of food for the rural worker increased 300 per cent. Jesús Silva Herzog, "Los Salarios de Nuestros Campesinos," *La Antorcha*, July 4, 1925. The British consul at Vera Cruz reported that the workers there were not participating fully in the prosperity of the period 1905-1911. He indicated about a 33-1/3 per cent reduction in working-class levels of living in the seven years. Cited in E. W. Kemmerer, *Inflation and Revolution* (Princeton: Princeton University Press, 1940), pp. 35-36.

3. "It is . . . my central hypothesis that aberrant behavior may be regarded sociologically as a symptom of dissociation between culturally prescribed aspirations and socially structured avenues for realizing these aspirations." Merton, *op. cit.*, p. 128. The Mexican Revolution offers the sociologist a fascinating opportunity to test this hypothesis. The Mexican society, in fact, during the civil war (1910-1921) probably came as close as any large modern group to achieving an advanced state of what Durkheim called *anomie*, or normlessness. Unfortunately, to pursue this idea in detail would take us too far off the course of our present investigation.

4. There is great temptation here, which must be resisted, to attempt to fit the Mexican social scene into Merton's scheme of "five types of adaptation" when aspirations are frustrated:

    I   Conformity
    II Innovation
    III Ritualism
    IV Retreatism
    V Rebellion

One thinks, for instance, of the greater hold of the church on women who, in the Spanish culture, find their place only "in the home," in other words, "*in* the society but not *of* it," (IV); the exaggerated etiquette of the Spanish "gentleman," which is generally confined to his peers, (III); the small, seminomadic Indian tribes which have physically carried out their retreat; the persistent playing of the lottery; the tremendous quantities of *pulque* consumed by the Mexican poor, etc. *Ibid.*, pp. 133-46.

    5. Nathaniel and Sylvia Weyl, *The Reconquest of Mexico* (New York: Oxford University Press, 1939), p. 26. This must be taken to mean that economic deterioration is both a necessary *and* a sufficient "cause" for social change. As a matter of fact, it may be neither.

    6. Charles Flandreau, *Viva México* (London: D. Appleton-Century Co., 1935), p. 61.

    7. Sociologists writing on social stratification in the United States during recent years have split between those stressing "subjective" and those stressing "objective" factors. The germs of such a split are contained in the writings of Marx and the Marxists as well as in Weber. Weber differentiates between classes which are stratified "according to their relations to the *production* and *acquisition* of goods" and status groups which are stratified "according to the principles of their *consumption* of goods as represented by their special 'styles of life.'" (Max Weber, "Capitalism and Rural Society in Germany," in *From Max Weber: Essays in Sociology*, eds. H. H. Gerth and C. Wright Mills [London: Kegan Paul, 1948], p. 193.) Centers reverses this distinction and makes class dependent on the subjective factors and uses strata in the way in which Weber uses class. (Richard Centers, *The Psychology of Social Classes* [Princeton: Princeton University Press, 1949], p. 27.) Weber added a third dimension to his stratification scheme—legal or political power (see Paul K. Hatt, "Stratification in the Mass Society," *American Sociological Review*, XV, 2 [April, 1950], 217). Kingsley Davis and Wilbert E. Moore add still another factor, the distribution of technical knowledge ("Some Principles of Stratification," *American Sociologist Review*, X, 2 [April, 1945], 247-48.)

    No matter whether one speaks of wealth, power, authority, prestige, or "life-chances," a small group at the top in the Mexico of 1910 practically monopolized the "objective" wealth and the "subjective" symbols. Our concern is the major social institutions in the structure of that situation.

    8. The 1895 data are analyzed in José E. Iturriaga, *La Estructura Social y Cultural de México* (México: Fondo de Cultura Económica, 1951), pp. 24-89. The method is described as primarily occupational but the technics of analysis are not given.

    9. Simpson, *op. cit.*, pp. 32, 33, thus summarizes several studies. There is some dispute among students of the period just before the revolution as to the distribution of the rural population between haciendas, large landed estates; ranchos, small farms; and landholding villages left from precolonial days. Tannenbaum (*The Mexican Agrarian Revolution*, pp. 30-37) holds that 51 per cent of the rural population would be included in the landholding

villages. Simpson believes this estimate to be far too high. The 1895 census results, which probably would not have changed significantly by 1910, show the following distribution of the rural working population:

	Per Cent
Peons (landless land-workers)	80.74
Owners of parcels of land	6.68
Rural artisans	3.23
Small store owners or peddlers	0.72
Miscellaneous	8.63
	100.00

(Iturriaga, *op. cit.*, p. 35.)

The crucial question is not exactly what proportion of landless persons existed. It is agreed that a sizable percentage of the total population was completely dependent upon a few others for access to the means of making a living. Even more important is the fact that several millions of the landless peasants had, within one or two generations, lost their or their forefathers' lands by force or fraud. (Simpson summarizes the five chief methods, *op. cit.*, pp. 31-33.)

10. This sketch of the agrarian structure is based on the following principal sources, as well as on dozens of interviews with persons who lived under the system described, and personal visits to most of the important areas of all but one state of the Mexican federation:

Molina Enríquez, "La Dictadura Porfiriana," in *La Revolución Agraria de México*, IV; "Proyecto de la Ley Agraria y el Discurso del Dip. Lic. Luis Cabrera," in Manuel Fabila, *Cinco Siglos de Legislación Agraria en México, 1493-1940* (México: Banco Nacional de Crédito Agrícola, 1941), pp. 218-42; Gruening, *op. cit.*, pp. 111-66; Tannenbaum, *The Mexican Agrarian Revolution, passim*; John Kenneth Turner, *Barbarous Mexico* (Chicago: Charles H. Kerr and Co., 1910), pp. 9-119.

11. See Charles S. Johnson, E. R. Embree, and W. W. Alexander, *The Collapse of Cotton Tenancy* (Chapel Hill: University of North Carolina Press, 1935), and Howard Kester, *Revolt Among the Sharecroppers* (New York: Covici, Friede, 1936). Tannenbaum writes of the hacienda store that "the ideal of good administration was to make such money as was paid out in wages return to the hacienda . . . at a profit," *The Mexican Agrarian Revolution*, p. 118.

12. Gruening reports a case in Hidalgo (popularized outside of Mexico by Serge Eisenstein in his film "Thunder Over Mexico") in which the leaders of the village were buried up to their shoulders and then ridden down by the *hacendado's* horsemen, *op. cit.*, p. 129.

13. Rafael Ramos Pedrueza, *La Lucha de Clases a Través de la Historia de México* (México: Secretaría de Educación Pública, 1936).

14. Sorokin and Zimmerman, *op. cit.*, p. 458.

15. Lynd, *Knowledge for What?*, p. 211.

16. Callcott, *op. cit.*, Chap. I, and J. Lloyd Mecham, "The Origins of Federalism in Mexico," *The Hispanic-American Historical Review*, XVIII, 2 (May, 1938), 164-82.

17. Frank Tannenbaum, "Personal Government in Mexico," *Foreign Affairs*, XXVII, 1 (October, 1948), 57. See also Alberto María Carreño, *La Evolución Económica de México en los Ultimos Cincuenta Años* (Mexico: Academia Nacional de Ciéncias "Antonio Alzate," 1937); Armando Servín, *La Evolución Técnica del Sistema Impositivo Federal* (México: Fondo de Cultura Económica, 1942), p. 7. Davis has shown how the feudal social order in Latin America has hampered the growth of democracy throughout the area. Kingsley Davis,

"Political Ambivalence in Latin America," *Journal of Legal and Political Sociology*, I, 1-2 (October, 1942), 127-50.

18. Henry B. Parkes, *A History of Mexico* (Boston: Houghton Mifflin Co., 1938), p. 287.

19. One example out of many of the interlocking of the political and rural feudal structure was reported by *El País*, a Catholic daily of Mexico City, on May 3, 1909, as the power of the dictator began to wane:

. . . the Secretary of Agriculture Don Olegario Molina conceded to the *hacendado* Don Olegario Molina the adjudication of these thousands of hectares as vacant land and the real governor of Yucatán, Don Olegario Molina, ordered possession given to the aforesaid *hacendado*, the denouncement having been made before Tomás Avila López, agent of the Secretaría of Agriculture, the head of which is Don Olegario Molina. (Gruening, *op. cit.*, p. 128.)

20. Frank A. Manuel, *The Politics of Modern Spain* (New York: McGraw-Hill Book Co., 1938), pp. 11-14; Thomas J. Hamilton, *Appeasement's Child: The Franco Regime in Spain* (New York: Alfred A. Knopf, 1943); Salvador de Madariaga, *Spain* (New York: Creative Age Press, 1943); Herbert L. Matthews, *The Yoke and the Arrows* (New York: Geo. Braziller, Inc., 1957).

21. Henry Lea, *History of the Spanish Inquisition* (London: The Macmillan Co., 1922), II, 322.

22. Gruening, *op. cit.*, p. 183, quoting various primary sources. The same richly documented reference is used in the following pages, unless otherwise noted.

23. See three volumes of Mora's writings and speeches published in the collection *El Liberalismo Mexicano*, edited by Martín Luis Guzman: "El Clero, la Milicia y las Revoluciones"; "El Clero, el Estado y la Economía Nacional"; and "El Clero, la Educación y la Libertad" (México: Empresas Editoriales, 1950 and 1951). For a sketch of the life and works of Mora, see W. Rex Crawford, *A Century of Latin American Thought* (Cambridge: Harvard University Press, 1944), pp. 247-50.

24. These and similar sentiments quoted in Callcott, *op. cit.*, Chaps. VI, VII, VIII.

25. *Restauración*, 8-9 de marzo, 1921; similar quotations may be found in Callcott, *op. cit.;* Weyl, *op. cit.*, chap. VI; Marjorie Clark, *Organized Labor in Mexico* (Chapel Hill: University of North Carolina Press, 1934), pp. 86-96; and in Gruening, *op. cit.*, *passim*.

26. Francisco Bulnes, *The Whole Truth About Mexico* (New York: M. Bulnes Book Co., 1916), pp. 116-17.

27. Gerth and Mills, *op. cit.*, pp. 43, 80.

28. See *infra*, p. 63.

29. Gabriel Ferrer de M., *Vida de Francisco I. Madero* (México: Secretaría de Educación Pública, 1945), pp. 7-21.

30. John Creelman, "President Díaz, Hero of the Americas," *Pearson's Magazine*, March, 1908, p. 241. Text, in Spanish, in *Documentos de la Revolución Mexicana* (México: Secretaría de Educación Pública, 1945), pp. 7-16.

31. The influence of the Masonic movement in Mexico has often been great, although its various orders have never had large numbers of followers. It has many times served "behind the scenes" to promote anticlerical and other unorthodox ideas. Sometimes it has served the interests of non-Mexicans, e.g., when the York rite group was financed by one ambassador and the Scottish by the other in the rivalry between the United States and Great Britain during the early days of the republic. Masons have been one of the favorite whipping

boys of political clericalism in Italy, Spain, and Mexico. Ernest Gruening reports: "In my conversations with members of the Mexican clergy they commonly applied the terms 'socialist,' 'Protestant,' 'atheistic,' 'Bolshevik,' and 'Masonic' indiscriminately to individuals or doctrines not endorsed by the church" (*op. cit.*, p. 220). Díaz "rode both horses"; he was a thirty-third degree Mason, Grand Master of a Masonic order, *and* a Roman Catholic! (Callcott, *op. cit.*, pp. 140, 142).

32. Jesús Silva Herzog, "Un Balance de la Revolución Mexicana," *Memoria del Segundo Congreso Mexicano de Ciencias Sociales* (México: Sociedad Mexicana de Geografía y Estadística, 1945), II, 474.

33. *Documentos de la Revolución Mexicana* (México: Secretaría de Educación Pública, 1945), pp. 25-30.

34. For text see *ibid.*, p. 43; for commentary, Charles Wilson Hackett, *The Mexican Revolution and the United States* (Boston: World Peace Foundation, 1926), p. 342.

35. One hundred thirty-four and a half million acres of public lands had been disposed of to private interests by Díaz at little or no return to the nation. Simpson, *op. cit.*, p. 28.

36. *El Imparcial*, 27 de julio, 1912, quoted in Molina Enríquez, *op. cit.*, IV, 167-68.

37. Rudolf Heberle defines a genuine social movement as "an attempt of certain groups to bring about fundamental changes in the social order, especially in the basic institutions of property and labor relationships." "Observations on the Sociology of Social Movements," *American Sociological Review*, XIV, 3 (June, 1949), 346-57.

38. Gruening, *op. cit.*, pp. 141-42.

39. *Documentos . . .* , pp. 60-65.

40. Rosa E. King, in *Tempest Over Mexico* (Boston: Little, Brown and Co., 1935), gives a sympathetic account of the Zapata movement in spite of the loss of her property because of it.

41. Gruening, *op. cit.*, pp. 96-97.

42. One of the great obstacles to the growth of democracy in Mexico is *liderismo*. Frank Tannenbaum writes of it: "The principle of government was a principle of loyalty to the little chief; the little chief, in turn, rendered loyalty to the still greater chief in the capital of the state or in the City of Mexico. - *The small group has always followed its local leader against anyone, even against the great leader*." (*Peace by Revolution* [New York: Columbia University Press, 1933], p. 96.)

43. On the Indian heritage, see G. C. Vaillant, *The Aztecs of Mexico* (New York: Doubleday, Doran & Co., 1944), p. 119, who writes that "In theory and practice Aztec society was democratic, and the communal ownership of productive property was its economic base." The Spanish antecedents are described by Simpson: " The core and heart of Mexico's agrarian reform is the ejido. The word ejido (pronounced á-heé-doe) is derived from the Latin *exire, exitum* 'to go out.' As originally used in Spain the term was applied to uncultivated lands held collectively on the outskirts (on the way out) of agrarian communities. In Mexico at the present time the word is used to refer to all types of lands which have been restored or granted to agricultural communities under the agrarian reform initiated in 1915. By extension, the word is used to designate the communities possessing such lands." (Simpson, *op. cit.*, pp. vii-viii.)

44. Molina Enríquez, *op. cit.*, V, 143-47.

45. "Proyecto de la Ley Agraria y el Discurso del Dip. Lic. Luis Cabrera," in Fabila, *op. cit.*

46. "In the case of restitution there is, logically, no indemnification. Land stolen from the original owners is restored to them. The fact that they are not forced to pay for the use they have made of the land speaks highly for Mexican revolutionary moderation." Gilberto Bosques, *The National Revolutionary Party of Mexico and the Six-Year Plan* (Mexico: National Revolutionary Party, 1937), p. 20.

47. Unfortunately there is no satisfactory study of the Cárdenas program as a whole. The first few years are covered in Weyl, *op. cit.*

48. "Presidential Farewell Address," quoted in *Tiempo*, 2 de septiembre, 1952.

49. Marte R. Gómez, "Los Riegos de México," *Problemas Agrícolas e Industriales de México*, II (1950), 35.

50. Investment in irrigation work during the Alemán six-year term was 2,103 million pesos, a quantity far above that spent in all previous revolutionary administrations *(Informe de Labores de la Secretaría de Recursos Hidráulicos* [México: Secretaría de Recursos Hidráulicos, 1951] and "Presidential Farewell Address," *op. cit.).*

51. Data for 1930, 1940, and 1950 from *Compendio Estadístico* (México: Secretaría de la Economía Nacional, 1951), p. 120; 1854 and 1910 figures from George McCutchen McBride, *The Land Systems of Mexico* (New York: American Geographical Society, 1923), p. 102.

52. Banco Nacional de Crédito Ejidal, *Informe 1951* (México: Banco Nacional de Crédito Ejidal, 1952), pp. 64-69.

53. United Nations, Economic and Social Council, Economic Commission for Latin America, *Recent Developments and Trends in the Mexican Economy* (New York: United Nations, E/CN, 12/217, Add. 8,26 March, 1951), p. 48.

54. Clark, *op. cit.*, pp. 3-22.

55. Iturriaga, *op. cit.*, pp. 43-46; Alfonso López Aparicio, *El Movimiento Obrero en México* (México: Editorial Jus., 1952), pp. 151-54.

56. Clark, *op. cit.*, p. 29.

57. *Ibid.*

58. Bosques, *op. cit.*, p. 34.

59. Weyl, *op. cit.*, pp. 239-40.

60. For recent events and estimates see Robert J. Alexander, *World Labor Today* (New York: League for Industrial Democracy, 1952); John Coe, "Recent Labor Developments in Mexico and the Caribbean," *Inter-American Economic Affairs*, March, 1948, pp. 15-70; and official periodicals of the Organización Regional Inter-Americana de Trabajadores (ORIT), the Confederación de Trabajadores de América Latina, and the American Federation of Labor—Congress of Industrial Organizations. ORIT is the Western Hemisphere regional body of the International Confederation of Free Trade Unions.

61. The percentage of the nonfarm labor force organized in Mexico and in the United States was almost the same—one quarter—in 1950. Mexico's labor force was shown as 8,240,063 by the 1950 census, of which 4,823,901 were occupied in agricultural pursuits. If organized labor included 777,000 (as reported in 1948), that was 9.4 per cent of the total, and 23 per cent of the nonagricultural. Labor organizations in the United States included 25 per cent of the total and 28 per cent of the nonagricultural in 1950. (*Compendio Estadístico*, 1951, p. 15; U. S. Census of Agriculture, *1950 Special Reports*, V, Part 6 [Washington: Government Printing Office, 1950], 12, 17.)

62. Francisco Pimentel, *Memoria sobre las Causas que han Originado la Situación Actual de la Raza Indígena de México y Medios de Remediarla*, pp. 202-3, quoted in Clark, *op. cit.*, p. 31.

63. Bulnes, *The Whole Truth About Mexico*, p. 308. The rate of exchange used to translate pesos into dollars at each reference throughout the study is the one which prevailed at the time referred to. The exchange rate of the peso by years from 1910 is shown in Appendix Table 37.

64. Kemmerer, *op. cit.*, pp. 60-61.

65. Official United States figures for the 1910-1920 decade indicate an immigration of 219,000 in this period. Comparison of the two censuses, however, shows that the increase in persons born in Mexico was 264,500. Undoubtedly Guatemala and other Central American countries and nearby Cuba also received some Mexican refugees during the civil war. See Kingsley Davis and Clarence Senior, "Immigration from the Western Hemisphere," *Annals of the American Academy of Political and Social Science*, CCLXII (March, 1949), 70-81.

66. Iturriaga, *op. cit.*, pp. 4, 32.

67. Kemmerer recalls the remark of John Witherspoon about a similar situation in the thirteen British colonies during the War for Independence. "Debtors," he wrote, "were often seen pursuing their creditors and paying them without mercy." *Op. cit.*, pp. 128-29.

68. *Supplements to Commerce Reports*, "Mexico," II, 32a (1914) (Washington: United States Department of Commerce, 1914), 1-2.

69. Data from Banco de México; International Bank for Reconstruction and Development, *The Economic Development of Mexico* (Baltimore: Johns Hopkins Press, 1953), Table 1; and United Nations, Statistical Office, *Statistics of National Income and Expenditure, 1953* (New York: United Nations, 1956), p. 3.

70. *Compendio Estadístico*, 1951, p. 293; *Anuario Estadístico*, 1953 (México: Secretaría de la Economía Nacional, 1954), p. 944.

71. United Nations, Statistical Office, *National Income and Its Distribution in Underdeveloped Countries* (New York, United Nations, 1951); *Statistics of National Income and Expenditure* (New York: United Nations, 1953).

72. International Bank for Reconstruction and Development, *The Economic Development of Mexico*, Table 7.

73. *Hispanic American Report*, X, 2 (February, 1957), 61.

74. Mexico's population was estimated by the National Bureau of Statistics as 31,426,190 in June, 1957, according to a United Press dispatch, *New York Times*, June 20, 1957.

75. This is indicated both by modern demographic experience generally, and an examination of the relation between birth and death rates for the periods cited above. If the birth and death rates for 1895-1900 were correct, there would have been a population loss of 0.02 per cent during the period. Instead, there was a population gain of 1.5 per cent. The first decade of the twentieth century would have registered a gain of only 0.08 per cent, but the actual increase was 1.09 per cent. The decade after the civil war (no demographic data are available for that eleven-year period) showed a similar contrast of 0.09 per cent versus 1.75 per cent. Improvements in the vital statistics system are indicated by closer coincidences for the next two decades (1931-1940 and 1941-1950), when there were discrepancies of only 1.17 per cent and 0.10 respectively. In- and out-migration have been fairly minor factors.

76. United Nations, *Demographic Yearbook, 1956* (New York: United Nations, 1957), pp. 634-43.

77. *Ibid.,* p. 687.

78. Whetten, *op. cit.,* pp. 332-33.

79. Louis Dublin, Lotka, A. J., and Spiegelman, M., *Length of Life* (New York: The Ronald Press Co., 1949), *passim.*

80. R. G. Burnight, N. L. Whetten, and B. D. Waxman, "Differential Rural-Urban Fertility in Mexico," *American Sociological Review,* XXI, 1 (February, 1956), 3-8.

81. United Nations, Economic and Social Council, *Preliminary Report on the World Social Situation* (E/CN, 5/267, 25 April, 1952), pp. 34-36; Julio Durán Ochoa, *Población* (México: Fondo de Cultura Económica, 1955), pp. 27-31.

82. *New York Times,* June 15, 1957; *Hispanic American Report,* X, 2 (February, 1957), 60.

83. Whetten, *op. cit.,* pp. 329-32; and *supra,* p. 35.

84. Parkes, *op. cit.,* p. 116.

85. Iturriaga, *op. cit.,* pp. 90-110; *Tiempo,* 3 de agosto, 1953.

86. Moore, *op. cit.,* p. 206.

87. See the book with that title by Weyl, *op. cit.*

88. Two recent studies indicate the kinds of problems arising when "modern" ideas and technology come to Indian villages: Robert Redfield, *A Village that Chose Progress* (Chicago: University of Chicago Press, 1950); and Oscar Lewis, *Life in a Mexican Village* (Urbana: University of Illinois Press, 1951).

89. Gilberto Loyo, "Ocupaciones e Ingresos de la Población Indígena de México," *Hechos y Problemas del Mexicano Rural* (México: Seminario Mexicano de Sociología, 1952), pp. 61-69.

90. *Ibid.,* p. 67.

91. United Nations Statistical Office, *National Income and Its Distribution in Underdeveloped Countries,* pp. 15-33.

92. Iturriaga, *op. cit.,* pp. 31-35.

93. *Ibid.,* pp. 63-79; Nathan L. Whetten, "The Rise of a Middle Class in Mexico," *Materiales para el Estudio de la Clase Media en la América Latina,* Vol. II (Washington: Unión Panamericana, 1950), pp. 1-29, and comments on it by Angel Palerm, "Notas sobre la Clase Media en México," *Ciencias Sociales,* abril-junio, 1952, pp. 18-27, and diciembre, 1952, pp. 129-35; Laszlo Radvanyi, "Mediciones de la Clase Media de la Ciudad de México," *La Sociología en México,* julio, 1951, pp. 17-21.

94. *Supra,* p. 28.

95. *Tiempo,* 8 de febrero, 1954.

96. Weyl, *op. cit.,* p. 354.

97. This section is based upon hundreds of clippings in the author's files, plus interviews, attendance at party conferences and conventions, residence in Mexico during two presidential elections, and other first-hand experience. References pertinent to the material include: Simpson, *op. cit.,* pp. 351-53; Whetten, *Rural Mexico,* pp. 523-59; Bosques, *op. cit.,* Tannenbaum, "Personal Government in Mexico," pp. 44-57.

98. Pedro Bosch García, *Indices de los Organismos de Intervención del Estado en la Vida Económica de México* (Montevideo, Consejo Interamericano de Comercio y Producción, 1946); Rosendo Rojas Coria, *Tratado de Cooperativismo Mexicano* (México: Fondo de Cultura Económica, 1953).

99. Anita Brenner, "The Mexican Renaissance," *Harpers*, January, 1951, pp. 173-82; Virginia Stewart, *45 Contemporary Mexican Artists* (Stanford: Stanford University Press, 1951).

100. Secretaría de Educación Pública, *Novela de la Revolución Mexicana* (México: Secretaría de Educación Pública, 1945); Carlos González Peña, *History of Mexican Literature* (Dallas: University of Texas Press, 1952); José Manuel Topete, *A Working Bibliography of Latin American Literature* (St. Augustine: Inter-American Bibliographical and Library Association, 1952), pp. 81-113.

101. Titles indicative of the scope of the *corrido* are: "The Glory of that Martyr to Democracy, Aquiles Serdán" (a newspaper editor killed by the Díaz forces in 1910); "The Uprising of Zapata" (1911); "The Death of Madero" (1913); "The Danger of American Intervention" (1914); "The Crimes of the Tyrant Huerta" (1914); "The Workers" (1914); "The True Ideals of the Revolution Promoted by Venustiano Carranza" (1914); "The Constitutional Convention" (1917); "The Tragic Death of Carranza" (1920); "The Surrender of Villa" (1920); "The Death of Obregón" (1928); "The Failure of the Military Rebellion" (1929); "The Corrido of Lázaro Cárdenas" (1934); and "The Expropriation of the Oil Wells" (1938). Jesús Romero Flores, *Corridos de la Revolución Mexicana* (México: El Nacional, 1941); see also Vicente T. Mendoza (ed.), *50 Corridos Mexicanos* (México: Secretaría de Educación Pública, 1944).

CHAPTER 3

1. *Actitud de la Cía. del Tlahualilo en las juntas de rivereños del Nazas, 1909;* Francisco Bulnes, *El Verdadero Díaz y la Revolución Mexicana*, and *La Cuestión del Tlahualilo* (Confidential memo, 1909); *Cía. Agrícola, Industrial, Colonizadora Limitada del Tlahualilo contra el gobierno federal de la República Mexicana. Juicio Entablado ante la 3a Sala de la Suprema Corte de Justicia de la Nación. Demanda—Contestación y contra-demanda-Réplica,* (1909); *Cía. agrícola, industrial, colonizadora, limitada del Tlahualilo versus el gobierno federal. Juicio ordinario. Alegatos que presenta el Sr. Lic. Don Jorge Vera Estañol como abogado especial del gobierno federal ante la tercera sala de la Suprema corte de justicia de la nación,* (1910); *Refutación . . . a los alegatos verbales de la Cía. Tlahualilo; Sentencia . . . de la Suprema Corte . . . en el caso de la Cía. Tlahualilo,* (1911); *Foreign Relations of the United States,* 1912, 312. 11/811, 1001; Jorge L. Tamayo, *Transformación de la Comarca Lagunera* (México: Academia Nacional de Ciencias "Antonio Alzate," 1941), p. 9; *Carlos Ortiz versus la Compañía agrícola industrial colonizadora limitada del Tlahualilo* (1891).

2. Many other differences will appear as an examination of the region continues. A convenient summary of characteristics of the Indian areas of Mexico is found in Howard Cline, "Mexican Community Studies," *The Hispanic-American Historical Review,* May, 1952, pp. 212-42. Some eighty studies made between 1922 and 1952 are cited.

3. Tamayo, *op. cit.,* pp. 16, 19; Enrique Nájera, *et al., Informe General de la Comisión de Estudios de la Comarca Lagunera* (México: Editorial Cultura, 1930), p. 288; Eduardo Guerra, *Torreón, Historia de La Laguna* (Torreón: 1932), pp. 302-9; Interviews with peasants and Torreón businessmen; Weyl, *op. cit.,* p. 219.

4. Fray Juan Agustín de Morfí, *Viaje de Indias y Diario del Nuevo México* *(1777-1778)* (México: Antigua Librería Robredo de J. Porrúa e'hijos, 1935), p. 138; Esteban L. Portillo, *Apuntes para la Historia Antigua de Coahuila y Texas* (Saltillo: Tip. "El Golfo de México" de S. Fernández, 1886), pp. 10-11.

5. Eduardo Guerra, "Bosquejo Histórico de la Comarca Lagunera 1739-1936," *Ciclo de Conferencias* (Torreón: Comité Americano de "Amigos de la Paz," 1939, mimeo.).

6. Esteban L. Portillo, *Catecismo Geográfico, Político e Histórico del Estado de Coahuila de Zaragoza* (Saltillo: Tipografía del gobierno en palacio, 1897), pp. 103-14.

7. Eduardo Guerra, "Bosquejo Histórico . . . "; Miguel O. de Mendizábal gives the total area owned by the Marqués as 7,500,000 *hectáreas* (18,525,000 a.); *El Universal*, 21 de agosto, 1943.

8. Guerra, *Torreón*, pp. 32-35.

9. Nájera, *op. cit.*, pp. 39-41, 43, 45, 49, 50. The valuations were made by the regional Chamber of Agriculture and accepted both by all the owners and the Coahuila state government as the tax base. Probably they were not excessively high.

10. Marte R. Gómez, *La Región Lagunera* (México: Sociedad Agronómica Mexicana, 1941), pp. 29, 34; Liga de Agrónomos Socialistas, *La Comarca Lagunera* (México: Liga de Agrónomos Socialistas, 1940), pp. 45-63.

11. Guerra, *Torreón*, pp. 55-59.

12. Portillo, *Catecismo Geográfico* . . . , pp. 116-20.

13. Marc Bloch, "Feudalism—European," *Encyclopedia of Social Sciences*, VI, 203-10; Henri Pirenne, *Economic and Social History of Medieval Europe* (New York: Harcourt, Brace & Co., 1937); Carl Stephenson, *Medieval Feudalism* (Ithaca: Cornell University Press, 1942).

14. Interviews with local people in 1937, 1939, 1940, 1941, 1943, and 1947.

15. Nájera, *op. cit.*, pp. 15-16.

16. *Ibid.*, p. 289.

17. Catholic Association for International Peace, *Latin America and the United States* (Washington: Catholic Association for International Peace, 1929), p. 21.

18. See Pirenne, *op. cit.*, pp. 62, 66, and 195, for similar arrangements in medieval times.

19. Gruening, *op. cit.*, p. 218.

20. *Ibid.*, p. 278.

21. Weyl, *op. cit.*, p. 147.

22. Banks were nonexistent in Mexico during the entire colonial period. Money was secured either from private lenders, from crop purchasers, or from the church, which was the biggest money lender and mortgage holder. The first real bank in Mexico was founded in 1864; the first strong one in 1884. The first state intervention in Mexican banking came in 1905 with the creation of an organization to supervise banks and credit operations. Mexico did not establish a central bank until 1925, which has since been operating as the Banco de México, S.A. Secretaría de Bienes Nacionales, *Directorio del Gobierno Federal* (México: Secretaría de Bienes Nacionales, 1949), pp. 433-50.

23. Miguel O. de Mendizábal, "La Reforma Agraria Desde el Punto de Vista Económico," *Revista de Economía*, 20 de junio, 1942, pp. 22-29.

24. *Reglamento provisional para la distribución de las aguas, del Rio Nazas,*

desde la presa de San Fernando en el estado de Durango hasta la Laguna de Mayrán en él de Coahuila, 1891; Distribución de las aguas del Río Nazas. Documentos adicionales, 1891; Reglamento para la distribución de las aguas del Río Nazas desde la presa de San Fernando en el estado de Durango hasta la presa de la Colonia en él de Coahuila, 1895; La Comarca Lagunera, pp. 439-40.

25. Gómez, La Región Lagunera, pp. 70, 81.

26. Francisco I. Madero, Estudio sobre la conveniencia de la construcción de una presa en el cañón de Fernández, para almacenar las aguas del río Nazas (San Pedro: Tipografía Benito Juárez, 1907).

27. La Comarca Lagunera, p. 36.

28. Diario Oficial de la Federación Mexicana, 1 de noviembre, 1935; Tamayo, op. cit., pp. 21-24.

29. Tamayo, op. cit., pp. 18-25; La Comarca Lagunera, pp. 37-45; Mexican Labor News, September 1, 1936.

CHAPTER 4

1. A. García Cubas, Cuadro de la Situación Económica Novo-Hispana en 1788 (México, 1906), pp. 66-67.

2. M. González Pérez, México y sus Capitales (México, 1906), p. 85.

3. Julio Riquelme Inda, "La Crisis Económica del Henequén," Boletín de la Sociedad Mexicana de Geografía y Estadística, XXXVII (1928), 63-64.

4. "U. S. Auto Imports Curbed by Mexico" the New York Times (August 4, 1956) reported as one of Mexico's reactions to cotton "dumping."

5. New York Times, October 9, 1953; Tiempo, 14 and 28 de septiembre, 1953; The State of Food and Agriculture in 1951 (Rome: Food and Agriculture Organization, 1951), pp. 68-71.

6. World Fiber Survey (Washington: Food and Agriculture Organization, 1949), p. 85.

7. José Fernando Ramírez, "La Fábrica de Tunal," El Museo Mexicano, I (1843), 121-28.

8. González Pérez, op. cit., pp. 137-40; García Cubas, op. cit., pp. 26-30; Guerra, Torreón, pp. 35-37.

9. United Nations, Economic and Social Council, Economic Commission for Latin America, Labor Productivity of the Cotton Textile Industry in Five Latin American Countries (E/CN 12/219, 12 May, 1951).

10. Boletín Americano, mayo, 1957, pp. 5, 9-16.

11. El Universal, 24 de noviembre, 1943.

12. Novedades, 2 de agosto, 1943.

13. International Bank, The Economic Development of Mexico, Table 80.

14. Competition for world cotton textile markets has become more severe in recent years. The United States dropped from first place in 1951 and 1952 to third place in the first half of 1953. Japanese and British exporters have nosed out the United States, while India fell only a few thousand yards behind this country to stand in a close fourth position. All four countries are not only far more efficient producers than Mexico; even more important, they are prepared to back their exports by subsidies. (See "U. S. Lags in Export of Cotton Textiles," New York Times, September 28, 1953, and "Cotton: U. S. Loses Ground in World Market," Business Week, March 10, 1956, pp. 128-29.)

15. Alfonso Madariaga, "Datos Históricos Acerca de la Aparición del Gusano Rosado . . . en la República Mexicana," *Agricultura*, I, 3 (1924), 12-44.

16. Nájera, *op. cit.*, p. 267.

17. Gómez, *La Región Lagunera*, p. 56.

18. *El Siglo de Torreón*, 29 de julio, 1943.

19. Nájera *op. cit.*, chap. IV; *La Comarca Lagunera*, pp. 170-74; Ing. Benjamín Franklin, in *Ciclo de Conferencias*, 1939, *op. cit.*

20. Nájera, *op. cit.*, p. 199.

21. "La Uva," *Boletín Mensual de la Dirección de Economía Rural*, septiembre, 1943, pp. 881-84.

22. Gonzalo González H., *El Trigo en México*, Parte V (México: Banco Nacional de Crédito Agrícola, 1939), p. 97; "El Abastecimiento Nacional de Trigo," *Revista de Economía*, 31 de octubre, 1943, pp. 8-9; *Plan de Movilización Agrícola de la República Mexicana* (México: Secretaría de Agricultura, 1943); *Boletín Mensual de la Dirección de Economía Rural*, diciembre, 1946, p. 1128.

23. Alfonso Contreras Arias, *El Trigo en México*, Parte II (México: Banco Nacional de Crédito Agrícola, 1939), pp. 159-60; *Ciclo de Conferencias*, 1939.

24. Gonzalo González H., *op. cit.*, p. 98; Alfonso González Gallardo, *El Trigo en México*, Parte IV (México: Banco Nacional de Crédito Agrícola, 1939), p. 114.

25. Gonzalo González H., *op. cit.*, p. 175.

26. *Ibid.*, pp. 170-71.

27. Gómez, *La Región Lagunera*, pp. 62-63.

28. *Excelsior*, 2 de septiembre, 1956.

29. *Padrón de Establecimientos Comerciales, 1939* (México: Dirección General de Estadística, 1939), pp. 8, 105; *Sexto Censo de Población de los Estados Unidos Mexicanos—Población Municipal* (México: Dirección General de Estadística, 1940), p. 3.

30. *Revista de Estadística*, abril, 1947, p. 320.

31. *El Siglo de Torreón*, annual review issues, 1939-1942.

32. Amado Prado, *Prontuario de Torreón*, (Torreón, 1899).

33. *Moody's Manual of Investments* (New York: Moody's Investors Service, 1943), pp. 2151-55.

34. *Mines Register*, 1941; *Mexican Yearbook, 1914* (London: McCorquodale & Co. Ltd., 1914); A. González de León, "Compañía Metalúrgica de Torreón," *Boletín de la Secretaría de Fomento*, 2ª Epoca, 3 (II) 8, pp. 394-97; Carlos Díaz Dufoo, *México y los Capitales Extranjeros* (México: Librería de la Vda. de Ch. Bouret, 1918), p. 321.

35. Ernesto Galarza, *La Industria Eléctrica en México* (México: Fondo de Cultura Económica, 1941), pp. 48-50, 78, 80-83; Gómez, *La Región Lagunera*, p. 25; *El Siglo de Torreón*, 5 de agosto, 1943; *Novedades*, 21 de julio, 1943; *El Universal*, 10 de agosto, 1943.

36. Diego G. López Rosado, *Atlas Histórico Geográfico de México* (México: El Nacional, 1940), p. 102.

37. D. Rafael Durán, "Derroteros Generales de los Departamentos del Imperio Mexicano," *Boletín de la Sociedad Mexicana de Geografía y Estadística*, Tomo XI, pp. 345-470.

38. Federico Bach, "The Nationalization of the Mexican Railroads," *Annals of Collective Economy*, IV (January-April, 1939), 1, 76-77; Simpson, *op. cit.*, pp. 522-26; Javier Sanchez Mejorada, "Communication and Transportation," *Annals of the American Academy of Political and Social Science*, CCXXXI (March, 1940), 78-93.

39. Tannenbaum, *The Mexican Agrarian Revolution*, p. 130.
40. *La Comarca Lagunera*, p. 71.
41. Data from Secretaría de Comunicaciones y Obras Públicas.
42. Guerra, *Torreón*, pp. 275, 278-79.

CHAPTER 5

1. Lázaro Cárdenas, *A Message to the Mexican Nation on the Solution of the Agrarian Problem of La Laguna* (Mexico: National Revolutionary Party, 1936), p. 9.
2. The first adequate land classification, alkalinity, and soil series maps were published in 1951, almost fifteen years after the expropriations: *Estudio Agrológico Detallado del Distrito de Riego en la Región Lagunera* (México: Secretaría de Recursos Hidráulicos, 1951), Tomo I, Tomo II.
3. Gómez, *La Región Lagunera*, pp. 29, 34; *La Comarca Lagunera, op. cit.,* pp. 45-53.
4. *Ibid.,* pp. 59-67; data supplied by Ing. J. Antonio Viadas, Agrarian Department Delegate in La Laguna, August 13, 1943.
5. Fabila, *op. cit.,* passim; Lucio Mendieta y Nuñez, *El Sistema Agrario Constitucional* (México: Librería de Porrua Hnos., 1940), pp. 10-11.
6. *Estudio Agrológico Detallado del Distrito de Riego en la Región Lagunera*, Tomo I, pp. 220-22.
7. For a journalistic account of Laguna peasants leaving their lands see Gonzalo Blanco Macías, "Traición en La Laguna," *Hoy*, 10 de octubre, 1953, pp. 6-8.
8. *Estudio Agrológico Detallado del Distrito de Riego en la Región Lagunera*, Tomo I, p. 174. See Figure 5 and pages 91-93 for examples of farms legally under separate ownership but actually under unified management. The *New York Times* reported on August 16, 1953, that the famed Hearst Babicora ranch in Chihuahua (117 miles long and 70 miles wide) had once been legally cut into eight divisions to ward off application of Mexico's agrarian laws.
9. The political theory back of this part of the *ejidal* structure seems to stem from Montesquieu's "checks and balances" as interpreted by the Mexican in his mistrust of others, particularly those near the exchequer.
10. The best recent short statements on this subject are Julia L. Wooster and Walter Bauer, *Agricultural Credit in Mexico* (Washington: Farm Credit Administration, 1943), and Kathryn H. Wylie, "Land Irrigation Policy in Mexico," *Foreign Agriculture*, October, 1946, pp. 138-46. (The latter unfortunately contains a fundamental misunderstanding of the cooperative ejido.) For criticisms of agricultural credit see Moisés de la Peña, "El Fracaso del Crédito Agrícola en México," *Revista de Economía*, 30 de noviembre, 1943, pp. 29-31; Lucio Mendieta y Nuñez, "El Vampiro Ejidal," and "El Desastre del Crédito Ejidal," *El Universal*, 6 and 20 de octubre, 1943.
11. This is only one of many allegations against the bank; see *infra,* pp. 139-43.
12. Banco Nacional de Crédito Ejidal, *Informe . . . Ejercicio de 1950* (México: 1951).
13. *Mexico City Post,* January 15, 1944.
14. Banco Nacional de Crédito Ejidal, *Informe*, 1946, 1950.
15. Gómez, *La Región Lagunera*, p. 50; Banco Nacional de Crédito Ejidal,

Informes, 1937-1950, and data in private correspondence; *Compendio Estadístico*, 1947, p. 543.

16. E.g., see Robert W. Hudgens, "Credit: Keystone of a Plan" in *Proceedings, Third Annual Conference on Agricultural Life and Labor* (Washington: National Conference on Agricultural Life and Labor, 1953), pp. 12-14.

17. Olaf F. Larson, "Rural Rehabilitation—Theory and Practice," *Rural Sociology*, XII, 3 (September, 1947), 223.

18. The banks are as follows: Banco Algodonero Refaccionario, Banco Capitalizador de Ahorros, Banco Capitalizador de América, Banco Capitalizador de Monterrey, Banco de la Laguna, Banco de México, Banco Industrial y Agrícola, Banco Mercantil y Capitalizador de Mazatlán, Banco Mexicano Refaccionario, Banco Nacional de Crédito Agrícola, Banco Popular de Edificación y Ahorros, Banco de Fomento Urbano, Banco Nacional de Crédito Ejidal, Banco Nacional de México, Banco General y Capitalizador, Crédito Industrial de Monterrey, Crédito Minero y Mercantil, Financiera y Fiduciaria de Torreón, Benito Rivera, Unión Lagunera de Crédito.

19. Baltasar Dromundo, "Aproximaciones a la verdad ejidal Lagunera," *El Universal*, 13 de febrero, 1941.

20. *El Universal*, 9 de julio, 1943.

21. *El Agricultor Lagunero*, 15 de enero, 1947, p. 1.

22. *Hispanic American Report*, August, 1953, p. 11.

23. *El Siglo de Torreón*, 1 de diciembre, 1954; 7 de octubre, 1956; Jorge L. Tamayo, "Presente y Futuro de la Comarca Lagunera," *Cuadernos del Círculo de Estudios Mexicanos*, agosto, 1957, p. 11.

24. Gómez, *La Región Lagunera*, pp. 70, 81.

25. The percentage had shifted slightly, against the ejidos, by 1954: private properties, 65 per cent; ejidos, 35 per cent.

26. Gómez, *La Región Lagunera*, pp. 9, 94.

27. Statement by Banco Ejidal to writer, May 21, 1937.

28. Alfonso G. Cadaval, "Descripción de las obras de la presa 'El Palmito,' " *Irrigación en México*, mayo-junio 1939, pp. 3-22; Comisión Nacional de Irrigación, *Memoria del Distrito de Riego de la Laguna* (México: Secretaría de Recursos Hidráulicos, 1951); Andrés García Quintero; "Curva de Gastos del Río Nazas aguas abajo de la presa 'El Palmito,' " *Irrigación en México*, mayo-junio, 1941, p. 179; Paul Waitz, "Las condiciones geológicas de las boquillas y vasos del curso del Río Nazas en el Cañón de Fernández y entre este y Torreón," *Irrigación en México*, septiembre-octubre, 1940, p. 29.

29. Gómez, *La Región Lagunera*, pp. 34, 45-47; *Informe* (Torreón: Unión de Sociedades de Crédito Colectivo Ejidal de la Comarca Lagunera, 1943), pp. 4-5.

30. Reports on the 1953-1954 crop year illustrate the point. The region received more rain than in ten years, both rivers flowed more amply than in seven years, and wells which had pumped dry again delivered water. Cotton production increased 42 per cent, wheat 63 per cent. The gross value of the two crops about doubled; from 353,243,500 pesos in 1952-1953 to 707,000,000 in 1953-1954. *El Siglo de Torreón*, 1 de diciembre, 1954.

31. Gómez, *La Región Lagunera*, p. 17.

32. *Nuevo Código Agrario* (México: Departamento Agrario, 1943), p. 128.

33. *Tiempo*, 3 de agosto, 1945. See also Porfirio García de León, Jr., "Fraccionamientos Simulados," *México Agrario*, noviembre-diciembre, 1939, pp. 205-14.

34. *Informe* (Torreón: Unión de Sociedades de Crédito Colectivo Ejidal

de la Comarca Lagunera, 1943), pp. 4-5.

35. *Tiempo*, 4 de mayo, 1945; *Informe, Unión Central . . . al quinto congresso ordinario* (Torreón, 21-23 de febrero, 1947) (typescript) Section 7.

36. *El Siglo de Torreón*, 11 and 17 de octubre, 1947.

37. Nájera, *op. cit.*, pp. 76-79; Guerra, "Bosquejo Histórico . . . ," p. 12.

38. *Memoria de la Primera Convención Nacional Algodonera* (México: 1935), pp. 83, 90-91. Unfortunately, the term "small" is not defined.

39. Isabel Kelly, *Notas Acerca de la Cultura Lagunera*, II (México: Instituto de Asuntos Interamericanos, 1954), 20-21.

40. Emilio López Zamora, "Problema Agrario de la Región Lagunera," *Problemas Económico-Agrícolas de México*, julio-septiembre, 1946, pp. 138-42.

41. *Novedades*, 13 de enero, 1944; Gómez, *La Región Lagunera*, p. 32.

42. It should be emphasized that no survey of the earnings of migratory labor has been made. The figures given were secured from various individuals and represent their best guesses.

43. Gómez, *La Región Lagunera*, pp. 54-56, 97-99; *La Comarca Lagunera*, pp. 173-74; *El Universal*, 15 de abril and 16 de agosto, 1941; *Diario Oficial*, 14 de abril, 1941; *El Agricultor Lagunero*, 15 de noviembre, 1946; *El Siglo de Torreón*, 5 and 6 de agosto, 1941, 17 de agosto, 1947; *La Opinión*, 3 de agosto, 1947.

CHAPTER 6

1. *Supra*, pp. 28-29.

2. See, for example, Henrik F. Infield and Koka Freier, *People in Ejidos*, (New York: Frederick A. Praeger, Inc., 1954), pp. 104-5.

3. *El Nacional*, 22 de julio, 1942; *Mexican Weekly News*, November 8, 1941.

4. Gómez, *La Región Lagunera*, pp. 41-45; *Novedades*, 31 de julio, 1943; *La Opinión*, 2 de agosto, 1943, and 31 de julio, 1941; *El Siglo de Torreón*, 3 de agosto, 1943, and 7 de octubre, 1941; *La Voz de México*, 11 de julio, 1943.

5. *El Universal*, 16 de agosto, 1952.

6. *Nuevo Código Agrario*, Art. 79; *Ciclo de Conferencias*, 1939, 1940, and 1941; Gómez, *La Región Lagunera*, pp. 42-44, 69-90; *Informe* (Torreón: Unión de Sociedades de Crédito Colectivo Ejidal de la Comarca Lagunera, 1943); *La Opinión*, 5 de agosto, 1941; *El Siglo de Torreón*, 5 de julio; López Zamora, *op. cit.*, pp. 132-33.

7. General Cárdenas attempted to bring the two groups together during his tour of the region in connection with the twentieth anniversary celebration of the expropriations (*La Opinión*, 8 de octubre, 1956; *El Siglo de Torreón*, 8 de octubre, 1956). No report of real progress has since been noted.

8. Ernesto Galarza, *Labor Trends and Social Welfare in Latin America* (Washington: Pan American Union, 1942), p. 128.

9. For valuable data on Mexican cooperative developments see Miguel García Cruz, "El Problema de las Cooperativas de Consumo," *Trabajo y Previsión Social*, IX, 38, 39, (marzo, abril, 1941), 75-84, 87-98; Joaquín Ramírez Cabañas, "The Tendencies of the Cooperative Movement in Mexico," *Annals of Collective Economy*, January-April, 1939, pp. 107-19; *Tiempo*, 20 de agosto, 1943.

10. The plant renewed operations in 1953, after modernization.

11. Banco Nacional de Crédito Ejidal, *Seguros Contra Riesgo de la Agri-*

cultura y Ganadería (México: Banco Nacional de Crédito Ejidal, 1945); *El Nacional*, 20 de mayo, 1940; *El Siglo de Torreón*, 21 de julio, 1943; *Torreón Agrícola-Industrial-Comercial* (Torreón: Cámara de Comercio, 1950), p. 5; *La Opinión*, 5 de marzo, 1942; *El Universal*, 11 de julio, 1943, 12 de junio, 1943; *Excelsior*, 14 de septiembre, 1957; *Informe del Consejo de Administración* (Torreón: Unión de Sociedades Locales de Crédito Colectivo Ejidal, febrero, 1947) (typed).

12. *El Siglo de Torreón*, 1 de diciembre, 1954.

13. Tamayo, *op. cit.*, pp. 16, 19; Nájera, *op. cit.*, p. 288; Guerra, *Torreón*, pp. 302-9; interviews with peasants and Torreón businessmen.

14. Leo Gruliow (ed.), *Current Soviet Policies* (New York: Frederick A. Praeger, 1953), *passim*.

15. Gómez, *La Región Lagunera*, pp. 54-56.

16. *Tiempo*, 30 de octubre, 1942, p. 29; 20 de agosto, 1943; 3 de agosto, 1943; *El Universal*, 23 de enero, 1941; 9 de noviembre, 1941; *El Norte*, 7 de agosto, 1943; *Mexican Labor News*, February 17, 1938.

17. See news stories and editorial comment in *El Siglo de Torreón* and *La Opinión* during a month beginning March 6, 1953, especially "Simbolismo de una Derrota" and "La Misma Gata?" *El Siglo*, 19 de marzo and 3 de abril, 1953. *Tiempo*, Mexico City newsweekly, carried the story in four successive issues starting March 13, 1953. Ing. Blanco was "kicked upstairs"; assigned a better-paid post in the main offices of the bank in Mexico City. He was later discharged, after public interest had died down.

18. *El Siglo de Torreón*, 28 de julio, 1942, 23 de julio, 1943, 3 de agosto, 1943; *Novedades*, 11 de julio, 1943; *El Universal*, 7 de julio, 1943; *La Jeringa*, 1 de agosto, 1943; *Diario Oficial*, 2 de agosto, 1943.

19. *La Opinión*, 1 de octubre, 1939, and 25 de julio, 1943; interviews with bank officials and peasant leaders.

20. Tannenbaum, *Peace by Revolution*, p. 97.

21. E.g., see David Loth, *Public Plunder: A History of Graft in America* (New York: Carrick and Evans, 1938), *passim*.

22. Gruening, *op. cit.*, pp. 10-13. See also John H. Parry, *The Sale of Public Office in the Spanish Indies Under the Hapsburgs* (Berkeley: University of California Press, 1953).

23. Francisco Rojas González, "La Institución del compadrazgo entre los Indios de México," *Revista Mexicana de Sociología*, V, 2 (1943), 101-2.

24. Lucio Mendieta y Nuñez, *La Administración Pública en México* (México: Imprenta Universitaria, 1942), pp. 276-87.

25. *Time*, September 14, 1953.

26. *Diario Oficial*, 30 de diciembre, 1939.

27. *New York Times*, December 2 and December 29, 1952; *Tiempo*, 9 de enero, 1953.

28. Whetten, *Rural Mexico*, pp. 542-54, cites a number of examples.

29. *New York Times*, March 4 and March 20, 1953.

30. Loth, *op. cit.*, *passim*.

31. P. A. Sorokin, *Society, Culture and Personality* (New York: Harper & Bros., 1947), pp. 70-91.

32. Difficulties between "bureaucrats" and farmers in a somewhat parallel situation in the United States are set forth in great detail in Edward C. Banfield, *Government Project* (Glencoe: Free Press, 1951). Puerto Rico's attempt to secure democratic participation in social reconstruction is explained in Earl Parker Hanson, *Transformation* (New York: Simon and Schuster,

1955), pp. 317-50; in Puerto Rico Planning Board, *Faith in People* (San Juan: Puerto Rico Planning Board, 1954); and in UNESCO, *Educación de la Comunidad en Puerto Rico* (Paris: UNESCO, 1952).

33. The survey used statistical units with the following values: children less than three years of age, 0.15; from 4 to 6, 0.40; from 7 to 10, 0.75; from 11 to 14, 0.90; women of 15 or over, 0.90; and men above 15, 1.00. *Anuario Estadístico, 1939*, p. 724.

34. Isabel Kelly, *Informe Preliminar del Proyecto de Habitación en La Laguna Ejido de El Cuije*, v. I, and *Notas Acerca de la Cultura Lagunera— Población y Subsistencia*, v. II (México: Instituto de Asuntos Interamericanos, 1954).

35. Data supplied by the Secretaría del Trabajo y Previsión Social, except for commercial employees in Torreón which were calculated from data in the *Primer Censo Comercial de los Estados Unidos Mexicanos* (México: Dirección General de Estadística, 1943).

36. *Tiempo*, 5 de noviembre, 1943, p. 12; 23 de marzo, 1945.

37. Secretaría del Trabajo y Previsión Social, *Salarios Mínimos Aprobados Para los Municipios . . . y que regirán durante los años de 1942 y 1943* (México: Secretaría del Trabajo y Previsión Social, 1941).

38. The discrepancy between the rise in *average* national income and consumption (*Supra*, p. 34) and the fall in certain occupations and areas will probably continue until Mexico has solved three major problems: (1) severe inequalities in distribution of income by class; (2) inefficiencies in trade and transportation; and (3) rural overpopulation. United Nations, Economic and Social Council, *Recent Developments and Trends in the Mexican Economy*, p. 5.

39. Data tabulated for this study by the Dirección General de Estadística.

40. For an account of a visit to this ejido, see Infield and Freier, *op. cit.*, pp. 113-23.

41. For an exceptionally able admission of the justice of the case made by the peasants, with an outline of the developments which followed the convention, see Joaquín Astorga Ochoa, "Informe General," *Ejidales*, mayo, 1939, pp. 11-34.

42. Later the title was shortened to Servicios Médicos Ejidales de la Comarca Lagunera. Data for 1950 and 1952 have been supplied by the statistical office of the organization in correspondence, but attempts to secure later data have proved fruitless.

43. J. J. Alcocer Campero, "Relaciones entre la Medicina Curativa y la Preventiva en los Servicios de Higiene Rural y Medicina Social en la Comarca Lagunera," *Higiene Rural y Medicina Social*, febrero-marzo, 1943, pp. 3-7.

44. Norman D. Humphrey, "Family Patterns in a Mexican Middletown," *The Social Service Review*, XXVI, 2 (June, 1952), 199-200; Oscar Lewis (*op. cit.*, p. 359) reports that "only an occasional woman in Tepoztlán has her child delivered by a doctor." It is interesting to note that in 1950 "over 99 per cent of all births" in New York City took place in hospitals; in 1930, the figure was 71.2 per cent. *New York Times*, February 22, 1951.

45. Humphrey, *op. cit.*, p. 199.

46. Lewis, *op. cit.*, pp. 353-54.

47. See Clarence Senior, "Women, Democracy and Birth Control," *The Humanist*, September-October, 1952, pp. 221-24, for examples of barriers and progress in overcoming them; also J. Mayone Stycos, "Family and Fertility in Puerto Rico," *American Sociological Review*, XVII, 5 (October, 1952),

572-80. A similar study in various regions of Mexico would be invaluable to supplement that of Lewis, which comes closer to the problem than any other anthropological study of Mexico.

48. *Tiempo*, 3 de agosto, 1953.

49. José Reyes Pimentel, *La Cosecha* (México: D.A.P.P., 1939); *El Universal*, 17 de noviembre, 1943; *Ciclo de Conferencias*, 1939, 1940, 1941.

50. Secretaría de Educación Pública, *Reglamento de la Parcela Ejidal Escolar* (México: Secretaría de Educación Pública, 1944).

51. From an unpublished typewritten report of Professor Arnulfo Ochoa Reyes, Director Federal de Educación en la Comarca Lagunera, 17 de julio, 1947.

52. Antonio Ballesteros, *Cómo se Organiza la Cooperación en la Escuela Primaria* (México: Ediapsa, 1940).

53. *Tiempo*, 28 de enero, 1944.

54. Isabel de Palencia, "Falange in the New World," *The Inter-American*, February, 1944, pp. 18-20.

55. The best treatment of *sinarquismo* known to this writer is found in Ch. XX of Whetten, *Rural Mexico*.

56. An interesting example of "extremes meeting" is provided by the advocacy of "family-sized farms" as the first plank in a platform advocated by the "Jacobin" Narciso Bassols, looked upon for years as one of the leading Communist thinkers of Mexico. "Estudiemos la cuestión agraria," *Revista de Economía*, 15 de enero, 1949, pp. 6-7. For something of Bassol's background see Weyl, *op. cit.*, pp. 114, 151.

57. Roberto Cossio y Cosio and Pedro Zuloaga, "Estudio sobre el Problema Agrario," n.d., no place of publication (*ca.* 1944-1945).

58. See, *inter alia, Tiempo*, 14 de noviembre, 1952; 16 de enero, 30 de enero, 11 de mayo, 1953, and 29 de octubre, 7 and 12 de noviembre, 1956; and *New York Times*, January 19 and 24, 1953.

CHAPTER 7

1. See Karl Sax, *Standing Room Only* (Boston: Beacon Press, 1955); and *World Population and Resources* (London: Political and Economic Planning, 1955).

2. *Supra*, p. 109.

3. The great damage done to the attempt of the Rural Resettlement Administration to organize and maintain a cooperative farm at Casa Grande, Arizona, when rootless "Okies" were included, is told by Edward C. Banfield, *op. cit.*, pp. 113-18.

4. Water Resources Policy Commission, *A Water Policy for the American People*, Vol. 1 (Washington: Government Printing Office, 1950), and Roy E. Huffman, *Irrigation Development and Public Water Policy* (New York: The Ronald Press Co., 1953).

5. *Supra*, p. 96.

6. Data for refining the birth and death rates for the region are not available. Existing data, for present purposes, and with their limitations in mind, are probably sufficiently close to the realities to merit use. Crude birth rates of 60 per 1,000 or above are looked upon with great suspicion by demographers. San Pedro's vital statistics show rates of 76.5, 72.5, 67.3, and others in or above the 60's for seven of the eleven years, 1940-1950! Such

figures might arise from a serious underestimation of the population. However, the 1940 and 1950 rates are based on census data and still show 67.5 (1940) and 57.4 (1950). It may be that babies whose births were not registered at the time of occurrence were later inscribed. Or, it may be that no dependable records are kept; figures being pulled out of sombreros for annual reports. Some local statistics offices visited by the writer incline him to the latter view. The fact that not all 48 states were admitted to the birth registration area of the United States until 1933 indicates that statistical accuracy in this field is sometimes late in developing. See T. Lynn Smith, *Population Analysis* (New York: McGraw-Hill Book Co., 1948), pp. 205-7.

7. United Nations, *Demographic Yearbook, 1952* (New York: United Nations, 1953), pp. 224-31.

8. Data from Dirección General de Estadística. Kingsley Davis and Ana Casís have analyzed the factors involved in such differentials in *Urbanization in Latin America* (New York: Milbank Memorial Fund, 1946). See also, "Urban Trends and Characteristics," United Nations, *Demographic Yearbook, 1956,* pp. 9-19.

9. Robert M. Woodbury, "Infant Mortality in the United States," *The Annals of the American Academy of Political and Social Science*, CLXXXVIII (1936), 94-106; United Nations, Economic and Social Council, *Preliminary Report on the World Social Situation*, pp. 13-15; Dublin, *op. cit.*, pp. 152, 155, 164.

10. United Nations, *Demographic Yearbook, 1952*, pp. 320-27.

11. Frank Notestein, "Population—The Long View" in Theodore W. Schultz (ed.), *Food for the World* (Chicago: University of Chicago Press, 1945).

12. International Bank, *op. cit.*, Table 24, charts 4A and 4B; Kathryn H. Wylie, in *Hispanic American Report*, X, 9 (October, 1957), 453; Banco Nacional de México, *Review of the Economic Situation of Mexico* (Mexico: Banco Nacional de México, July, 1956).

13. *Tiempo*, 7 de septiembre, 1953, pp. 16-30. Succeeding annual reports have reverted to the theme of "the race between population and production," as it was phrased in the 1956 message. *Excelsior*, 2 de septiembre, 1956. For data and an analysis of the movement of farm workers to the United States, see Luis Yañez-Pérez, *Mecanización de la Agricultura Mexicana* (México: Instituto Mexicano de Investigaciones Económicas, 1957), pp. 59-71.

14. Gilberto Loyo, *La Política Demográfica de México* (México: Partido Nacional Revolucionario, 1935), pp. xv, 14, 21.

15. Richard Hofstadter, *Social Darwinism in American Thought* (Boston: Beacon Press, 1955), p. 177.

16. *Excelsior*, 10 de marzo-10 de mayo, 1952.

17. Edmundo Flores, "Mesa Redonda sobre Agricultura," *Revista de Economía*, enero, 1952, p. 29.

18. See R. L. Cohen, *The Economics of Agriculture* (New York: Pitman Publishing Corporation, 1949), pp. 71-72; "Few Farm Jobs for Farm Youth," *New York Times*, March 10, 1957.

19. *Supra*, pp. 96, 167-68.

20. Types of mechanization were determined from an index worked out by a Banco Ejidal official for the 284 ejidos working with the agency in 1939. Ejidos in which up to one-third of all major farming operations were performed by self-propelled or tractor-drawn mechanical equipment were listed as "lightly mechanized"; the next third, "medium"; and the top third, "heavy." Carlos Torres Cordera, Jefe, Sección de Estudios Económicos (Typescript) 1939.

21. Cohen, *op. cit.*, p. 125. Boulding dislikes the phrase "diminishing

returns" and prefers "the law of eventually diminishing marginal physical productivity" or, better, a "law of eventually diminishing average physical productivity" (Kenneth E. Boulding, *Economic Analysis*, [New York: Harper & Bros., 1948], pp. 500-6). Although data are not available in such form as to allow the construction of input-output tables or productivity schedules, the basic story is told clearly by Table 18.

22. Franz Oppenheimer, Henry George, Marx, and Engels and their theories are treated succinctly in Eduard Heimann, *History of Economic Doctrines* (New York: Oxford Press, 1945), chap. VI, and in John Ise, *Economics* (New York: Harper & Bros., 1946), chap. XXXI. Henry George in *Progress and Poverty* (1879) and *Social Problems* (1883) placed the exclusive emphasis on necessity to "make land common property" in the solution of social problems; see *Social Problems* (New York: Doubleday, Page and Co., 1911), p. 203.

23. *La Comarca Lagunera*, chap. VI and p. 423.

24. John Temple Graves, "The Cotton Industry—Past, Present, Future," *Think*, November, 1947, pp. 16-20; Cruz Venstrom, "Experience in 1945 with Mechanical Cotton Pickers in California" (Washington: United States Department of Agriculture, Bureau of Agricultural Economics, October, 1946) (mimeographed), p. 1; "Farm Technology and Labor," *Labor Market and Employment Security*, June 3, 1953, pp. 21-24; "Technology Takes Over the Farm—and the Farmer," *Business Week*, June 6, 1953, pp. 116-26; Harold A. Pedersen, "Mechanized Agriculture and the Farm Laborer," *Rural Sociology*, XIX, 1 (March, 1954), 143-51.

25. "Technology Makes a New Gain in Cotton," *New York Times*, October 31, 1953.

26. *Excelsior*, 20 de febrero, 1952.

27. *New York Times*, January 28, 1952; *Tiempo*, 27 de mayo, 1953, 31 de agosto, 1953, and 4 de enero, 1954; *Excelsior*, 23 de junio, 1953; *Tiempo*, 8 de febrero, 1954.

28. *Tiempo*, "Lucha contra la sequía," 31 de octubre, 1952.

29. *Excelsior*, 20 de febrero, 1952; *Novedades*, 25 de enero, 1953.

30. *El Siglo de Torreón*, 1 de mayo, 1953. Another emergency program was announced in June 1957 after La Laguna's "worst recorded heat wave." *New York Times*, June 15, 1957; *Excelsior*, 16 de junio, 1957.

31. Moisés T. de la Peña, "Problemas Demográficos y Agrarios," *Problemas Agrícolas e Industriales de México*, II, 3-4 (1950), 315.

32. The figure for the United States (1950), was 39.9 per cent; the U.S.S.R., 57.5 per cent (1926); France, 44.8 per cent (1954); Colombia, 33.4 per cent (1951); Finland, 49.2 per cent (1950); Great Britain, 46.2 per cent (1951); Japan, 43.6 per cent (1950); Argentina, 40.6 per cent (1947). The Mexican censuses have showed the following ratios of economically active to the total population:

1900	33.6
1910	34.7
1921	34.1
1930	31.2
1940	29.7
1950	32.4

Year Book of Labour Statistics, 1956 (Geneva: International Labour Organization, 1956), pp. 6-7.

33. Data furnished by the Dirección General de Estadística.

34. United Nations, *Economic Survey of Latin America, 1949* (New York: United Nations, 1951), p. 483.

35. Infield and Freier, *op. cit.*, pp. 116-17.
36. Kelly, *Informe Preliminar del Proyecto de Habitación* . . . , I, 3-6.

CHAPTER 8

1. *Supra*, p. 12.
2. C. E. Eisinger, "The Influence of Natural Rights and Physiocratic Doctrine on American Agrarian Thought during the Revolutionary Period," *Agricultural History*, January, 1947, pp. 13-23; Henry W. Siegel, *Land Tenure Policies at Home and Abroad* (Chapel Hill: University of North Carolina Press, 1941), chaps. I and II; Marshall Harris, *Origin of the Land Tenure System in the United States* (Ames: Iowa State College Press, 1953), *passim*.
3. Gruening, *op. cit.*, p. 27.
4. Weyl, *op. cit.*, *passim*.
5. Fabila, *op. cit.*, pp. 1-58; Fernando González Roa, four chapters on the agrarian question in Mexico from *Las Cuestiones Fundamentales de Actualidad en México*, translated by Gustavo E. Archilla (New York: W.P.A. and Columbia University, 1937); Antonio Gómez Robledo, *The Bucareli Agreements and International Law* (Mexico: The National University of Mexico Press, 1940), pp. 49-80, 105-16; Lucio Mendieta y Nuñez, *El Problema Agrario de México*, *passim*, and *El Sistema Agrario Constitucional*, chap. I (Mexico: Librería de Porrua Hnos., 1937); Simpson, *op. cit.*, chap. I-IV.
6. See, for many examples, C. K. Meek, *Land Law and Customs in the Colonies* (New York: Oxford University Press, 1946), *passim*, and *Caribbean Land Tenure Symposium* (Port of Spain: Caribbean Research Council, 1946).
7. *Agricultural Act, 1947*, 10 & 11 Geo. VI, Ch. 48 (London: H. M. Stationery Office, 1947). For a news account of the working of the Act, see "Britain Evicts 100 from Farms for Ineptness," *New York Post*, June 10, 1956.
8. United Nations, *Progress in Land Reform* (New York: United Nations, Department of Economic Affairs, 1954), chap. III.
9. Ise, *op. cit.*, p. 455. See also Charles Abrams, *Revolution in Land* (New York: Harper & Bros., 1939); A. N. Chandler, *Land Title Origins, A Tale of Force and Fraud* (New York: Robert Schalkenbach Foundation, 1945); Seba Eldridge, *Development of Collective Enterprise* (Lawrence: University of Kansas Press, 1943); Leonard A. Salter, Jr., "Do We Need a New Land Policy?" *Journal of Land and Public Utility Economics*, November, 1946, pp. 309-20.
10. *Supra*, p. 12.
11. *Supra*, chap. II.
12. *Supra*, p. 138.
13. *New York Times*, November 15, 1953.
14. Emilio López Zamora, "El Crédito Ejidal," *Problemas Económico-Agrícolas de México*, julio-septiembre, 1946, pp. 143-49.
15. *La Comarca Lagunera*, pp. 203-30; Whetten, *Rural Mexico*, pp. 226-31.
16. Margaret Jarman Hagood, *Statistics for Sociologists* (New York: Henry Holt and Co., 1941), chaps. XVII, XX.
17. It may be assumed that if the method of ejido organization and its successful functioning were the major factor in differential yields between ejidos and private properties, the variation in yields would be as great within zones among ejidos as the variation between zones among ejidos. (The zones tend to be more or less homogeneous in soil composition, and even in availability of water.) This combination of assumption and fact leads us to set up

what is conventionally known as a null hypothesis, i.e., that the differentials are due to the *ejidal* form of organization.

An analysis of variance was done for the productivity per *hectárea* in wheat per ejido, and the productivity per *hectárea* in cotton per ejido. It was clear in the productivity figures for both wheat and cotton that the variation between zones was much greater than the variation within zones. The P value for this between-zone variation equaled less than .0001. The null hypothesis is rejected decisively by these comparisons.

On the other hand, a similar null hypothesis testing the relationship between the number of tractors per ejido and productivity in cotton was not rejected because the P value fell between the 5 per cent and 1 per cent levels of significance.

18. Ernesto Galarza, *La Industria Eléctrica en México*, pp. 124-26, contains a useful sketch of municipal developments. Simpson, Gruening, and Tannenbaum have written on local government problems.

19. Modesto C. Rolland, *El Desastre Municipal en la República Mexicana* (México: n.d.), p. 123.

20. García Cubas, *op. cit.*, pp. 21, 28-30, 33, 36-38.

21. Secretaría de la Economía Nacional, *El Problema de las Alcabalas*, (México: 1941); "Reformas a Nuestros Sistemas Impositivos-Alcabalas y Contribución Federal," *Revista de Economía*, 20 de junio, 1942, pp. 19-21; *El Siglo*, 28 de julio, 1943; *El Universal*, 31 de agosto, 1943; *Financial Week in Mexico*, December 26, 1953, p. 9.

22. Armando Servín, *op. cit.*, p. 13.

23. *Anuario Estadístico*, 1941, p. 916; *Compendio Estadístico*, 1951, pp. 281-82; Eduardo Bustamente, "Los Sistemas tributarios de los estados," *Revista de Economía*, 15 de abril, 1950, pp. 124-27.

24. *Anuario Estadístico*, 1941, p. 198; United Nations, *Demographic Yearbook, 1956*, pp. 694-711.

25. *Tiempo*, 7 de septiembre, 1953.

26. Simpson, *op. cit.*, p. 579.

27. *Tiempo*, 8 de febrero, 1954.

28. The same wave killed what had come close to being the first agricultural extension service in Mexico. See Jorge de Alba, "En nuestro país la organización de la extensión agrícola aún no ha principiado," *Chapingo*, IV, 35 (30 de septiembre, 1949), 33.

29. *El Nacional*, 28 de mayo, 1939; *Tiempo*, 11 de enero, 1954.

30. For some examples in the field of United States political cartooning see *Salon of American Humorists: A Political and Social Pageant from the Revolution to the Present Day* (New York: College Art Association, 1933), and Henry Ladd Smith, "The Rise and Fall of the Political Cartoon," *The Saturday Review*, May 29, 1954, pp. 7-9, 28-29. For other examples see daily newspapers in recent months.

31. Howard Cline points out that 65 per cent of all such studies between 1922 and 1952 dealt with Yucatán, Quintana Roo, Chiapas, and Oaxaca: *op. cit.*, pp. 212-42. These states cover 13 per cent of the national territory and include about 10 per cent of Mexico's inhabitants. *Compendio Estadístico*, 1951, pp. 66, 73-74.

32. Redfield, *op. cit.*, especially pp. 109,119. From the less isolated state of Jalisco comes a similar report: Norman D. Humphrey, "The Cultural Background of the Mexican Immigrant," *Rural Sociology*, XIII (September. 1948), 253-55.

33. *Ibid.*, p. 253.

34. Lewis, *op. cit.*, p. 292.
35. Another report by Humphrey underlines the father's demand for respect and obedience: "The father . . . may strike a grown and even married son without retaliatory action." Humphrey, "Family Patterns," pp. 195-201.
36. José María Luis Mora, *México y sus Revoluciones* (México: Editorial Porrúa, 1950), Tomo I, p. 69; Bulnes, *El Verdadero Díaz.* pp. 171-91; Salvador Quevedo y Zubieta, *El Caudillo,* cited by A. Molina Enríquez, *Los Grandes Problemas Nacionales* (México: Imp. de A. Carranza e Hijos, 1909), pp. 67-69. See also the feeling of being victims of nepotism reported by industrial workers to Moore, *op. cit.*, p. 270.
37. Iturriaga, *op. cit.*, p. 124.
38. For examples, see Iturriaga, *op. cit.*, p. 237; Carlos A. Echánove Trujillo, "La Mentalidad de la Población Indígena de México," *Hechos y Problemas del México Rural* (México: Seminario Mexicano de Sociología, 1952), pp. 24-44.
39. Lasswell, *op. cit.*, pp. 21-22.
40. "Ethics Inquiry Bluntly Scores Executive, Congress, Public," *New York Times,* October 18, 1951; "Fight on Frauds in its Thirtieth Year," *New York Times,* October 12, 1952; "Corruption, Disaster and Inertia in Eleven Communities Met by Citizen-inspired Action," *National Municipal Review,* February, 1954, pp. 65-80; *Directory of Organizations and Individuals Professionally Engaged in Governmental Research, 1956-1957* (New York: Governmental Research Organization, 1956); Phillip Monypenny, "The Control of Ethical Standards in the Public Service," *The Annals of the American Academy of Political and Social Science,* CCXCVII (January, 1955), 98-104.
41. R. H. Tawney, *Equality* (London: George Allen and Unwin, Ltd., 1929), p. 38.
42. Floyd Dotson, "A Note on Participation in Voluntary Associations in a Mexican City," *American Sociological Review,* XVIII, 4 (August, 1953), 380-86.
43. Anita Brenner, "Mexico," *Holiday,* March, 1947, p. 122.
44. These and many similar opinions are reported by William L. Schurz in Chapter III, "The Spaniard," of his book *This New World* (New York: E. P. Dutton & Co., 1954). See also Julia Córdova de Braschi, "La Psicología Española Vista por Ortega y Gasset," *Asomante,* octubre-diciembre, 1954, pp. 33-42.
45. Quoted in Whetten, *Rural Mexico,* pp. 544-45.
46. Jesús Silva Herzog, *op. cit.*, I, 498-99.
47. Rodrigo García Treviño, *Precios, Salarios y Mordidas* (México: Editorial América, 1953).
48. For illustration of the situation in Spain, see René de Visme Williamson, *Culture and Policy* (Knoxville: University of Tennessee Press, 1949), pp. 18-30.
49. March 9, 1953.
50. *Supra,* pp. 138, 188.
51. 23 de marzo, 1954.
52. United Nations, *Progress in Land Reform* (1954), p. 2. See also, United Nations, *Progress in Land Reform-Second Report* (New York: United Nations, 1956).
53. See "Is the United States Neglecting Land Reform in its Foreign Policy?", *University of Chicago Round Table,* No. 811, October 25, 1953; and "Jefferson and Land Reform," *ibid.,* No. 837, April 25, 1954.
54. "Bolivia Land Reform is Aided by U. S. Loan," *New York Times,* December 11, 1953.
55. "First World Land Tenure Problems Conference," *op. cit.*, p. 19; Inter-

238 NOTES (PAGES 208-212)

national Bank for Reconstruction and Development, *Fourth Annual Report,* 1948-1949, p. 2.

56. Lyford P. Edwards, *The Natural History of Revolution* (Chicago: University of Chicago Press, 1927), p. 38.

57. For an analysis of a recent agrarian movement see Lowry Nelson, *Land Reform in Italy* (Washington: National Planning Association, 1956), *passim.*

58. Frank A. Pearson and Floyd A. Harper, *The World's Hunger* (Ithaca: Cornell University Press, 1945), p. 49.

59. Josué de Castro, *The Geography of Hunger* (Boston: Little, Brown & Co., 1952), p. 25.

60. V. I. Lenin, *Collected Works* (New York: International Publishers Co., 1930), XX, Book 1, 117, 144.

61. Wendell C. Gordon, *The Economy of Latin America* (New York: Columbia University Press, 1950), p. 49.

62. Henrik F. Infield, "Social Control in a Cooperative Society," *Sociometry,* V, 3 (1942); Henrik F. Infield and Ernest Dichter, "Who is Fit for Cooperative Farming?", *Applied Anthropology,* II, 2-3 (1943); Henrik F. Infield and Joseph B. Maier, *Cooperative Group Living* (New York: Koosis and Co., 1950).

63. Davis points out that Latin American experience brings out the difference between political and social democracy, "the dependence of one upon the other, and the perversion of one in the absence of the other." Kingsley Davis, "Political Ambivalence in Latin America," p. 127.

Appendix

TABLE 23
LAND DISTRIBUTED, NUMBER OF EJIDOS AND EJIDATARIOS
MEXICO — 1916-1954

Year	Number of Ejidos	Ejidatarios Receiving Land	Area Hectáreas
1916	2	182	1,246
1917	57	12,016	64,208
1918	69	19,715	66,564
1919	85	19,478	57,117
1920	121	25,812	192,791
1921	179	36,552	552,130
1922	84	18,086	177,848
1923	203	48,500	465,329
1924	293	58,650	520,274
1925	442	86,174	880,624
1926	357	68,246	853,369
1927	471	82,575	835,090
1928	397	64,592	604,066
1929	865	126,317	1,850,532
1930	499	60,367	582,691
1931	365	40,262	660,268
1932	177	16,462	249,349
1933	362	42,885	538,167
1934	1,223	115,254	1,509,029
1935	1,300	110,286	1,923,457
1936	2,542	194,427	3,985,700
1937	2,802	199,292	5,808,979
1938	2,049	118,336	3,472,226
1939	1,484	94,779	2,203,685
1940	1,170	54,520	2,680,657
1941	721	25,674	1,315,122
1942	542	23,148	1,312,501
1943	527	20,295	794,031
1944	433	18,186	760,689
1945	358	11,868	589,865
1946	187	11,541	514,428
1947	335	16,163	657,658
1948	371	14,586	664,822
1949	315	15,066	655,228
1950	284	13,824	691,134
1951	255	11,391	148,986
1952	166	3,614	311,457
1953	194	8,679	344,791
1954	217	9,892	419,232
Total	22,503	1,917,692	39,915,340

Source: Departamento Agrario, *Memorias,* 1945-46; Departamento Agrario, Sección de Estadística, 1955.

239

TABLE 24
Ownership of Irrigated Land, by Sizes
La Laguna
1928*

Municipios	Less Than 247 Acres	247-1,235 Acres	1,236-2,470 Acres	2,471-12,350 Acres	12,351-24,700 Acres	More Than 24,700 Acres	Total
Torreón	5	15	3	5	0	0	28
San Pedro	34	28	21	13	1	3	100
Matamoros	0	3	5	7	0	0	15
Gómez Palacio	1	13	2	11	0	1	28
Lerdo	2	5	3	3	0	0	13
Mapimí	0	1	0	0	0	1	2
Totals	42	65	34	39	1	5	186

Source: *Informe General de la Comisión de Estudios de la Comarca Lagunera*, p. 51.

*These data apply only to properties within the Nazas basin.

[240]

TABLE 25

PROPERTIES LEASED, RENTED, OR SHARECROPPED
BY MUNICIPIO, NUMBER, AREA, AND VALUE
LA LAGUNA
1928*

Municipio	Number	Per Cent	Area	Per Cent	Value 000's Pesos	Per Cent
Torreón	18	60.0	155,736	88.7	2,235	82.4
San Pedro	38	28.8	379,108	15.0	10,822	70.5
Matamoros	7	46.6	50,129	64.3	1,731	60.4
Gómez Palacio	22	78.6	278,006	89.3	2,201	85.4
Lerdo	0	—	—	—	—	—
Mapimí	0	—	—	—	—	—
Totals	85	38.3	862,979	22.9	16,989	63.6

Source: *Informe General de la Comisión de Estudios de la Comarca Lagunera*, p. 76.

*These data apply only to properties within the Nazas basin.

TABLE 26

PROPERTIES WORKED OR ADMINISTERED BY OWNERS
BY MUNICIPIO, NUMBER, AREA, AND VALUE
LA LAGUNA
1928*

Municipio	Number	Per Cent	Area	Per Cent	Value 000's Pesos	Per Cent
Torreón	12	40.0	19,869	11.3	476	17.6
San Pedro	96	71.2	2,147,492	85.0	4,532	29.5
Matamoros	8	53.4	27,863	35.7	1,138	39.6
Gómez Palacio	6	21.4	33,296	10.7	378	14.6
Lerdo	13	100.0	507,667	100.0	1,123	100.0
Mapimí	2	100.0	119,513	100.0	2,099	100.0
Totals	137	61.7	2,855,700	77.1	9,746	36.4

Source: *Informe General de la Comisión de Estudios de la Comarca Lagunera*, p. 76.

*These data apply only to properties within the Nazas basin.

TABLE 27

MEXICAN COTTON PRODUCTION
AREA, YIELD: PRINCIPAL REGIONS
1944-1945, 1949-1950, AND 1953-1954

(crop years)

Region	Area Hectáreas			Yield per Hectárea Kilograms			Production Metric Tons		
	1944-1945	1949-1950	1953-1954	1944-1945	1949-1950	1953-1954	1944-1945	1949-1950	1953-1954
Laguna region	134,103	121,930	140,170	321	443	382	43,104	56,401	53,545
Mexicali Valley, B.C.	61,884	125,154	197,214	236	410	463	14,625	51,313	91,310
Matamoros, Tamps.	91,845	305,000	223,658	243	263	325	22,310	80,215	72,689
Juárez Valley, Chih.	13,301	36,200	34,557	243	404	401	3,239	10,580	13,843
Delicias, Chih.	29,023	36,650	54,791	198	377	398	5,744	13,806	21,807
Don Martín, N.L.	15,701	29,300	18,850	280	324	396	4,399	9,493	6,842
Sonora-Sinaloa	15,100	96,540	184,794	212	322	413	3,208	31,101	76,360
All others	4,859	19,760	27,564	197	360	348	957	7,110	9,579

Source: Dirección de Economía Rural, Secretaría de Agricultura.

TABLE 28

WHEAT: TYPES OF CULTIVATION
COSTS, YIELD, AND PROFIT
LA LAGUNA

(in pesos)

	Cost per Hectárea	Yield per Hectárea	Profit per Hectárea	Cost per Metric Ton	Profit per Metric Ton
1. Flooding and one supplementary irrigation by wells, and cultivation by mules	204.31	1.20	65.69	145.26	54.74
2. Flooding and two supplementary irrigations by wells, and use of mules and tractors	209.24	1.40	70.76	149.46	50.54
3. Flooding by river, no supplementary irrigation, and use of mules and tractors	141.53	.95	48.47	148.98	51.02
4. Flooding by river, two supplementary irrigations by wells, and mules and tractors	228.47	1.40	96.53	130.76	69.24
5. Flooding by river, two supplementary irrigations by wells and mules alone	190.13	1.40	89.87	135.81	64.19
6. Flooding by river, one supplementary irrigation by well and use of mules and tractor	171.83	1.30	88.17	132.18	67.82
7. Flooding by river, two supplementary irrigation wells, use of mules and tractors	207.25	1.40	112.75	119.47	80.53

Source: Gonzalo González H., *El Trigo en México,* Parte V, pp. 98-106; chap. VII.

TABLE 29

WHEAT: COSTS OF VARIOUS OPERATIONS
FLOODING BY RIVER, TWO IRRIGATIONS BY PUMPS
AND USE OF TRACTOR AND MULES
LA LAGUNA

(in pesos)

Operations	Cost per Hectárea	Days Work per Hectárea		
		Man	Mule	Machine
Prepare Seedbed				
Cleaning and repairing ditches and borders	14.10	6.0	4.0	2.0
Cleaning fields, gathering and burning weeds and stubble	6.75	4.0	.5	.2
Plowing	14.01	.7	—	.4
Discing	4.71	.2	—	.1
Deep plowing	15.96	4.0	8.0	4.0
Harrowing	2.08	.3	1.3	.3
Subtotal	57.61	15.2	13.8	7.0
Seeding				
Seed, 60 kilos. (132 lbs.) at 25 centavos (5.1 cents) each	15.00	—	—	—
Furrowing	14.92	4.0	6.0	4.0
Rolling	2.27	.3	1.3	.3
Subtotal	32.19	4.3	7.3	4.3
Irrigation				
Flooding	4.56	2.0	—	2.0
Two ditch irrigations by pump	48.09	3.0	—	.8
Subtotal	52.65	5.0	—	2.8
Harvest and Marketing				
Cutting and Stacking	15.30	10.0	—	10.0
Collecting sheaves	4.31	1.5	1.0	.5
Threshing	8.69	1.0	—	.1
Baling straw	7.18	.7	—	.1
Hauling	3.15	.2	—	.1
Subtotal	38.63	13.4	1.0	10.8
Total	181.08	37.9	22.1	24.9

Source: Gonzalo González H., *El Trigo en México,* Parte V, p. 102.

Note: Taxes, at 5% of the value of the production; social fund and other community charges, at 8%; and interest, at 10% of loans figured on an 8-month basis, add 47.41 pesos. The total then is 228.47 pesos (See Type 4, Table 28).

TABLE 30

WHEAT: COSTS OF VARIOUS OPERATIONS
FLOODING BY RIVER AND USE OF TRACTORS
AND MULE-DRAWN EQUIPMENT
LA LAGUNA
(*in pesos*)

Operation	Cost per Hectárea	Days Work per *Hectárea*		
		Man	Mule	Machine
Prepare Seedbed				
Cleaning and repairing ditches and borders	14.10	6.0	4.0	2.0
Cleaning fields, gathering and burning weeds and stubble	6.75	4.0	.5	.1
Plowing	14.01	.7	—	.4
Discing	7.71	1.0	4.0	1.0
Deep plowing	15.96	4.0	8.0	4.0
Harrowing	2.08	.3	1.0	.3
Subtotal	60.61	16.0	17.8	7.8
Seeding				
Seed, 60 kilos. (132 lbs.) at 25 centavos (5.1 cents) each	15.00	—	—	—
Furrowing	7.98	2.0	4.0	2.0
Rolling	6.94	2.0	2.0	2.0
Subtotal	29.92	4.0	6.0	4.0
Irrigation				
Flooding	4.56	2.0	—	2.0
Harvesting				
Cutting and threshing sheaves (combin.)	16.41	3.0	—	2.1
Hauling	1.58	.1	—	.1
Subtotal	22.55	5.1	—	4.2
Total	113.08	25.1	23.8	16.0

Source: Gonzalo González H., *El Trigo en México*, Parte V, p. 101.

TABLE 31

DISTRIBUTION OF CREDIT SOCIETIES
BY AREAS WORKED AND MEMBERSHIP
LA LAGUNA

1937-1938

Average Area per Member	Number of Societies	Number of Members
Less than one *hectárea*	7	421
From 1.1 to 1.5 *hectáreas*	12	1,306
1.6 to 2.0	13	2,216
2.1 to 2.5	27	4,270
2.6 to 3.0	59	8,036
3.1 to 3.5	52	4,710
3.6 to 4.0	46	5,954
4.1 to 4.5	29	1,580
4.6 to 5.0	8	409
5.1 to 5.5	9	634
5.6 to 6.0	5	264
6.1 to 6.5	9	424
6.6 to 7.0	0	0
More than 7.0	7	398
Total	283	30,622

Source: La Comarca Lagunera, pp. 233-34.

TABLE 32
Number of Buildings and Percentages by Materials
Coahuila, Durango, and La Laguna
1929, 1939, and 1950

	Total Buildings			Adobe			Daubed Reed			Wood			Reed*			Other		
	1929	1939	1950	1929	1939	1950	1929	1939	1950	1929	1939	1950	1929	1939	1950	1929	1939	1950
Coahuila	88,622	110,601	141,282	69,384	81,534	112,362	1,252	3,410	1,818	8,515	7,538	6,844		6,804	292	9,471	11,315	19,963
				78.3	73.72	79.5	1.4	3.11	1.3	9.6	6.81	4.8		6.15	0.2	10.7	10.2	14.2
Durango	81,727	99,829	120,252	69,394	81,722	103,981	859	2,130	754	6,798	8,454	8,415		3,394	78	4,676	4,129	7,024
				84.9	81.86	86.5	1.0	2.11	0.6	8.3	8.51	7.0		3.40	0.1	5.8	4.1	5.8
La Laguna Gómez Palacio	8,204	10,817	16,816	7,627	9,594	15,018	59	338	153	176	109	1		334	14	342	442	1,630
				92.9	88.6	89.3	0.8	3.2	4.5	2.1	1.1	—		3.1	0.4	4.2	4.0	48.0
Lerdo	3,342	4,034	5,551	3,021	3,543	5,081	141	28	28	41	80	68		166	43	139	217	331
				90.3	87.8	91.5	4.3	0.7	0.5	1.2	1.9	1.2		4.2	0.8	4.2	5.4	6.0
Mapimí	4,240	2,456	3,057	3,361	1,947	2,797	61	12	78	549	191	45		147	1	269	159	136
				79.2	79.2	91.5	1.4	0.5	2.8	13.0	7.8	1.6		6.0	—	6.4	6.5	4.9
Matamoros	4,260	5,349	7,496	4,103	4,676	7,072	22	70	38	41	107	49		431	34	94	65	303
				96.3	87.4	94.3	0.6	1.3	0.5	0.9	2.0	0.7		8.0	0.5	2.2	1.3	4.0
San Pedro	10,049	9,012	12,434	9,218	7,901	11,596	208	408	103	290	256	56		309	45	333	138	634
				91.7	87.6	93.3	2.0	4.6	0.8	2.9	2.8	0.5		3.5	0.3	3.4	1.5	5.1
Torreón	12,079	16,062	28,966	10,403	12,944	22,917	143	339	246	173	246	313		368	15	1,360	2,165	5,475
				86.1	80.5	79.1	1.2	2.1	0.8	1.4	1.6	1.1		2.3	0.1	11.3	13.5	18.9
Viesca	1,516	2,200	2,542	1,417	1,574	2,256	6	77	62	53	85	63		337	4	40	127	157
				93.4	71.5	88.7	0.4	3.6	2.4	3.5	3.8	2.5		15.3	0.2	2.7	5.8	6.2

Source: Dirección General de Estadística.

*For 1929, Reed included in Other

[247]

TABLE 33

HOUSING, DRINKING WATER SUPPLY
MEXICO, COAHUILA, DURANGO, AND LA LAGUNA
1939 AND 1950

	1939		1950	
	Total Buildings	Per Cent Without Water Service	Total Buildings	Per Cent Without Water Service
Mexico	3,884,582	62.0	5,259,208	8.2
Coahuila	110,601	53.7	141,282	5.4
Durango	99,829	59.9	120,252	8.6
La Laguna				
Gómez Palacio	10,817	41.4	16,883	0.7
Lerdo	4,034	62.9	5,484	10.3
Mapimí	2,456	47.8	2,797	7.2
Matamoros	5,349	79.0	7,496	4.3
San Pedro	9,012	59.7	12,434	3.4
Torreón	16,062	42.4	28,966	5.1
Viesca	2,200	66.0	2,542	3.9

Source: Censo de Edificios, 1939: Dirección General de Estadística, 1950.

TABLE 34

CHURCH BUILDINGS
MEXICO, COAHUILA, AND DURANGO
1929 AND 1939

	Roman Catholic	Per Cent of Change	Protestant	Per Cent of Change
		+ or —		+ or —
Mexico				
1929	12,774		686	
1939	13,488	+5.6	512	−25.3
Coahuila				
1929	183		62	
1939	165	−9.8	42	−32.2
Durango				
1929	302		23	
1939	271	−10.2	12	−47.8

Source: Censos de Edificios, 1929 and 1939.

TABLE 35

COTTON INVESTMENT AND OPERATIONS
LAGUNA EJIDOS WITH LIGHT MECHANIZATION
1939

Operation	Man-days Work per 100 Hectáreas	Investment per 100 Hectáreas (in pesos)
Dry plowing	400	1,196
Cleaning and repairing ditches and borders	300	264
Cleaning field	600	—
Flooding	200	—
First discing	50	315
Plowing	400	1,196
Second discing	50	315
Seed	—	1,375
Disinfection of seed	2	34
Furrowing	150	449
Seeding	150	302
Rolling	20	73
Hoeing	300	—
Thinning	500	—
Hoeing	500	—
Weeding	400	—
First cultivation	66	107
Weeding	600	—
Second cultivation	100	147
Well irrigation	225	2,305
Third cultivation	150	239
Pest control	50	325
Picking	1,000	—
Transport to gin	50	113
Ginning	—	1,998
Insurance	—	200
Classification	—	50
Taxes	—	1,496
Water	—	50
Administration and general expenses	360	2,974
Interest	—	1,308
Total	6,623	16,831*

Source: Unpublished study of 284 collective credit societies by Carlos Torres Cordera, Jefe, Sección de Estudios Económicos, Banco Nacional de Crédito Ejidal, Torreón, 1939.

*Includes forage, tractor and truck fuel, lubricants, amortization, and repairs.

TABLE 36

PROFITS FROM COTTON CULTIVATION
DISTRIBUTED BY BANCO EJIDAL
1937-1938 TO 1954-1955

(crop years)

Crop Year	Profits Distributed
1937-1938	$ 1,163,542.30
1938-1939	1,081,176.54
1939-1940	1,777,276.67
1940-1941	692,011.99
1941-1942	2,532,955.08
1942-1943	7,489,723.59
1943-1944	11,840,120.47
1944-1945	1,580,485.26
1945-1946	3,732,244.96
1946-1947	4,725,306.21
1947-1948	6,049,738.94
1948-1949	10,412,047.78
1949-1950	13,217,459.80
1950-1951	24,276,498.20
1951-1952	6,144,324.60
1952-1953	1,935,344.00
1953-1954	5,932,145.66
1954-1955	45,578,423.38

Source: Banco Nacional de Crédito Ejidal, Agencia en Torreón.

TABLE 37

AVERAGE ANNUAL EXCHANGE RATE
PESOS TO DOLLARS
1927-1957

Year	Average Rate
1927	2.116
1928	2.078
1929	2.075
1930	2.122
1931	2.431
1932	3.170
1933	3.530
1934	3.600
1935	3.599
1936	3.600
1937	3.600
1938	4.515
1939	5.181
1940	5.401
1941	4.857
1942	4.854
1943	4.851
1944	4.856
1945	4.855
1946	4.855
1947	4.859
1948	5.725
1949	8.011
1950	8.643
1951	8.647
1952	8.629
1953	8.615
1954	11.332
1955	12.500
1956	12.500
1957	12.500

Source: Anuario Estadístico de los Estados Unidos Mexicanos, 1954.
México: Secretaría de Economía, Dirección General de Estadística, 1957.

Bibliography

BOOKS AND PAMPHLETS

ABRAMS, Charles. *Revolution in Land.* New York: Harper & Bros., 1939.
ALEXANDER, Robert J. *Communism in Latin America.* New Brunswick: Rutgers University Press, 1957.
————. *World Labor Today.* New York: League for Industrial Democracy, 1952.
ALLEN, Devere. *What Europe Thinks About America.* Hinsdale, Ill.: Henry Regnery Co., 1948.
ASIATIC REGIONAL CONFERENCE, INTERNATIONAL LABOUR ORGANIZATION. *Economic Background of Social Policy.* New Delhi: International Labour Organization, 1947.
BALLESTEROS, Antonio. *Como se Organiza la Cooperación en la Escuela Primaria.* México: Ediapsa, 1940.
BANFIELD, Edward C. *Government Project.* Glencoe: Free Press, 1951.
BAUER, Walter. *Agricultural Credit in Mexico.* Washington: Farm Credit Administration, 1943.
BLANCO MACÍAS, Gonzalo. *La Laguna y Su Desarrollo Bajo el Sistema Colectivo de Trabajo.* Torreón: (no pub.), 1940.
BOSCH GARCÍA, Pedro. *Indices de los Organismos de Intervención del Estado en la Vida Económica de México.* Montevideo: Consejo Interamericano de Comercio y Producción, 1946.
BOSQUES, Gilberto. *The National Revolutionary Party of Mexico and the Six-Year Plan.* Mexico: National Revolutionary Party, 1937.
BOULDING, Kenneth E. *Economic Analysis.* New York: Harper & Bros., 1948.
BOWLES, Chester. *American Politics in a Revolutionary World.* Cambridge: Harvard University Press, 1956.
————. *The New Dimensions of Peace.* New York: Harper & Bros., 1955.
BRANDT, Karl. *The Reconstruction of World Agriculture.* New York: W. W. Norton & Co., 1945.
BUCHANAN, Norman S., and LUTZ, F. A. *Rebuilding the World Economy.* New York: Twentieth Century Fund, 1947.
BULNES, Francisco. *El Verdadero Díaz y la Revolución Mexicana.* México: E. Gómez de la Puente, 1920.
————. *The Whole Truth About Mexico.* New York: M. Bulnes Book Co., 1916.
CALLCOTT, Wilfrid Hardy. *Liberalism in Mexico, 1857-1929.* Stanford: Stanford University Press, 1931.
CÁRDENAS, Lázaro. *A Message to the Mexican Nation on the Solution of the Agrarian Problem of La Laguna.* Mexico: National Revolutionary Party, 1936.
CARREÑO, Alberto María. *La Evolución Económica de México en los Ultimos Cincuenta Años.* México: Academia Nacional de Ciéncias "Antonio Alzate," 1937.
CATHOLIC ASSOCIATION FOR INTERNATIONAL PEACE. *Latin America and the United States.* Washington: Catholic Association for International Peace, 1929.
CENTERS, Richard. *The Psychology of Social Classes.* Princeton: Princeton University Press, 1949.
CHANDLER, A. N. *Land Title Origins, A Tale of Force and Fraud.* New York: Robert Schalkenbach Foundation, 1945.

CHANG, P. K. *Agriculture and Industrialization.* Cambridge: Harvard University Press, 1941.

CHAPIN, F. Stuart. *Experimental Designs in Sociological Research.* New York: Harper & Bros., 1947.

CHÁVEZ OROZCO, Luis. *Historia Económica y Social de México.* México: Secretaría de Educación Pública, 1935.

CLARK, Marjorie. *Organized Labor in Mexico.* Chapel Hill: University of North Carolina Press, 1934.

COHEN, R. L. *The Economics of Agriculture.* New York: Pitman Publishing Corporation, 1949.

CONTRERAS ARIAS, Alfonso. *El Trigo en México.* Parte II. México: Banco Nacional de Crédito Agrícola, 1939.

CORIA, Rosendo Rojas. *Tratado de Cooperativismo Mexicano.* México: Fondo de Cultura Económica, 1953.

COSSIO Y COSIO, Roberto, and ZULOAGA, Pedro. *Estudio sobre el Problema Agrario* (*ca.* 1944-1945)n.d., no place of publication.

CRAWFORD, W. Rex. *A Century of Latin American Thought.* Cambridge: Harvard University Press, 1944.

DAVIS, Kingsley. *Human Society.* New York: Macmillan Co., 1949.

————, and CASÍS, Ana. *Urbanization in Latin America.* New York: Milbank Memorial Fund, 1946.

DE CASTRO, Josué. *The Geography of Hunger.* Boston: Little, Brown & Co., 1952.

DE MADARIAGA, Salvador. *Spain.* New York: Creative Age Press, 1943.

DE MORFÍ, Fray Juan Agustín. *Viaje de Indias y Diario del Nuevo México (1777-1778).* México: Antigua Librería Robredo de J. Porrúa e hijos, 1935.

DEWEY, John. *Freedom and Culture.* New York: G. P. Putnam's Sons, 1939.

DÍAZ DUFOO, Carlos. *México y los Capitales Extranjeros.* México: Librería de la Vda. de Ch. Bouret, 1918.

Documentos de la Revolución Mexicana. México: Secretaría de Educación Pública, 1945.

DOUGLAS, William O. *Strange Lands and Friendly People.* New York: Harper & Bros., 1951.

DUBLIN, Louis, LOTKA, A. J., and SPIEGELMAN, M. *Length of Life.* New York: The Ronald Press Co., 1949.

DUNN, Robert W. *American Foreign Investments.* New York: B. W. Huebsch and the Viking Press, 1927.

DURÁN OCHOA, Julio. *Población.* México: Fondo de Cultura Económica, 1955.

ECHÁNOVE TRUJILLO, Carlos A., "La Mentalidad de la Población Indígena de México," *Hechos y Problemas del México Rural.* México: Seminario Mexicano de Sociología, 1952.

EDWARDS, Everett E., "American Agriculture — the First 300 Years," *An Historical Survey of American Agriculture.* Washington: Department of Agriculture, 1941, pp. 171-276.

EDWARDS, Lyford P. *The Natural History of Revolution.* Chicago: University of Chicago Press, 1927.

ELDRIDGE, Seba. *Development of Collective Enterprise.* Lawrence: University of Kansas Press, 1943.

FABILA, Manuel. *Cinco Siglos de Legislación Agraria en México, 1493-1940.* México: Banco Nacional de Crédito Agrícola, 1941.

FERRER DE M., Gabriel. *Vida de Francisco I. Madero.* México: Secretaría de Educación Pública, 1945.

FISCHER, Louis. *Empire.* New York: Duell, Sloan & Pearce, 1943.

FLANDREAU, Charles. *Viva México*. London: D. Appleton-Century Co., 1935.
FRANK, Lawrence K. *Society as the Patient*. New Brunswick: Rutgers University Press, 1948.
GALARZA, Ernesto. *La Industria Eléctrica en México*. México: Fondo de Cultura Económica, 1941.
————. *Labor Trends and Social Welfare in Latin America*. Washington: Pan American Union, 1942.
GARCÍA CUBAS, A. *Cuadro de la Situación Económica Novo-Hispana en 1788*. México: 1906.
GARCÍA TREVIÑO, Rodrigo. *Precios, Salarios y Mordidas*. México: Editorial América, 1953.
GEORGE, Henry. *Progress and Poverty*. New York: Doubleday, Page and Company, 1879.
————. *Social Problems*. New York: Doubleday, Page and Company, 1911.
GERTH, H. H., and MILLS, C. Wright (eds.). *From Max Weber: Essays in Sociology*. London: Kegan Paul, 1948.
GÓMEZ, Marte R. *La Región Lagunera*. México: Sociedad Agronómica Mexicana, 1941.
GÓMEZ ROBLEDO, Antonio. *The Bucareli Agreements and International Law*. Mexico: The National University of Mexico Press, 1940.
GONZÁLEZ GALLARDO, Alfonso. *El Trigo en México*. Parte IV. México: Banco Nacional de Crédito Agrícola, 1939.
GONZÁLEZ H., Gonzalo. *El Trigo en México*. Parte V. México: Banco Nacional de Crédito Agrícola, 1939.
GONZÁLEZ PEÑA, Carlos. *History of Mexican Literature*. Dallas: University of Texas Press, 1952.
GONZÁLEZ PÉREZ, M. *México y sus Capitales*. México: 1906.
GONZÁLEZ ROA, Fernando. *Las Cuestiones Fundamentales de Actualidad en México*. Translated by Gustavo E. Archilla. New York: W.P.A. and Columbia University, 1937.
————. *The Mexican People and Their Detractors*. New York: Latin American News Association, 1916.
GOOCH, Donald W. *World Land Reform*. Washington: U. S. Department of Agriculture, 1951.
GORDON, Wendell C. *The Economy of Latin America*. New York: Columbia University Press, 1950.
GRISWOLD, A. Whitney. *Farming and Democracy*. New York: Harcourt, Brace and Co., 1948.
GRUENING, Ernest. *Mexico and Its Heritage*. New York: Century Co., 1928.
GRULIOW, Leo (ed.). *Current Soviet Policies*. New York: Frederick A. Praeger, 1953.
GUERRA, Eduardo. *Torreón, Historia de La Laguna*. Torreón: 1932.
HACKETT, Charles Wilson. *The Mexican Revolution and the United States*. Boston: World Peace Foundation, 1926.
HAGOOD, Margaret Jarman. *Statistics for Sociologists*. New York: Henry Holt and Co., 1941.
HAMILTON, Thomas J. *Appeasement's Child: The Franco Regime in Spain*. New York: Alfred A. Knopf, 1943.
HAMMOND, J. L., and HAMMOND, Barbara. *The Rise of Modern Industry*. New York: Harcourt, Brace & Co., 1937.
HANSON, Earl Parker. *Transformation: The Story of Modern Puerto Rico*. New York: Simon and Schuster, 1955.
HARRIS, Marshall. *Origin of the Land Tenure System in the United States*.

Ames: Iowa State College Press, 1953.

HEIMANN, Eduard. *History of Economic Doctrines.* New York: •Oxford Press, 1945.

HEWES, Lawrence I., Jr. *Japan — Land and Men, the Story of Land Reform in Japan.* Ames: Iowa State University Press, 1955.

HOFSTADTER, Richard. *Social Darwinism in American Thought.* Boston: Beacon Press, 1955.

HUFFMAN, Roy E. *Irrigation Development and Public Water Policy.* New York: The Ronald Press Co., 1953.

HUTTON, Graham. *We Too Can Prosper.* London: Allen and Unwin, 1953.

INFIELD, Henrik F., and FREIER, Koka. *People in Ejidos.* New York: Frederick A. Praeger, Inc., 1954.

————, and MAIER, Joseph B. *Cooperative Group Living.* New York: Koosis and Co., 1950.

Informe del Consejo de Administración, Torreón: Unión de Sociedades Locales de Crédito Colectivo Ejidal, 1947.

INTERNATIONAL BANK FOR RECONSTRUCTION AND DEVELOPMENT. *The Economic Development of Mexico.* Baltimore: Johns Hopkins Press, 1953.

ISE, John. *Economics.* New York: Harper & Bros., 1946.

ITURRIAGA, José E. *La Estructura Social y Cultural de México.* México: Fondo de Cultura Económica, 1951.

JACOBY, Erich. *Agrarian Unrest in Southeast Asia.* New York: Columbia University Press, 1949.

JAFFE, A. J., and STEWART, Charles D. *Manpower Resources and Utilization.* New York: John Wiley & Sons, 1951.

JOHNSON, Charles S., EMBREE, E. R., and ALEXANDER, W. W. *The Collapse of Cotton Tenancy.* Chapel Hill: University of North Carolina Press, 1935.

KEMMERER, E. W. *Inflation and Revolution.* Princeton: Princeton University Press, 1940.

KESTER, Howard. *Revolt Among the Sharecroppers.* New York: Covici, Friede, 1936.

KING, Rosa E. *Tempest Over Mexico.* Boston: Little, Brown & Co., 1935.

KIRKPATRICK, Evron M. *Target: The World.* New York: Macmillan Co., 1956.

LAIDLER, Harry W. *Social-Economic Movements.* New York: Thomas Y. Crowell Co., 1949.

LASKER, Bruno. *Human Bondage in Southeast Asia.* Chapel Hill: University of North Carolina Press, 1950.

LASSWELL, Harold D. *The World Revolution of Our Time: A Framework for Basic Policy Research.* Stanford: Stanford University Press, 1951.

LEA, Henry. *History of the Spanish Inquisition,* Vol. II. London: The Macmillan Co., 1922.

LENIN, V. I. *Collected Works,* Vol. XX. New York: International Publishers Co., 1930.

LEWIS, Oscar. *Life in a Mexican Village.* Urbana: University of Illinois Press, 1951.

LIGA DE AGRÓNOMOS SOCIALISTAS. *La Comarca Lagunera.* México: Liga de Agrónomos Socialistas, 1940.

LOOMIS, C. P., and BEEGLE, J. A. *Rural Social Systems.* New York: Prentice-Hall, Inc., 1950.

LÓPEZ APARICIO, Alfonso. *El Movimiento Obrero en México.* México: Editorial Jus., 1952.

LÓPEZ ROSADO, Diego G. *Atlas Histórico Geográfico de México.* México: El Nacional, 1940.

LORWIN, Lewis L. *Labor and Internationalism.* New York: The Macmillan Co., 1929.

LOTH, David. *Public Plunder: A History of Graft in America.* New York: Carrick and Evans, 1938.

LOYO, Gilberto. *La Política Demográfica de México.* México: Partido Nacional Revolucionario, 1935.

_____. "Ocupaciones e Ingresos de la Población Indígena de México," *Hechos y Problemas del Mexicano Rural.* México: Seminario Mexicano de Sociología, 1952.

LYND, Robert S. "Foreword" to Robert Brady, *Business as a System of Power.* New York: Columbia University Press, 1943.

_____. *Knowledge for What?* Princeton: Princeton University Press, 1946.

MADERO, Francisco I. *Estudio sobre la conveniencia de la construcción de una presa en el cañón de Fernández, para almacenar las aguas del río Nazas.* San Pedro: Tipografía Benito Juárez, 1907.

MALENBAUM, Wilfred. *The World Wheat Economy, 1865-1939.* Cambridge: Harvard University Press, 1953.

MANUEL, Frank A. *The Politics of Modern Spain.* New York: McGraw-Hill Book Co., 1938.

MATTHEWS, Herbert L. *The Yoke and the Arrows.* New York: Geo. Braziller, Inc., 1957.

McBRIDE, George McCutchen. *The Land Systems of Mexico.* New York: American Geographical Society, 1923.

MEEK, C. K. *Land Law and Customs in the Colonies.* New York: Oxford University Press, 1946.

MENDIETA Y NUÑEZ, Lucio. *El Problema Agrario de México.* México: Librería de Porrua Hnos., 1937.

_____. *El Sistema Agrario Constitucional.* México: Librería de Porrua Hnos., 1940.

_____. *La Administración Pública en México.* México: Imprenta Universitaria, 1942.

MENDOZA, Vicente T. (ed.). *50 Corridos Mexicanos.* México: Secretaría de Educación Pública, 1944.

MERRIAM, Charles E. *The New Democracy and the New Despotism.* New York: McGraw-Hill Book Co., 1939.

MERTON, Robert K. *Social Theory and Social Structure.* Glencoe: Free Press, 1949.

MITCHELL, C. Clyde. *Land Reform in Asia.* Washington: National Planning Association, 1952.

MOLINA ENRÍQUEZ, Andrés. *La Revolución Agraria de México.* 5 vols. México: Talleres Gráficos del Museo Nacional de Arqueología, Historia y Etnografía, 1933-1937.

_____. *Los Grandes Problemas Nacionales.* México: Imp. de A. Carranza e Hijos, 1909.

MOORE, W. E. *Economic Demography of Eastern and Southern Europe.* Geneva: League of Nations, 1945.

_____. *Industrialization and Labor.* Ithaca: Cornell University Press, 1951.

MORA, José María Luis. "El Clero, el Estado y la Economía Nacional," *El Liberalismo Mexicano.* Edited by Martín Luis Guzman. México: Empresas Editoriales, 1950.

_____. "El Clero, la Educación y la Libertad," *El Liberalismo Mexicano.* Edited by Martín Luis Guzman. México: Empresas Editoriales, 1950.

_____. "El Clero, la Milicia y las Revoluciones," *El Liberalismo Mexicano.*

Edited by Martín Luis Guzman. México: Empresas Editoriales, 1950.

————. *México y sus Revoluciones*. Tomo I. México: Editorial Porrúa, 1950.

MORGAN, Arthur E. (ed.). *Bottom-Up Democracy*. Yellow Springs, Ohio; Community Service, Inc., 1954.

MOSHER, Arthur T. *Technical Cooperation in Latin-American Agriculture*. Chicago: University of Chicago Press, 1957.

MUNSON, Henry L. *European Beliefs Regarding the United States*. New York: Common Council on American Unity, 1949.

NÁJERA, Enrique, et al. *Informe General de la Comisión de Estudios de la Comarca Lagunera*. México: Editorial Cultura, 1930.

NATIONAL PLANNING ASSOCIATION. *America's New Opportunities in World Trade*. Washington: National Planning Association, 1944.

NELSON, Lowry. *Land Reform in Italy*. Washington: National Planning Association, 1956.

PARKES, Henry B. *A History of Mexico*. Boston: Houghton Mifflin Co., 1938.

PARRY, John H. *The Sale of Public Office in the Spanish Indies Under the Hapsburgs*. Berkeley: University of California Press, 1953.

PARRY, J. H., and SHERLOCK, P. M. *A Short History of the West Indies*. London: Macmillan & Co., Ltd., 1956.

PARSONS, Talcott. *Essays in Sociological Theory*. Glencoe: Free Press, 1949.

————. *The Social System*. Glencoe: Free Press, 1951.

————. *The Structure of Social Action*. Glencoe: Free Press, 1949.

PEARSON, Frank A., and HARPER, Floyd A. *The World's Hunger*. Ithaca: Cornell University Press, 1945.

PERLOFF, Harvey. *Puerto Rico's Economic Future*. Chicago: University of Chicago Press, 1950.

PIRENNE, Henri. *Economic and Social History of Medieval Europe*. New York: Harcourt, Brace & Co., 1937.

Plan de Movilización Agrícola de la República Mexicana. México: Secretaría de Agricultura, 1943.

POLANYI, Karl. *The Great Transformation*. New York: Rinehart & Co., 1944.

POLITICAL AND ECONOMIC PLANNING. *World Population and Resources*. London: Political and Economic Planning, 1955.

POOL, Ithiel de Sola, et al. *Symbols of Democracy*. Stanford: Stanford University Press, 1952.

PORTILLO, Esteban L. *Apuntes para la Historia Antigua de Coahuila y Texas*. Saltillo: Tip. "El Golfo de México" de S. Fernández, 1886.

————. *Catecismo Geográfico, Político e Histórico del Estado de Coahuila de Zaragoza*. Saltillo: Tipografía del gobierno en palacio, 1897.

PRADO, Amado. *Prontuario de Torreón*. Torreón: 1899.

PUERTO RICO PLANNING BOARD. *Faith in People*. San Juan: Puerto Rico Planning Board, 1954.

RAMOS PEDRUEZA, Rafael. *La Lucha de Clases a Través de la Historia de México*. México: Secretaría de Educación Pública, 1936.

REDFIELD, Robert. *A Village That Chose Progress*. Chicago: University of Chicago Press, 1950.

————. *The Folk Culture of Yucatan*. Chicago: University of Chicago Press, 1941.

REYES PIMENTEL, José. *La Cosecha*. México: D.A.P.P., 1939.

ROLLAND, Modesto C. *El Desastre Municipal en la República Mexicana*. México: (n.d.).

ROMERO FLORES, Jesús. *Corridos de la Revolución Mexicana*. México: El Nacional, 1941.

ROSSITER, Clinton. *The First American Revolution.* New York: Harcourt, Brace & Co., 1953.

ROSTOTZEFF, M. *The Social and Economic History of the Roman Empire.* Oxford: Clarendon Press, 1926.

SADY, Emil J. *The United Nations and Dependent Peoples.* Washington: The Brookings Institution, 1956.

Salon of American Humorists: A Political and Social Pageant from the Revolution to the Present Day. New York: College Art Association, 1933.

SAX, Karl. *Standing Room Only.* Boston: Beacon Press, 1955.

SCAFF, Alvin H. *The Philippine Answer to Communism.* Stanford: Stanford University Press, 1955.

SCHULTZ, Theodore W. (ed.). *Food for the World.* Chicago: University of Chicago Press, 1945.

SCHURZ, William L. *This New World.* New York: E. P. Dutton & Co., 1954.

SECRETARÍA DE EDUCACIÓN PÚBLICA. *Novela de la Revolución Mexicana.* México: Secretaría de Educación Pública, 1945.

SELZNICK, Philip. *TVA and the Grass Roots.* Berkeley: University of California Press, 1949.

SERVÍN, Armando. *La Evolución Técnica del Sistema Impositivo Federal.* México: Fondo de Cultura Económica, 1942.

SIEGEL, Henry W. *Land Tenure Policies at Home and Abroad.* Chapel Hill: University of North Carolina Press, 1941.

SIMPSON, Eyler N. *The Ejido — Mexico's Way Out.* Chapel Hill: University of North Carolina Press, 1937.

SMITH, T. Lynn. *Population Analysis.* New York: McGraw-Hill Book Co., 1948.

SOROKIN, P. A. *Social and Cultural Dynamics.* Vol. 3. New York: American Book Co., 1937.

————. *Society, Culture and Personality.* New York: Harper & Bros., 1947.

————, and ZIMMERMAN, C. C. *Principles of Rural-Urban Sociology.* New York: Henry Holt & Co., 1929.

SOULE, George, *et al. Latin America in the Future World.* New York: Farrar & Rinehart, 1945.

STEBBINS, Richard P. *The United States in World Affairs.* New York: Harper & Bros., 1956.

STEINBECK, John. *The Grapes of Wrath.* New York: The Viking Press, Inc., 1939.

STEPHENSON, Carl. *Medieval Feudalism.* Ithaca: Cornell University Press, 1942.

STERNBERG, Fritz. *The Coming Crisis.* New York: The John Day Co., 1947.

STEWART, Virginia. *45 Contemporary Mexican Artists.* Stanford: Stanford University Press, 1951.

SULZBERGER, C. L. *The Big Thaw.* New York: Harper & Bros., 1956.

SYDNOR, Charles S. *Gentlemen Freeholders.* Chapel Hill: University of North Carolina Press, 1952.

TAMAYO, Jorge L. *Transformación de la Comarca Lagunera.* México: Academia Nacional de Ciencias "Antonio Alzate," 1941.

TANNENBAUM, Frank. *The Mexican Agrarian Revolution.* New York: The Macmillan Co., 1929.

————. *Mexico—The Struggle for Peace and Bread.* New York: Alfred A. Knopf, 1950.

————. *Peace by Revolution.* New York: Columbia University Press, 1933.

TAWNEY, R. H. *The Agrarian Problem in the Sixteenth Century.* New York: Longmans, Green & Co., 1912.

————. *Equality.* London: George Allen and Unwin, Ltd., 1929.

TOPETE, José Manuel. *A Working Bibliography of Latin American Literature.* St. Augustine: Inter-American Bibliographical and Library Association, 1952.

Torreón: Agrícola-Industrial-Commercial. Torreón: Cámara de Comercio, 1950.

TURNER, John Kenneth. *Barbarous Mexico.* Chicago: Charles H. Kerr and Co., 1910.

UNITED NATIONS. *Progress in Land Reform.* New York: United Nations, Department of Economic Affairs, 1954.

————. *Statistics of National Income and Expenditure, 1953.* New York: United Nations, 1956.

VAILLANT, G. C. *The Aztecs of Mexico.* New York: Doubleday, Doran & Co., 1944.

WARD, Barbara. *The West at Bay.* New York: W. W. Norton & Co., 1948.

WATER RESOURCES POLICY COMMISSION, *A Water Policy for the American People.* Vol. I. Washington: Government Printing Office, 1950.

WEYL, Nathaniel, and WEYL, Sylvia. *The Reconquest of Mexico.* New York: Oxford University Press, 1939.

WHETTEN, Nathan L. *Rural Mexico.* Chicago: University of Chicago Press, 1948.

WILLIAMSON, René de Visme. *Culture and Policy.* Knoxville: University of Tennessee Press, 1949.

WINFIELD, Gerald F. *China, the Land and the People.* New York: William Sloane Associates, 1948.

WOOSTER, Julia L., and BAUER, Walter. *Agricultural Credit in Mexico.* Washington: Farm Credit Administration, 1943.

YAÑEZ-PÉREZ, Luis. *Mecanización de la Agricultura Mexicana.* México: Instituto Mexicano de Investigaciones Económicas, 1957.

ZOLA, Emile. *Earth.* New York: Grove Press, 1955.

PERIODICALS, ARTICLES, UNPUBLISHED MATERIAL

ALCOCER CAMPERO, J. J. "Relaciones entre la Medicina Curativa y la Preventiva en los Servicios de Higiene Rural y Medicina Social en la Comarca Lagunera," *Higiene Rural y Medicina Social,* febrero-marzo, 1943, pp. 3-7.

ALEMÁN, Miguel. "Presidential Farewell Address." *Tiempo,* 2 de septiembre, 1952.

BACH, Federico. "The Nationalization of the Mexican Railroads," *Annals of Collective Economy,* IV (January-April, 1939), 70-93.

BANCO NACIONAL DE MÉXICO. *Review of the Economic Situation of Mexico.* México: Banco Nacional de México, July, 1956.

BASSOLS, Narciso. "Estudiemos la cuestión agraria," *Revista de Economía,* 15 de enero, 1949, pp. 6-7.

BIERSTADT, Robert. "An Analysis of Social Power," *American Sociological Review,* XV (December, 1950), 730-38.

BLOCH, Marc. "Feudalism — European," *Encyclopedia of Social Sciences,* VI, 203-10.

BOLETÍN AMERICANO. New York: Federación Internacional de Asociaciones de Trabajadores Textiles, mayo, 1957.

BOLETÍN MENSUAL DE LA DIRECCIÓN DE ECONOMÍA RURAL, septiembre, 1943; diciembre, 1946.

BRENNER, Anita. "The Mexican Renaissance," *Harpers,* January, 1951, pp. 173-82.

————. "Mexico," *Holiday,* March, 1947, p. 122.

BURNIGHT, R. G., WHETTEN, N. L., and WAXMAN, B. D. "Differential Rural-Urban Fertility in Mexico," *American Sociological Review*, XXI, 1 (February, 1956).

Business Week, March 1, 1956.

CALLENDER, Harold. "False Picture of U. S. Abroad Held to Antedate Red Efforts," *New York Times*, April 24, 1950.

CLINE, Howard. "Mexican Community Studies," *The Hispanic-American Historical Review*, May, 1952, pp. 212-42.

COE, John. "Recent Labor Developments in Mexico and the Caribbean," *Inter-American Economic Affairs*, March, 1948, pp. 15-70.

CREELMAN, John. "President Díaz, Hero of the Americas," *Pearson's Magazine*, March, 1908, p. 241.

DAVIS, Kingsley. "Political Ambivalence in Latin America," *Journal of Legal and Political Sociology*, I, 1-2, (October, 1942).

————, and SENIOR, Clarence. "Immigration from the Western Hemisphere," *Annals of the American Academy of Political and Social Science*, CCLXII (March, 1949), 70-81.

DE ALBA, Jorge. "En nuestro país la organización de la extensión agrícola aún no ha principiado," *Chapingo*, IV, 35 (30 de septiembre, 1949), 33.

DE BRASCHI, Julia Córdova. "La Psicología Española Vista por Ortega y Gasset," *Asomante*, octubre-diciembre, 1954.

DE LA PEÑA, Moisés T. "Problemas Demográficos y Agrarios," *Problemas Agrícolas e Industriales de México*, II, 3-4 (1950), 315.

DE MENDIZÁBAL, Miguel O. "La Reforma Agraria Desde el Punto de Vista Económica," *Revista de Economía*, 20 de junio, 1942, pp. 22-29.

Distribución de las aguas del Río Nazas. Documentos adicionales, 1891.

DOTSON, Floyd. "A Note on Participation in Voluntary Associations in a Mexican City," *American Sociological Review*, XVIII, 4 (August, 1953), 380-86.

DROMUNDO, Baltasar. "Aproximaciones a la verdad ejidal Lagunera," *El Universal*, 13 de febrero, 1941.

DURÁN, D. Rafael. "Derroteros Generales de los Departamentos del Imperio Mexicano," *Boletín de la Sociedad Mexicana de Geografía y Estadística*, Tomo XI, pp. 345-470.

EISINGER, C. E. "The Influence of Natural Rights and Physiocratic Doctrine on American Agrarian Thought during the Revolutionary Period," *Agricultural History*, January, 1947, pp. 13-23.

Ejidales, mayo, 1939.

El Agricultor Lagunero, 15 de noviembre, 1946; 15 de enero, 1947.

El Nacional, 28 de mayo, 1939; 20 de mayo, 1940.

El Norte, 7 de agosto, 1943.

El Siglo de Torreón, Annual review issues, 1939-1942; 5 de julio, 1940; 5 de agosto, 1941; 6 de agosto, 1941; 7 de octubre, 1941; 28 de julio, 1942; 21 de junio, 1943; 23 de julio, 1943; 28 de julio, 1943; 3 de agosto, 1943; 5 de agosto, 1943; 17 de agosto, 1947; 11 de octubre, 1947; 17 de octubre, 1947; 31 de mayo, 1953; 3 de abril, 1953; 1 de mayo, 1953; 1 de diciembre, 1954; 7 de octubre, 1956; 8 de octubre, 1956.

Excelsior, 20 de febrero, 1952; 10 de marzo to 10 de mayo, 1952; 23 de junio, 1953; 2 de septiembre, 1956; 16 de junio, 1957; 14 de septiembre, 1957.

The Financial Times of London, March 9, 1953.

Financial Week in Mexico, December 26, 1953.

"First World Land Tenure Problems Conference and Report of Its Steering Committee," *Land Economics*, XVIII, 1 (February, 1952), 77.

FLORES, Edmundo. "Mesa Redonda sobre Agricultura," *Revista de Economía,* enero, 1952, p. 29.

GARCÍA CRUZ, Miguel. "El Problema de las Cooperativas de Consumo," *Trabajo y Previsión Social,* IX, 38, 39 (marzo, abril, 1941), 75-84, 87-98.

GARCÍA DE LEÓN, Porfirio, Jr. "Fraccionamientos Simulados," *México Agrario,* noviembre-diciembre, 1939, pp. 205-14.

GÓMEZ, Marte R. "Los Riegos de México," *Problemas Agrícolas e Industriales de México,* II (1950), 35.

GRAVES, John Temple. "The Cotton Industry — Past, Present, Future," *Think,* November, 1947, pp. 16-20.

Hispanic American Historical Review, XVIII, 2 (May, 1938).

Hispanic American Report, August, 1953; February, 1957; October, 1957.

Hispano Americano, 8 de febrero, 1954.

Hoy, 10 de octubre, 1953.

HUMPHREY, Norman D. "Family Patterns in a Mexican Middletown," *The Social Service Review,* XXVI, 2 (June, 1952), 199-200.

——————. "The Cultural Background of the Mexican Immigrant," *Rural Sociology,* XIII (September, 1948), 253-55.

INFIELD, Henrik F. "Social Control in a Cooperative Society," *Sociometry,* V, 3 (1942).

——————, and DICHTER, Ernest. "Who is Fit for Cooperative Farming?" *Applied Anthropology,* II, 2-3 (1943).

Informe . . . de la Unión Central . . . al quinto congreso ordinario, Torreón, 21-23 de febrero, 1947 (typescript).

Irrigación en México, mayo-junio, 1939; septiembre-octubre, 1940; mayo-junio, 1941.

La Jeringa, 1 de agosto, 1943.

La Opinión, 1 de octubre, 1939; 31 de julio, 1941; 5 de agosto, 1941; 5 de marzo, 1942; 25 de julio, 1943; 2 de agosto, 1943; 3 de agosto, 1947; 1-31 de marzo, 1953; 8 de octubre, 1956.

La Voz de México, 11 de julio, 1943.

LARSON, Olaf F. "Rural Rehabilitation — Theory and Practice," *Rural Sociology,* XII, 3 (September, 1947), 223.

LOUIS, Paul. "Agrarian Movements in Rome," *Encyclopedia of the Social Sciences,* I (1938), 494-95.

LUBIN, Isador. "Hope of the Hungry Millions," *New York Times Magazine,* February 10, 1952, pp. 18, 49, 52, 54.

MADARIAGA, Alfonso. "Datos Históricos Acerca de la Aparición del Gusano Rosado . . . en la República Mexicana," *Agricultura,* I, 3 (1924), 12-44.

MECHAM, J. Lloyd. "The Origins of Federalism in Mexico," *The Hispanic-American Historical Review,* XVIII, 2 (May, 1938), 164-82.

MENDIETA Y NUÑEZ, Lucio. "El Vampiro Ejidal," and "El Desastre del Crédito Ejidal," *El Universal,* 6 and 20 de octubre, 1943.

Mexican Labor News, September 1, 1936; February 17, 1938.

Mexican Weekly News, November 8, 1941.

Mexican Yearbook, 1914. London: McCorquodale & Co. Ltd., 1914.

Mexico City Post, January 15, 1944.

Mines Register, 1941.

MONYPENNY, Phillip. "The Control of Ethical Standards in the Public Service," *The Annals of the American Academy of Political and Social Science,* CCXCVII (January, 1955), 98-104.

Moody's Manual of Investments. New York: Moody's Investors Service, 1943.

National Municipal Review, February, 1954.

New York Post, June 10, 1956.

New York Times, February 22, 1951; October 18, 1951; January 28, 1952; February 10, 1952; April 8, 1952; October 12, 1952; December 2, 1952; December 29, 1952; March 4, 1953; March 20, 1953; August 16, 1953; September 28, 1953; October 9, 1953; October 31, 1953; December 11, 1953; October 26, 1954; April 17, 1955; April 23, 1955; December 28, 1955; August 4, 1956; March 10, 1957; April 6, 1957; June 15, 1957; June 20, 1957.

OCHOA REYES, Arnulfo. "Informe del Director de Educación Federal en la Comarca Lagunera" (typescript) 1947.

PALENCIA, Isabel de. "Falange in the New World," *The Inter-American,* February, 1944.

PALERM, Angel. "Notas sobre la Clase Media en México," *Ciencias Sociales,* abril-junio, 1952, pp. 18-27, and diciembre, 1952, pp. 129-35.

PEDERSEN, Harold A., "Mechanized Agriculture and the Farm Laborer," *Rural Sociology,* XIX, 1 (March, 1954), 143-51.

Problemas Económico-Agrícolas de México, julio-septiembre, 1946.

RADVANYI, Laszlo. "Mediciones de la Clase Media de la Ciudad de México," *La Sociología en México,* julio, 1951, pp. 17-21.

RAMÍREZ, José Fernando. "La Fábrica de Tunal," *El Museo Mexicano,* I (1843), 121-28.

RAMÍREZ CABAÑAS, Joaquín. "The Tendencies of the Cooperative Movement in Mexico," *Annals of Collective Economy,* January-April, 1939, pp. 107-19.

Restauración, 8-9 de marzo, 1921.

Revista de Economía, 20 de junio, 1942; 31 de octubre, 1943; 30 de noviembre, 1943; 15 de enero, 1949; 15 de abril, 1950.

Revista de Estadística, abril, 1947.

RIQUELME INDA, Julio, "La Crisis Económica del Henequén," *Boletín de la Sociedad Mexicana de Geografía y Estadística,* XXXVII (1928), 63-64.

ROJAS GONZÁLEZ, Francisco. "La Institución del compadrazgo entre los Indios de México," *Revista Mexicana de Sociología,* V, 2 (1943), 101-2.

ROMÁN, Julia. "Historia de los Ferrocarriles de México," *Anales del Museo Nacional de Arqueología, Historia y Etnografía,* Tomo VIII, pp. 389-448.

SALTER, Leonard A., Jr. "Do We Need a New Land Policy?" *Journal of Land and Public Utility Economics,* November, 1946, pp. 309-20.

SANCHEZ MEJORADA, Javier. "Communication and Transportation," *Annals of the American Academy of Political and Social Science,* CCXXXI (March, 1940), 78-93.

SENIOR, Clarence. "Disequilibrium Between Population and Resources: The Case of Puerto Rico," *Conservation of Natural Resources.* Washington: Department of State, 1949, pp. 143-49.

————. "Women, Democracy and Birth Control," *The Humanist,* September-October, 1952, pp. 221-24.

SILVA HERZOG, Jesús. "Los Salarios de Nuestros Campesinos," *La Antorcha,* July 4, 1925, p. 474.

SMITH, Henry Ladd. "The Rise and Fall of the Political Cartoon," *The Saturday Review,* May 29, 1954.

STYCOS, J. Mayone. "Family and Fertility in Puerto Rico," *American Sociological Review,* XVII, 5 (October, 1952), pp. 572-80.

Supplements to Commerce Reports, "Mexico," II, 32a (1914). Washington: U. S. Department of Commerce, 1914, pp. 1-2.

TANNENBAUM, Frank. "Personal Government in Mexico," *Foreign Affairs,* XXVII, 1 (October, 1948), 44-57.

Tiempo, 3 de agosto, 1953; 14 and 28 de septiembre, 1953; 8 de febrero, 1954; 29 de octubre, 1956; 7 de noviembre, 1956; 12 de noviembre, 1956.

Time, September 14, 1953.

Torres Cordera, Carlos. Typescript. Torreón: 1939.

University of Chicago Round Table, No. 811, October 25, 1953; No. 837, April 25, 1954.

Whetten, Nathan L. "The Rise of a Middle Class in Mexico," *Materiales para el Estudio de la Clase Media en la América Latina*, Vol. II. Washington: Unión Panamericana, 1950, pp. 1-29.

Woodbury, Robert M. "Infant Mortality in the United States," *The Annals of the American Academy of Political and Social Science*, CLXXXVIII (1936), 94-106.

Woytinsky, W. S. "India Facing Destiny," *The New Leader*, August 13, 1956.

Wylie, Kathryn H. "Land Irrigation Policy in Mexico," *Foreign Agriculture*, October, 1946, pp. 138-46.

Public Documents and Reports

Agricultural Act, 1947. London: H. M. Stationery Office, 1947.

Allera, Heriberto, "Survey," typescript, Torreón, 1932.

Anuario Estadístico de los Estados Unidos Mexicanos. México: Secretaría de la Economía Nacional, 1938, 1940, 1952, 1953, 1954.

Caribbean Land Tenure Symposium. Port of Spain: Caribbean Research Council, 1946.

Censo de Edificios. México: Dirección General de Estadística, 1929-1939.

Censo General. México: Dirección General de Estadística, 1900, 1940, 1950.

Ciclo de Conferencias. Torreón: Comité Americano de "Amigos de la Paz," 1939, 1940, 1941 (mimeographed).

Clasificación de Sociedades. Torreón: Banco Nacional de Crédito Ejidal, 30 de mayo, 1946.

Comisión Nacional de Irrigación. *Memoria del Distrito de Riego de la Laguna*. México: Secretaría de Recursos Hidráulicos, 1951.

Compendio Estadístico. México: Secretaría de la Economía Nacional, 1947, 1951, 1953.

Conclusiones de Manizales. Des Moines: National Catholic Rural Life Conference, 1953.

De León, A. González. "Compañía Metalúrgica de Torreón," *Boletín de la Secretaría de Fomento*, 2a Epoca 3(II)8.

Departamento Agrario. *Memoria*. México: Departamento Agrario, 1945, 1946.

Diario Oficial de la Federación Mexicana. 1 de noviembre, 1935; 30 de diciembre, 1939; 14 de abril, 1941; 2 de agosto, 1943.

Directory of Organizations and Individuals Professionally Engaged in Governmental Research, 1956-1957. New York: Governmental Research Organization, 1956.

Estudio Agrológico Detallado del Distrito de Riego en la Región Lagunera, Tomos I, II. México: Secretaría de Recursos Hidráulicos, 1951.

Faith in People. San Juan: Puerto Rican Planning Board, 1954.

Food and Agriculture Organization of the United Nations. *Report of the Director General, 1950-51*. Rome: Food and Agriculture Organization, 1951.

————. *Report on the Center on Land Problems in Asia and the Far East*. Rome: Food and Agriculture Organization, 1955.

————. *Report on the Latin-American Seminar on Land Problems.* Rome: Food and Agriculture Organization, 1953.

————. *The State of Food and Agriculture in 1951.* Rome: Food and Agriculture Organization, 1951.

————. *World Fiber Survey.* Washington: Food and Agriculture Organization, 1949.

————. *Yearbook of Food and Agriculture, 1950.* Rome: Food and Agriculture Organization, 1950.

GREAT BRITAIN, COLONIAL OFFICE. *Bibliography of Published Sources Relating to African Land Tenure.* London: His Majesty's Stationery Office (Colonial No. 258), 1950.

GUERRA, Eduardo. "Bosquejo Histórico de la Comarca Lagunera 1739-1936," *Ciclo de Conferencias.* Torreón: Comité Americano de "Amigos de la Paz," 1939 (mimeographed).

HUDGENS, Robert W. "Credit: Keystone of a Plan," *Proceedings, Third Annual Conference on Agricultural Life and Labor.* Washington: National Conference on Agricultural Life and Labor, 1953, pp. 12-14.

Informe. Torreón: Unión de Sociedades de Crédito Colectivo Ejidal de la Comarca Lagunera, 1943.

Informe de Labores de la Secretaría de Recursos Hidráulicos. México: Secretaría de Recursos Hidráulicos, 1951.

Informe Ejercicio de 1949. México: Banco Nacional de Crédito Agrícola y Ganadero, 1950.

Informes. México: Banco Nacional de Crédito Ejidal, 1937-1951.

INTERNATIONAL BANK FOR RECONSTRUCTION AND DEVELOPMENT. *Fourth Annual Report, 1948-1949.* Washington: 1949.

INTERNATIONAL LABOUR ORGANIZATION. *World Labour Report, 1953.* Geneva: International Labour Organization, 1953.

————. *Yearbook of Labour Statistics, 1956.* Geneva: International Labour Organization, 1956.

JACOBY, Erich H. *Inter-relationship between Agrarian Reform and Agricultural Development.* Rome: Food and Agriculture Organization, 1953.

KELLY, Isabel. *Informe Preliminar del Proyecto de Habitación en La Laguna Ejido de El Cuije,* v. I. México: Instituto de Asuntos Interamericanos, 1954.

————. *Notas Acerca de la Cultura Lagunera — Población y Subsistencia,* v. II. México: Instituto de Asuntos Interamericanos, 1954.

Land Reform — A World Challenge. Washington: Department of State, 1952.

Legislación Agraria Mexicana. Banco Nacional de Crédito Ejidal. México: 1938.

Memoria de la Primera Convención Nacional Algodonera. México: 1935.

Memoria de la Secretaría de la Economía Nacional. México: 1943.

Memoria del Segundo Congreso Mexicano de Ciéncias Sociales. México: Sociedad Mexicana de Geografía y Estadística Vol. I, 1945.

MÉXICO. *Reglamento provisional para la distribución de las aguas del Río Nazas, desde la presa de San Fernando en el estado de Durango hasta la Laguna de Mayrán en él de Coahuila,* 1891.

MÉXICO. *Reglamento para la distribución de las aguas del Río Nazas desde la presa de San Fernando en el estado de Durango hasta la presa de la Colonia en él de Coahuila,* 1895.

Nuevo Código Agrario. México: Departamento Agrario, 1943.

Padrón de Establecimientos Comerciales, 1939. México: Dirección General de Estadística, 1939.

Primer Censo Comercial de los Estados Unidos Mexicanos. México: Dirección General de Estadística, 1943.

RAPER, Arthur F., *et al. The Japanese Village in Transition.* Tokyo: General Headquarters, Supreme Commander for the Allied Powers, 1950.

RUIZ CORTINES, Adolfo. *Annual Report to Congress.* Mexico: 1953.

SECRETARÍA DE AGRICULTURA. *Plan de Movilización Agrícola de la República Mexicana.* México: Secretaría de Agricultura, 1943.

SECRETARÍA DE BIENES NACIONALES. *Directorio del Gobierno Federal.* México: Secretaría de Bienes Nacionales, 1949.

SECRETARÍA DE LA ECONOMÍA NACIONAL. *El Problema de las Alcabalas.* México: 1941.

_____. *El Salario Mínimo, 1946-47.* México: Secretaría de la Economía Nacional, 1947.

SECRETARÍA DE EDUCACIÓN PÚBLICA. *Reglamento de la Parcela Ejidal Escolar.* México: Secretaría de Educación Pública, 1944.

SECRETARÍA DEL TRABAJO Y PREVISIÓN SOCIAL. *Salarios Mínimos Aprobados Para los Municipios . . . y que regirán durante los años de 1942 y 1943.* México: Secretaría del Trabajo y Previsión Social, 1941.

Sexto Censo de Población de los Estados Unidos Mexicanos — Población Municipal. México: Dirección General de Estadística, 1940.

SILVA HERZOG, Jesús. "Un Balance de la Revolución Mexicana," *Memoria del Segundo Congreso Mexicano de Ciencias Sociales.* Tomos I, II. México: Sociedad Mexicana de Geografía y Estadística, 1945.

UNESCO. *Educación de la Comunidad en Puerto Rico.* Paris: UNESCO, 1952.

UNITED NATIONS. *Demographic Yearbook, 1952.* New York: United Nations, 1953.

_____. *Demographic Yearbook, 1956.* New York: United Nations, 1957.

_____. *Economic Survey of Latin America, 1949.* New York: United Nations, 1951.

_____. *Progress in Land Reform. Second Report.* New York: United Nations, 1956.

UNITED NATIONS, ECONOMIC AND SOCIAL COUNCIL, ECONOMIC COMMISSION FOR LATIN AMERICA. *Labor Productivity of the Cotton Textile Industry in Five Latin American Countries.* E/CN, 12/219, 12 May, 1951.

_____. *Preliminary Report on the World Social Situation.* E/CN, 5/267, 25 April, 1952.

_____. *Recent Developments and Trends in the Mexican Economy.* E/CN, 12/217, 26 March, 1951.

UNITED NATIONS, STATISTICAL OFFICE. *National Income and Its Distribution in Underdeveloped Countries.* New York: United Nations, 1951.

_____. *Statistics of National Income and Expenditure.* New York: United Nations, 1953.

UNITED STATES CENSUS OF AGRICULTURE, *1950 Special Reports.* Vol. V, Washington: Government Printing Office, 1950.

VENSTROM, Cruz. "Experience in 1945 with Mechanical Cotton Pickers in California." Washington: United States Department of Agriculture, Bureau of Agricultural Economics, October, 1946 (mimeographed).

AGRARIANISM, 2-9, 10, 47, 52, 53, 59, 89-117, 127, 136, 206-212
Agriculture, 3, 10, 28, 33, 53
Alemán, Miguel, 27, 99, 141
Alfalfa, 78, 115
Animals, 28-29, 53
Army, 17-18
Artists, 44, 45
Avila Camacho, Manuel, 27, 99
Azuela, Mariano, 44

BANKING, 26, 29, 82, 91, 96-106, 224n22, 228n18
Banco Nacional de Crédito Ejidal, 91, 96, 99-103, 105, 108, 113, 116, 119, 120, 122, 125-128, 132, 133, 136-139, 142, 148, 160, 188, 193, 196, 198
Beans, 10, 77, 78, 144
Births, 33, 36, 37, 149, 153, 154, 169-171, 221n75, 232n6
Bureaucracy, 41, 42
Bus lines, 86

CABRERA, Luis, 25
Calles, Plutarco E., 25, 31, 43, 52
Cárdenas, Lázaro, 26, 31, 65, 66, 90, 112, 118, 121, 136, 141, 142, 149, 154, 155, 184, 188, 197
Carranza, Venustiano, 24, 25, 30
Catholic Church, 4, 18, 19, 22, 58-61, 163, 164
Cattle, 53
Census, 33, 35, 36, 39, 167
Charlot, Jean, 44
Charts. See Maps
Chickens, 115, 121
Cía. Algodonera e Industrial, 54
Clothing, 73, 81, 143
Clubs, 59, 87, 203
Colonization, 50
Commerce, 53, 80-83
Communists, 7, 125, 126, 131, 134, 164, 188
Compañía Agrícola, 49, 50
Constitution, 8, 16, 20, 30, 47, 63, 155, 164

Cooperatives, 128, 129
Corn (maize), 10, 77, 78, 129, 130, 144
Corrido (song), 45
Cortines, Adolfo Ruiz, 31, 99, 141, 205
Cotton, 10, 16, 20, 47, 61, 66, 69-73, 79, 91, 99, 103, 113, 115, 116, 123, 125, 132, 134, 135, 138, 139, 176, 189, 191, 192, 225n14, 249, 250
Covarrubias, Miguel, 44
Credit, 99-106, 121, 124, 128, 132, 160, 161, 190, 192
Culture, 204-208

DEMOCRACY, 11, 12, 18, 19, 89, 117, 118, 142, 173, 182, 212
Díaz, Porfirio, 13-19, 20-22, 29, 30, 47, 50, 51, 136, 165, 215n2
Diseases and Pests, 52, 56, 76, 77, 116, 117, 121, 131, 134, 137, 149-153
Doctors, 149--154
Dotación, 26
Droit du seigneur, 16, 183
Drunkenness, 130

ECONOMICS, 35, 55, 127, 133, 134, 172
Education, 38, 58, 59, 101, 119, 120, 124, 127, 130-132, 135, 140, 148, 153-162, 197, 199
Ejidos (group farms), vi, 25, 26, 55, 65, 91, 93, 95-99, 106, 112-114, 119, 120, 129-131, 133, 143, 144, 148, 150, 157, 161, 164, 168, 174, 180, 181, 186-188, 193, 198, 211, 219n43, 235n17
Electric power, 31, 84, 85, 103, 122, 133
Employment, 35, 178-180
Exports, 35
Expropriation, 10, 26, 30, 66, 79, 87, 89, 90, 93, 136, 149, 195

FAMILY, 200, 201
Famine, 33, 52

Farm groups. See ejidos
Feudalism, vi, 56, 58, 89, 118, 182, 183, 202
Figs, 78
Finance, 52, 53, 61, 105, 127, 194. See also Credit
Fire arms, 196
Flax, 72
Food, 34, 35, 143
Foreign policy, 31; influence, 49
Fuel, 85
Furniture, 147

GEOGRAPHY, 35, 67, 68
Gil, Portes, 31
Goats, 115
Gómez, Federico, 35
Gómez, Marte R., 148
Graft, 136-143, 203, 205
Grapes, 78, 99, 115, 128
Guillermo Purcell y Cía., 54
Guzmán, Henríquez, 126
Guzman, Martín Luis, 44

HACENDADOS, 15, 51, 52, 136, 137, 147, 155, 166, 186, 218n19
Hacienda, 15, 91
Health, 121, 130, 131, 135, 149-154
Henequén, 69
Hidalgo, Miguel, 25, 165
Hospitals, 56, 150, 151
Household appliances, 147
Housing, 40, 41, 56, 58, 59, 103, 116, 135, 147-149, 156
Huerta, Victoriano, 30, 47

IDEOLOGIES, 24, 25, 52, 91, 210
Income, national, 34; peasant, 132, 133, 144, 195
Industry, 55, 83-85
Inflation, 33, 34
Institutions, 89
Insurance, crop, 134, 135
Intellectuals, 25, 125
Irrigation, 50, 51, 55, 61, 62, 64, 68, 69, 78, 91, 93, 95, 99, 106-112, 132, 136, 162, 168, 191, 209, 211, 220n50

JÚAREZ, Benito, 165

LABOR code, 58. See also Unions
Laguna: area, 49; experiment launched, 89; location, 47, 49; scope, 11

Land, 1, 5, 6, 15, 24-28, 52, 54, 90, 91, 94-96, 112-116, 168, 184, 185, 219n43, 220n46
Lasswell, Harold, viii, 12, 19, 215n29
Latifundia, vi, 53
Lavín, Santiago, 54
Laws, 25, 31, 94
Life expectancy, 37
López y Fuentes, Gregorio, 44
Lynd, Robert S., viii, 11, 16

MACHINERY, 29, 51, 73, 78, 91, 99, 101, 103, 121-124, 129-131, 133, 173-176, 191, 192, 233n20
Macías, Gonzalo B., 138
Madero, Francisco I., 20-24, 30, 47, 63, 158
Magdaleno, Mauricio, 45
Maize. See Corn
Manufacturing, 33, 103
Maps and charts: Canals, 62; Laguna, 48; Land Tenure, 92; Railroads, 57; Water Flow of Río Nazas, 64
Masonic order, 22, 218n31
Melons, 78
Merton, Robert K., viii, 8, 14, 197, 215ns 3&4
Mexican Indians, 25
Mexico City, 15, 23, 158
Migration, 33, 52, 178, 179, 221n65
Mining, 31, 33, 83, 84
Molina Enríquez, Andrés, 25
Money, 33
Monopoly, 16-18, 43, 140, 222n97
Morale, 125
Morones, Luis, 45
Mules, 124
Municipios (counties), 49, 80, 81, 157, 158, 194, 195

NUEVA Italia, 27
Nueva Lombardía, 27
Newspapers and Magazines, 20, 158

OROZCO, José Clemente, 25, 44
Orózco y Jiménez, Archbishop Francisco, 19

PEACHES, 78
Peasants, 24, 25, 28, 47, 120, 125, 127, 133, 139, 219n42
Pigs, 121
Political questions, 16, 17, 97, 127, 133

Population, 33, 34, 37-39, 166-181, 209, 216n9, 221n65, 234n32
Postal service, 87
Press, freedom of, 20
Property relocation, 110-112

RACE, 202
Radio, 87, 147, 160
Railroads, 30, 31, 55-57, 86-87
Rayon, 73, 75, 76
Religion, 162-165. See also Catholic Church
Revolts, peasant, v, 52
Revolution, Mexican, vi, 8, 10, 13-14, 21-23, 42-46, 183, 184
Rivera, Diego, 40, 44, 45
Rivers: Aguanaval, 63; El Oro, 108; Nazas, 50, 56, 63, 64, 136; Ramos, 108
Rodríguez, Abelardo, 65

SÁNCHEZ Navarro family, 53
San Luis Potosí plan, 23
Schools. See Education
Sharecropping, 7, 58, 61, 241
Sheep, 51
Shepherd's Corner, 53, 112
SICA, 122
Siquerios, David Alfaro, 44, 45
Skills, 196, 197
Social services, 135, 151
Social system, 14, 216n7
Sorokin, P. A., 142, 214n13
Sports, 130, 131, 135
Squash, 77
Steel, 33
Stores, retail, 81-83, 97, 128, 129
Strikes, 65, 66
Sugar, 33, 72, 143
Superstition, 130, 131

TABLES: animals, 28, 29; average monthly income, 40; birth and death rates, 36, 169, 170, 171; buildings, 247, 248; census, 36; class structure, 41; cotton, 70, 71, 77, 189,

192, 242, 249, 250; credit societies, 246; employment, 179; finance, 102, 251; house appliances, 147; land, 27, 28, 54, 95, 96, 239-241; literacy, 155, 157; loans, 104; machinery, 29; mechanization, 174; national income, 34; population, 3, 38, 39; profits, 115; schools, 156, 159; unattended deaths, 149; wages, 145, 146; wheat, 79, 190, 192, 243-245
Taxes, 16-17, 73, 194, 195, 205
Telephones, 31
Textiles, 33, 69, 72, 74, 75, 225n14
Tlahualilo Land and Colonization Co., 50, 51, 54, 55, 61
Toledano, Vicente Lombardo, 126
Tomatoes, 78
Torreón, 48, 49, 53, 55-56
Torres Bodet, Jaime, 161
Transportation, 35, 53, 59, 85-88
Trees, fruit, 77, 99
Tuberculosis. See Diseases and Pests
Typhoid. See Diseases and Pests

UNIONS, vi, 29-32, 65, 74, 125-128, 220ns60, 61
Urban workers, 29
Urdiñola, Francisco de, 53

VEGETABLES, 99, 143, 144
Venereal disease, 152
Vice, 130, 152
Villa, Pancho, 20, 24, 25, 47

WAGES, 40, 143, 144-146
War: Civil, 32-34, 47; Independence, 53
Wheat, 47, 77-80, 91, 101, 115, 125, 132, 134, 189-192
Women, 129-131
Wool, 73
Writers, 44, 45

ZAPATA, Emiliano, 23-25
Zimmerman, C. C., 214n13
Zuloaga, widow of, 136